29.95
9/14

THE MARKETPLACE OF ATTENTION

THE MARKETPLACE OF ATTENTION

How Audiences Take Shape in a Digital Age

James G. Webster

The MIT Press
Cambridge, Massachusetts
London, England

MIT Press books may be purchased at special quantity discounts for business or sales promotional use. For information, please email special_sales@mitpress.mit.edu.

This book was set in Gentium and Futura by the MIT Press. Printed and bound in the United States of America.

Library of Congress Cataloging-in-Publication Data

Webster, James G.
The marketplace of attention : how audiences take shape in a digital age / James G. Webster.
    pages   cm
Includes bibliographical references and index.
ISBN 978-0-262-02786-1
1. Mass media—Audiences. I. Title.
P96.A83W428   2014
302.23—dc23
2014003869

10   9   8   7   6   5   4   3   2   1

To the kindness of friends and strangers

CONTENTS

PREFACE

When I finished my bachelor's degree in psychology I needed to find work. Although I was interested in media, I wasn't really qualified to do anything. Nevertheless, I stumbled into a job in audience research at Children's Television Workshop. At the time, the Workshop produced *Sesame Street* and *The Electric Company* and was celebrated for blending information with entertainment. Flushed with their success in children's television, the Workshop decided to produce a health show for adults that would revolutionize the nation's health practices the way *Sesame Street* had revolutionized the way kids learned their ABCs. I was hired to study viewer reactions to the new program.

That show, called *Feeling Good,* premiered in prime time opposite a lineup of expensively produced network television programs. From day one, there were problems. Most notably, very few people watched *Feeling Good,* and those who did already knew what the show had to teach them. *Feeling Good* lasted for one tortuous season, but it left me with a question I've been thinking about ever since. How do audiences take shape?

That question seems more pressing today than at any time in the past. Digital media present people with many ways to spend their time. They can choose among an endless number of outlets, ranging from the broadcast networks that denied *Feeling Good* a prime-time audience to websites of every imaginable kind. They can create their own media. They can share anything that's digital with friends or strangers around the world. But how do people actually use all these newfound resources, and why do they coalesce around some things and not others?

There is a broad consensus that the way people allocate their attention will go a long way toward determining digital media's social impact. But there are wildly different expectations about how audiences will take shape. Some writers believe that we're witnessing the dawn of a partici-patory society in which people will engage diverse ideas and revel in the best that the culture has to offer. Others envision a world in which people, guided by their own prejudices or insidious filtering technologies, will be segregated into niches or echo chambers. Some think our use of media will enrich us; others fear it will tear us apart.

The Marketplace of Attention is my attempt to sort through these com-peting claims and expectations and to provide a durable framework for understanding the forces that shape people's encounters with media. To do that, I draw on research and theory from several academic disciplines as well as studies done by and for the media. Some of this work has been around for decades and continues of offer useful insights. Other work is quite new. And some is described here for the first time. But, to the best my knowledge, this wide-ranging assortment has never been integrated into a single assessment of audience behavior and its implications for society.

To elaborate a bit, the middle chapters synthesize a large literature on the predispositions and habits of media users, the audience-making strat-egies of the media, and the methods and biases of media measures, includ-ing audience ratings and recommender systems, which often depend on "big data." The book then reviews what the best evidence tells us about audience fragmentation and other patterns of media use. The concluding chapters draw on all that theory and evidence to offer a new framework that explains how these forces interact to shape public attention and the marketplace of ideas.

I've written the book with three types of readers in mind. The first are fellow academics—particularly those who value an interdisciplinary approach. The second are people who work in or with the media—partic-ularly those who would like to step back and "see the forest" instead of the trees. The third are members of the general public—particularly those with a serious interest in media and how digital technologies are likely to affect popular culture and the public sphere. The book is not intended to be a how-to manual in audience manipulation—neither I nor anyone else has perfected that recipe. It is intended to offer readers a robust, lasting way to think about audiences and the many factors that produce public attention. For my readers, I've tried to be as concise, well-organized, and plainspoken as possible. But you, of course, will be the judge of that.

In writing this book, I'm doubly fortunate to have been on the faculty of Communication Studies at Northwestern University. First, communication is a relatively new academic discipline that tends to be an interdisciplinary enterprise. We have no reservations about taking the best that sociology, economics, political science, marketing, or computer science has to offer and turning it to our own ends. By breaking down disciplinary boundaries, we can see things from different angles and build on what others have done. Second, at Northwestern in particular, I'm surrounded by smart, engaged faculty members and students who have helped me enormously. In addition to a healthy "hall culture," we regularly meet to discuss our work or hear from some of the most innovative minds in the field. All of this makes for a challenging, collegial atmosphere.

The Northwestern faculty members who have helped me along the way include Jeremy Birnholtz, Nosh Contractor, Jack Doppelt, Stephanie Edgerly, Jim Ettema, Darren Gergle, Paul Hirsch, Paul Leonardi, Larry Lichty, Amy Lu, Ed Malthouse, Dan O'Keefe, Don Schultz, Aaron Shaw, Michelle Shumate, Cristina Tilley, Ellen Wartella, and Chuck Whitney. Other colleagues in academe and industry who offered support and counsel include Patrick Barwise, Bob Entman, Natali Helberger, David LeRoy, Russ Neuman, Joe Turow, and Jack Wakshlag. I am particularly grateful to Pablo Boczkowski, Aymar Christian, Eszter Hargittai, Phil Napoli, and the anonymous reviewers who read large swaths of the manuscript in various stages of development. Their comments helped shape the substance and tone of the book.

I also owe a special thank-you to Patricia Phalen of George Washington University. As I began work on this book, she and I were finishing a new edition of *Ratings Analysis: Audience Measurement and Analytics*.[1] The requirements of book production extend well beyond writing. There are permissions to obtain, sources to track down, copy to edit, and so on. Pat relieved me of those chores, so I could concentrate on the book before you now.

Those who are involved in graduate education know that, oftentimes, students are a particularly important source of insight. They're typically younger, so they have a different perspective on digital technologies, which for them don't seem like "new" media at all. With doctoral students, you often spend hours thinking through and executing research projects. Three of my recent students, Tom Ksiazek, Su Jung Kim, and Harsh Taneja, were particularly helpful in making this book a reality. Two other doctoral students, Anke Wonneberger and Michael LaCour, weren't "mine" but shared their work in progress with me, much to my benefit. Research by these young scholars shows up throughout the book, especially in the chapter on "Audience Formations."

A number of institutional affiliations have contributed, either directly or indirectly, to the work in the pages that follow. In addition to the collegial support and leave time provided by Northwestern University, I've benefitted from consulting relationships with Nielsen and Turner Broadcasting. They have, in fact, provided analyses that appear in "Audience Formations." In some instances, I've reproduced figures I first published in journals, and a few brief passages in this book have appeared in modified form in their pages.[2] I would especially like to thank the MIT Press and its editors for their support and guidance.

Finally, I thank my family. My sons have recently graduated from college. One works in "digital analytics" and the other in consulting (apparently they were qualified to do something). Much like my students, they offer me their own take on digital media. My wife, Debra, whom I met in graduate school, has seen me through good times and bad. She does not "suffer fools gladly," but generally indulges her absentminded professor husband. Without the support of friends and family this book would not have been possible.

1 THE MARKETPLACE OF ATTENTION

Digital media offer people countless choices. They can spend their time with hundreds of television networks, thousands of expensively produced films and TV shows, and a seemingly endless supply of websites, videos, and tweets. Some of these offerings are intended for large audiences; others are more narrowly directed to friends and followers. But almost without exception, their creators want attention. With it, they hope to amuse, build social capital, make money, or change the course of human events. Without it, their efforts are of little consequence. Media need an audience before they can achieve a purpose. And to find that audience, they must compete with one another in the marketplace of attention.

But the supply of human attention is limited. There are only so many people and so many hours in the day. This constraint is an inescapable feature of the marketplace. As more media compete for attention, the audiences they seek become relatively scarce. It's a zero sum game that dooms most offerings to obscurity, so understanding the forces that shape public attention is more important than ever. For media makers, it's the key to success. For the rest of us, it provides a keener sense of how digital technology might affect everything from politics and popular culture.

In fact, most observers agree that emerging patterns of media use will have profound economic and social implications. But they have very different notions about how the marketplace of attention works and very different ideas about what kind of a world it's likely to produce. Some claim that users are now in charge and celebrate their newfound ability to control the media environment.[1] They see the death of hit-driven culture and the birth of a cultural democracy that is no longer dominated by commercial interests. Others fear that people will use the abundance of digital media to avoid what they dislike and retreat into enclaves of comfortable, like-minded speech.[2] Or worse yet, they see people as unwitting pawns who are segregated by data-driven systems into "reputation silos" or "filter bubbles."[3] They fear that digital media are eroding the common cultural forum of mass media and promoting social polarization. In one world digital media liberate us to achieve our fullest potential. In the other, they tear us apart.

Why are there such differences in popular commentaries and serious scholarship on the social impact of digital media? Perhaps it's to be expected. Communication revolutions often play to our hopes and fears.[4] They create what one sociologist called "constitutive moments," in which the stakes for society are high but the outcomes are uncertain.[5] This wouldn't be the first time a new generation of media has triggered predictions that, in retrospect, seem overwrought.

In the fourth century BCE, Plato fretted that the "new" technology of writing would encourage forgetfulness and weaken people's minds.[6] In the first half of the twentieth century, critics were convinced that film and radio would manipulate the passions and opinions of gullible mass publics.[7] And in the early 1970s, the so-called blue-sky period of cable television, pundits expected a revolution in everything from entertainment to shopping to democracy.[8] So "new media" and hyperbolic expectations often go hand in hand.

Still, differences of opinion about the current revolution are pronounced, especially when it comes to how people are likely to use digital media. How can thoughtful, well-informed writers have such divergent views on the nature and implications of the new media environment? There seem to be three culprits at work.

First, most writers want to tell a memorable story. The easiest way to do that is to adopt a provocative, intuitively appealing premise and focus on the particulars that prove the point. The problem with this approach is that the marketplace of attention is a complicated system with lots of moving parts. It doesn't lend itself to simple narratives, which for any writer is a challenge. As my colleagues have realized, "Complex findings do not cater to punchy headlines and thus seldom receive the same level of attention as apocalyptic warnings."[9]

Second, the impulse to simplify things produces treatments that latch on to one piece of the new media environment, analyze it, and imply that it characterizes the whole. The hopeful accounts emphasize people's inclination to share, the increased availability and reach of social media platforms, or the "wisdom of crowds" captured in recommender systems. The bleaker accounts focus on people's penchant for selective exposure, the operation of filtering technologies, or the media's increasing ability to target specific groups or individuals. But when you fail to consider all the component parts, it's easy to miss how different forces can counteract one another.

Finally, many authors buttress their arguments with a combination of theory and anecdote. Those theories might prescribe how people ought to behave or predict how people are expected to behave. Either can produce satisfying, coherent arguments, but they don't necessarily tell us how people *actually do behave*. Anecdotes, although helpful, don't paint a complete picture. In most treatments, the shortage of accurate, empirical descriptions of audience behavior is a serious shortcoming.

This book tries to remedy at least some of those problems by incorporating all the factors that shape audiences into one comprehensive system—the marketplace of attention. It recognizes that although digital media empower people in important ways, individuals are not the sole masters of their destiny. Media systems "push" things at us, often in ways we scarcely notice. Contrary to most theories of choice, these encounters can cultivate preferences that would not otherwise exist. And increasingly, data orchestrate the process. Data-driven systems, including recommendations and audience ratings, are the lenses through which users and the media see the marketplace. But these optics are never distortion free. They have biases that favor certain outcomes and they pull public attention in different directions.

The forces of cultural production and consumption conspire to produce an environment that is at once diverse and concentrated. Although no two people will have the same diet of media, across the population there is a surprising commonality to what we see and hear. Far from retreating into enclaves or living in parallel worlds, audiences circulate across media offerings. These overlapping patterns create a public sphere that is centered but far more fluid than what we're used to. To understand how this happens, let's begin by noting a few inescapable features of the digital media environment.

Digital Media

Although digital media are constantly changing, three things about the digital environment are clear. First, media content and services are proliferating at such a rapid rate that the volume of material is essentially unlimited. Second, media, both old and new, are increasingly available on demand via fully integrated digital networks that allow users to move easily from one thing to the next. Third, the total supply of human attention available to consume those offerings has an upper bound. The widening gap between limitless media and limited attention makes it a challenge for anything to attract an audience.

Perhaps the most astonishing thing about digital media is their numerical abundance. It's one thing about which there is universal agreement. There are plenty of eye-popping statistics on the totals, such as the number of tweets (five hundred million a day),[10] the new videos on YouTube (one hundred million hours uploaded every minute),[11] or the sheer number of words we generate each day (enough to fill all the books in the US Library of Congress).[12]

These numbers will undoubtedly have been eclipsed by the time you read this. The point is, the world is awash in digital media, more is being created every second, and most of it doesn't go away. Furthermore, it's increasingly easy to get.

Not so long ago, media content was wed to particular modes of distribution. If you wanted to see a film, you went to a movie theater. If you wanted to read the news, you went to a newsstand or waited for it to be delivered to your doorstep. If you wanted to watch a television program, you went home and waited for the broadcast. But digital media are "interoperable."[13] They break down the barriers of time and place.

Today, 90 percent of US households subscribe to cable or satellite services and almost as many have Internet access.[14] They attach any number of devices—DVRs, video games, computers, tablets, and smartphones—to those networks to get what they want when they want it. Users might see a movie trailer on their smartphone, watch the film "on demand" on HDTV or their iPad, and perhaps tweet about it or recommend it to others on Facebook. People move easily from one platform to the next and anything that's digitized can move with them.

The combination of abundance and seamless access underlies many of the plot lines that we'll consider in the following pages. It has certainly shaken established media industries. At best, it's causing them to reinvent themselves and at worst it threatens utter "chaos."[15] It has posed formidable challenges to the way we measure, and therefore understand, media use.[16] And perhaps most important, it has fueled the notion that at long last the "consumer is king." The rhetoric of "audience autonomy" and "anywhere anytime" media consumption permeates business and academe alike.[17] As a Columbia University report on "postindustrial journalism" noted, "Observing a world where the members of the audience had become more than recipients of information, the scholar Jay Rosen of New York University coined the phrase "The People Formerly Known as the Audience" to describe the ways in which previously quiescent groups of consumers had become creators and annotators and judges and conduits for information."[18] Because media users now seem to hold all the cards, many believe that understanding them is the key to understanding the marketplace of attention.

But people still have limits. And one barrier that is non-negotiable is the hours in a day. In 1960, the average American spent 7.4 hours consuming information (i.e., TV, radio, print, etc.). By 2008, the daily average had jumped 60 percent to11.8 hours a day—and that didn't even include media use at work.[19] Television, in one form or another, still accounts for about half the time we spend with media and shows no sign of a decline. The latest from Nielsen is that Americans watch over 4.5 hours a day of live TV and another half an hour of time-shifted programming (e.g., DVRs).[20] Reports of the amount of time people spend "online" or with mobile devices are more varied because of different definitions and methods of measurement. Some claim the combined total equals time spent with TV,[21] although that number seems a bit inflated. Still, with a majority of Americans—and much of the world—now using smartphones,[22] it's not hard to imagine a time when media use will fill almost every waking hour.[23]

To keep up, more and more people find time by multitasking. There's plenty of evidence that people engage in "concurrent media use."[24] Whereas yesterday's television viewers might have occasionally read something as they watched, now they're keeping an eye on their tablets and smartphones.[25] They're also using platforms such as Facebook and Twitter while watching television; something the British call "media meshing."[26] In just one year between 2012 and 2013 there was a 38 percent increase in the number of TV-related tweets.[27]

Because of all that multitasking, tallies of time spent with media can be deceptive. But exact numbers aren't as important as the larger realization that we're simply running out of time. As Harvard's Yochai Benkler noted, "One of the primary remaining scarce resources in the networked environment is user time and attention."[28]

Attention

The realization that media would eventually overwhelm our ability to pay attention is hardly new. In the early 1970s, Nobel laureate Herbert Simon famously observed, "a wealth of information creates a poverty of attention, and a need to allocate that attention efficiently among the overabundance of information sources that might consume it."[29] In a world increasingly dependent on digital media, the poverty of attention has important consequences. Although public attention is often indispensable to the exercise of economic, political, or social influence, it's harder to come by.

This scarcity has encouraged talk of a new "attention economy," in which the allocation of attention is of central importance.[30] As Cass Sunstein argued, "one of the most important of all commodities, in the current situation, is people's attention. That is what companies are endlessly competing to obtain. Much activity on the Internet, by those interested in profits and other goods, is designed to produce greater attention, even if only for a moment. If a company or a political candidate can get attention from 300,000 people for as little as two seconds, it will have accomplished a great deal."[31] In a similar vein, another scholar argued, we should "assume that, in an information economy, the real scarce commodity will always be human attention and that attracting that attention will be the necessary precondition of social change. And the real source of wealth."[32] I'll have more to say about the value of attention in the following pages, but before I do that, I should clarify how this book approaches the subject of attention.

As you might imagine, attention has become something of a hot topic. It's the subject of several recent books. But they approach attention from different angles. At the risk of oversimplifying things, human attention is generally studied in one of two ways. Some treatments focus on how individuals deal with all of the stimuli that now bombard them. Others focus on the social or economic implications of widespread *public* attention.

The first approach is a micro-level conceptualization. It sees the world through the eyes of an individual media user. Because our surroundings are loaded with media that compete for our attention, researchers will often ask questions, such as how do people juggle multiple inputs, how do their eyes move from one piece of content to the next, and how do their brains process information?[33] Sometimes the goal is to design a better interface.[34] Sometimes it's to assess how we cope with everything at our disposal and whether that's likely to empower us or do us in. Perhaps unsurprisingly, these books also run the gamut from hopeful to despairing accounts of what's happening.[35]

The second approach is to think of attention as a macro-level phenomenon. These accounts see large collectives of people who are drawn together or divided by media. They ask a different set of questions, such as why do some things become popular whereas others go unnoticed or what factors shape patterns of cultural consumption? Sometimes the purpose is to help institutions manage audiences. Sometimes it's to assess where society is headed. And, as we've seen, there's very little consensus about the latter.

Although these two approaches aren't wholly separate, the emphasis in this book is on attention as a macro-level phenomenon. Micro-level factors are sometimes useful in providing insights, but they're rarely enough. It's only when multitasking and habits of mind scale up to form audiences that they are relevant to understanding the attention economy.[36]

You may have noticed by now that I use the terms *audience* and *public attention* more or less interchangeably. Many scholars draw careful distinctions between publics and audiences.[37] My failure to differentiate between the two may strike some as cavalier, but in today's environment I see little difference.

By the sixteenth century, the word *audience* had come to mean an "assembly of listeners." It has now been used to describe readers, moviegoers, radio listeners, TV viewers, website visitors, and the fans of particular people or genres. Modern audiences have traditionally been seen as groups of consumers who choose a particular media product or outlet. Often, those transactions have straightforward financial consequences. In that sense, the term *audience* sometimes has commercial connotations.

When the "assembly of listeners" is a group of citizens following a story or person in the news, the phenomenon is often described as *public attention.* Public attention is less routinely turned into cash, although it is often parleyed into financial gain or political advantage. In an age when celebrities and politicians tweet their followers and social media help direct people to news and entertainment, the distinction between building audiences and attracting public attention is murky at best.

Either way, an assembly of listeners has value, in part because it opens the door for further influence. Advertisers are the most practiced at exploiting those openings. One common model for orchestrating influence is described by the "hierarchy of effects." In its simplest form, it says advertising works by moving prospects through stages, from cognitions (e.g., becoming aware or learning) to affects (e.g., liking or desiring) to action (e.g., buying a product or voting for a candidate).[38] But the entire process begins by reaching people with a message. It begins by marshaling public attention.

In advertising, that attention comes at a well-defined price. Worldwide, advertisers spend roughly $500 billion a year to reach an audience. Although the United States is still the single biggest spender, in the last few years most of the growth has been in Asia and Latin America.[39] And, as you would expect, spending on digital media is rapidly gaining ground on more traditional outlets. Although governments once provided large subsidies to public broadcasters, advertising now supports much of the world's media, both online and off. But ad spending is just the tip of the iceberg. It fails to capture the true scope and value of public attention in two important ways.

First, most attention occurs outside advertising markets. People read books, go to movies, listen to music, watch TV, visit websites, and engage on social networks. In doing so, they encounter ideas that go well beyond the media's commercial content. Public attention coalesces around all kinds of people, places, and things. Such audiences can be difficult to manage, particularly in a digital media environment. As Benkler noted, "while money is useful in achieving visibility, the structure of the Web means that money is neither necessary nor sufficient to grab attention—because the networked information economy, unlike its industrial predecessor, does not offer simple points of dissemination and control for purchasing assured attention."[40] One of the challenges of the attention economy, then, is that the coin of the realm is hard to amass and quantify. As business writers Davenport and Beck put it, "there's no New York Attention Exchange, but ... anyone who wants to sell something or persuade someone to do something has to invest in the attention markets."[41]

Second, all of these attempts value public attention as a gateway to further influence. But that's only one, rather limiting, way to think about the consequences of audience formation. It's illustrative of what's been called a "transmission" view of communication. As one noted scholar suggested, we could just as well see communication as a "ritual" that "is directed not toward the extension of messages in space, but the maintenance of society in time ... ; not the act of imparting information or influence but the creation, representation, and celebration of shared even if illusory beliefs ... one that centers on the sacred ceremony that draws persons together in fellowship and commonality."[42]

Digital media are rife with events, large and small, in which the coming together of audiences confers meaning and purpose on those occasions. At one end of the spectrum, they include "media events" that interrupt the flow of daily life, inspire a ceremonial reverence, and can attract the "largest audiences in the history of the world."[43] The Olympics, presidential inaugurations, royal weddings and funerals, and the events of 9/11 have all spawned such massive virtual gatherings. At the other end of the spectrum, assemblies might include friends "checking in" to watch and share comments about their favorite TV show or people who circulate a link in an effort to bring something to wider notice. Large or small, audiences go a long way toward defining the spaces within which media objects and ideas circulate. Public attention can define their reach and, perhaps, their cultural significance.

Audiences have always been a component of how academics think about media. One of the pioneers in the field argued that the study of communication could be reduced to asking, "Who says what in which channel to whom with what effect?"[44] This way of thinking emerged against the backdrop of World War II, well after one particular "media regime" had taken hold in the United States. As Bruce Williams and Michael Delli Carpini described it, that regime featured "the centralization of newspaper ownership, the beginnings of radio, and the nationalization of advertising and marketing, thus reducing the number and diversity of media voices at the same time that the reach of remaining voices was greatly extended."[45]

With so few options competing for public attention, answering the "whom" part of the question wasn't much of a challenge. Stories on the front pages of newspapers and national magazines were guaranteed readership. If something was on a broadcast network, it reached a mass audience. With everyone choosing from the same limited menu, the theories needed to explain who was in the audience were fairly simple. But those explanations don't work very well in today's media environment. As that report on postindustrial journalism noted, "General ignorance of how people consume information was not an issue when the industrial model prevailed, but in today's fragmented and fraying world, knowledge of how audiences consume information, and whether what you write, record, or shoot reaches the people whom you want to see it, becomes critical."[46]

As we'll see in the pages that follow, answering the "whom" question has become a real challenge. In my view, the theories we've used to explain how people encounter media haven't kept pace with the fragmented and fraying world of digital media. To really understand how audiences take shape, we need to consider all the forces now at play in the media marketplace.

The Marketplace

This book offers a novel theoretical framework for thinking about the marketplace, one that highlights the interplay of people and the media resources that surround them. Here, I summarize the major components of the marketplace, each of which comprises a chapter in its own right. The first players are media users. They provide the raw material that fuels the attention economy. The second are the media themselves. These include all the providers that lay claim to public attention and the practices they use to achieve that end. The third are media measures. These are increasingly important tools that institutions and individuals use to make sense of and manage the digital media environment.

Theoretical Considerations

Audience formation is one of many complex social behaviors that have occupied social scientists for generations. Theorists have tried to explain these behaviors by attributing them to various causes. Historically, there have been two predominant schools of thought. The first credits social behavior to individual "agents" exercising their free will. The second attributes behaviors to larger structures such as social institutions. People who have studied audiences sort out along these lines. Some are inclined to explain audience formation as the result of individual predispositions. Others attribute it to the structural resources that enable media use.[47]

The well-known sociologist Anthony Giddens labeled these traditional schools of thought subjectivism and objectivism, respectively. And he found each wanting. In his judgment, neither agency nor structure alone could explain the constitution of society. In fact, the two were inseparable. Agents appropriated the structural resources available to them, and in doing so they reproduced and reshaped those very structures. According to Giddens, agency and structure were mutually constituted, bound together in what he called a "duality."[48]

Language is an example of a duality. Individuals are born into a structured world of words and linguistic conventions. Although they are free to abandon that world, they generally use it to achieve their own ends. They say what they want to say. As they do that, they reproduce and change the language that enables their agency. This is a "structurational" way to explain the evolution and durability of language and, more broadly, society itself. It also works quite well for explaining audience formation.

For example, media users confront a digital environment loaded with ready-made structures. They have television networks, video on demand, websites, social media, and search engines at their disposal. These are the resources they use to do what they want. Those structures, however, aren't rigid. They constantly adapt to the actions of their users. Networks change their schedules, canceling some shows and cloning others. Search engines move different sites to the top of their rankings. New topics trend on Twitter. Those changes, in turn, affect the actions of users. And so it goes. The marketplace of attention is a structurational world if ever there was one, and it's the theoretical framework I find most useful in explaining how the marketplace of attention works because it can accommodate all the pieces of the puzzle.[49] We'll return to the topic of structuration in chapter 6.

But be forewarned. Thinking about audience formation in this way is a challenge for two interrelated reasons. One has to do with attributing causation, such as figuring out what determines exposure to media. The other has to do with the "level of analysis," a subject I touched on previously. Most of us are drawn to straightforward explanations of whatever it is we're observing. That's probably why those schools of thought that attribute everything to agency or everything to structure have been so durable. In a structurational approach, causation is oftentimes hard to pin down. Instead, we confront many instances of reciprocal causation—which is a social scientist's version of the "chicken or egg" question. Is a website popular because Google recommends it or does Google recommend it because it's popular? In the real world, the interplay of media and audiences generally defies simple one-way explanations.

A related problem comes from the level of analysis. The most intuitively appealing way to think about audiences is as collections of individuals. This micro-level approach sees media use from the perspective of the individual user. Because we all have experience playing that role, it's easy for us to imagine what makes other people tick. The fact that digital technologies seem to have put users in control makes this way of seeing users all the more appealing to theorists. For them, if you want to understand audience behavior, all you have to do is understand individual predispositions and appetites. This approach is very much in keeping with subjectivist traditions. It encourages us to believe that audiences result from the sum of the choices made by newly empowered agents.

The alternative is to imagine audiences as something more than the sum of their parts. They are markets, publics, or networks given to mass behaviors that aren't readily apparent at the micro-level of analysis. This macro-level approach is more typical of the way institutions see audiences. It's certainly a more abstract and less intuitive way to think about people. And to many it seems unnatural and unhealthy. The noted cultural critic Raymond Williams once argued that "there are in fact no masses; there are only ways of seeing peoples as masses."[50] He was right in his belief that masses exist in the minds of onlookers and are in that sense artificial. Still, once they're recognized, they can take on a life of their own.

This happens in two ways. First, institutions see and respond to media users not as individuals but as audiences. This is what my colleagues at Northwestern have called the "institutionally effective audience."[51] It's constructed, usually through measurement, as a way for institutions to try to manage media users, but it ends up giving audiences considerable clout. As MIT's Ethan Zuckerman pointed out, "The use of analytics by gatekeepers grants a new form of power to the audience."[52] In the marketplace of attention, it is measured audiences not individual agents that are most likely to change the system.

Second, social media and digital networks enable interactions among users that produce mass behaviors, such as herding or information cascades, which aren't easy to explain at a micro level. As Duncan Watts, a sociologist and senior researcher at Microsoft Research wrote, "you could know everything about individuals in a given population—their likes, dislikes, experiences, attitudes, beliefs, hopes, and dreams—and still not be able to predict much about their collective behavior."[53] To understand the marketplace of attention, you have to be adept at moving between levels of analysis.

Media Users

Although understanding users won't tell us everything we want to know, they're still an important component of the marketplace. It's the users, after all, who ultimately constitute public attention. They're generally seen, by academics and professionals alike, as purposeful actors who know a good deal about the media at their disposal.[54] That, at any rate, is a common portrait of the typical media user, and it's in keeping with traditional notions of agency.

A great many things contribute to how those agents act. They include each user's psychological predispositions, their social networks, and the structures of their everyday lives. Of these, the most extensive academic literature deals with the psychology of media choice. Many disciplines identify people's predispositions as the principle or sole causes of their actions. Depending on which discipline you invoke, media choices are conceptualized as a function of program type preferences,[55] attitudes and beliefs,[56] moods and hedonic impulses,[57] needs,[58] or simply tastes.[59]

Each person's media choices are further shaped by his or her social networks. Researchers have long noted the power of face-to-face encounters to affect a person's actions. Most people belong to many groups (e.g., family, friends, social or business organizations). These groups will often have an "opinion leader" who is active in directing members' attention to some things and not others.[60] Today, digital media extend traditional face-to-face encounters to larger virtual networks, amplifying the effects of people's preferences. For example, social media often help people coalesce into like-minded communities leading them to media products and messages that resonate with group norms and, perhaps, reinforcing their predispositions.[61]

Although digital platforms enable people to use media anywhere at any time, that hypothetical freedom is often trumped by larger social structures. Historically, most media use has been deeply ingrained in the rhythms of day-to-day life. Time and again, we see predictable patterns of seasonal and hourly media use that betray equally predictable patterns of work and recreation.[62] Although new media have the potential to alter those practices, more often they are harnessed in service of how we live our lives.[63] The structural features of social life—when we work, where we live, what languages we speak, our socioeconomic status—aren't swept away with each new technology. Day-to-day life constitutes a remarkably stable, if mundane, force that shapes when and how audiences are likely to form.

So, each individual's use of media is shaped by his or her preferences, affiliations, and life circumstances. Users assess the available resources and choose among them in an effort to achieve their purpose, whatever that might be. In that sense, their actions are rational. But digital media present purposeful, reasoning agents with a dilemma. Their ability to act rationally is "bounded"[64] in two important ways. First, the vastness of the digital environment makes it impossible for any one person to know all the options at his or her disposal. Second, media products are "experience goods" subject to "infinite variety."[65] People can't fully know the nature of any new offering, and whether it will provide the desired gratification, until they've used it.

The user's dilemma isn't new. It's just getting much more complicated. For many years, people have coped with what seemed like an overabundance of choice by paring down their options to a smaller, more manageable "repertoire" of preferred sources.[66] They've also used "heuristics," or rules of thumb, to quickly categorize, assess, and choose among available resources.[67]

Today, digital media offer people a host of new tools to cope with their options. Search and recommendation systems are everywhere. They're indispensable for navigating the media environment. As the *New York Times* noted, "People are overwhelmed at how crowded the Internet has become—Google says there are 30 trillion Web addresses, up from 1 trillion five years ago —and users expect their computers and phones to be smarter and to do more for them. Many of the new efforts are services that people do not even think of as search engines."[68]

But as we'll see, recommender systems, no matter how sophisticated, are never completely neutral. And they can render even the savviest media users susceptible to influence. Indeed, the media environment that we rely on isn't just a menu from which we pick and choose. Most media providers want something from their audience. They will often try to manage users, sometimes in ways that are difficult to discern.

The Media

Media offer people the resources they use to achieve their purposes. Traditionally, media industries and governments have provided the infrastructures and programming that have made that possible. These institutions have their own reasons for doing so. Their goals might include enlightening the public, which has been the tradition in public service broadcasting; indoctrinating citizens, which has been the practice of totalitarian regimes; or profiting from media consumption, which is the objective in commercial systems. But no matter their goals, to achieve them, they must create and maintain an audience.

The number of media providers has now grown with the explosion of "user-generated content." These images and commentaries are often delivered via social media and content-sharing sites such as YouTube or Instagram. Although some of this activity supports fairly conventional interpersonal relationships,[69] a large portion of it shares the motives of traditional media institutions. That is, the new content providers hope their offerings will enlighten, indoctrinate, or make a profit. Beyond that, they might also seek "benefits to reputation"[70] or simple notoriety. To achieve their purposes, these "micro-celebrities" need an audience.[71] So, with the exception of people engaged in genuinely interpersonal communication, all media providers seek public attention.

Achieving that goal involves making media *and* making audiences. The resources that are devoted to making media vary dramatically. Some, such as Hollywood blockbusters or prime-time network television programs, can be enormously expensive to produce. Others, such as blogs or home-made videos are cheap, except for the cost of hardware and their creator's time. No matter the investment, all digital media share two attributes.

First, nothing you put in to a media product guarantees its success. It's notoriously difficult to predict whether creative works will appeal to an audience. This was famously described by the Hollywood writer William Goldman as the "nobody knows" phenomenon.[72] Media makers work in a world of considerable uncertainty and use strategies to mitigate their risks, including replicating what's worked before.

Second, digital media are what economists call "public goods."[73] Once they're created, they can be endlessly reproduced and consumed without diminishing the supply. That motivates media makers to distribute their wares as widely as possible or to find ways to repackage and repurpose what they already own. It also enables people to share existing media without cost. One result of these conservative production and distribution practices is to make the digital media marketplace less diverse than its sheer numerical abundance might suggest.

But none of that matters if the media goods and services in question fail to attract an audience. The media have to find their audiences and there are two strategies for doing that. These are sometimes called the "pull" and "push" models of audience building. In the *pull* model, audiences seek out media. Offerings such as movies or TV shows or websites are made available in the hopes that people will reach out and grab them. For creators with an established following or offerings on popular outlets, pull alone might do the trick. But most media aren't so fortunate. In the *push* model, the media find the audience. The classic example is an advertiser with a message. Rather than hoping that people with seek them out, advertisers spend billions of dollars making sure you get their messages. Advertisers construct their audiences and, given enough money, they can be spectacularly successful in bringing things to public attention.

Pull and push are conceptual extremes. Usually, these strategies work in tandem. Even successful movie franchises, featuring well-known stars, spend liberally to promote a sequel. Ambitious bloggers will use search engine "optimization" to drive traffic to their sites. And increasingly, advertisers are colonizing social media to engage brand loyalists who can't seem to get enough. To succeed in the marketplace of attention, media providers use every trick in the book.

But just as users confront a growing dilemma, so too do the media. They can't sell or manage what they can't see. Their audiences are dispersed in time and space, using media where and when they please. Some platforms that deliver media leave no trace of the users. Others produce masses of data that have to be mined for insights. Virtually all forms of media benefit from measurement systems in some way, and for most tracking and authenticating their audiences is essential. In fact, the media and ordinary users need measurement to operate effectively in digital environments.

Media Measures

Users provide the attention and media the resources that construct the digital media environment. But what machinery makes the construction possible? How do agents and structures actually manage to reproduce and change the marketplace? Media measures play a pivotal role in orchestrating this process. They enable the media to see users. With that knowledge, they can adapt to and exploit their audiences. Failures are quickly identified and remedied. Opportunities are seized and managed to their advantage. Alternatively, the measures offered by recommender systems enable users to see each other. Summaries of what others have said or done help guide the actions of users that, in the aggregate create or deny the public attention to which institutions respond.

Historically, measurement systems have been tools of commercially supported media. Ratings services made it possible for radio, then television, and now the web to respond to and profit from their audiences. These measures are now commonplace in virtually all developed media systems around the world, even those not driven by commercial imperatives. They serve institutions and are a prime example of what sociologists have called "market information regimes." Such regimes "are the medium through which producers observe each other and market participants make sense of their world."[74]

But institutions are no longer alone in needing to make sense of the marketplace. The overwhelming abundance of digital media has spawned a second genre of media measures. These "user information regimes" include search and recommendation systems. They make it possible for users to find what they want and, in the process, direct their attention. In either event, metrics are the lens through which users and the media make sense of the digital marketplace.

As we'll see, market and user information regimes have a lot in common, including the fact that they never offer a completely independent or neutral view of the marketplace. They are always constructed by and for human beings. The people who use those measures want them to do certain things, whether it's describing the buying habits of an audience or delivering personalized search results. As one industry analyst noted, "There is a lot of pressure on search engines to deliver more customized, more relevant results.... We need answers, solutions, whatever intel we were searching for."[75]

The measure makers respond accordingly, but only within the limits of their own resources. As in any research enterprise, they make decisions about how to collect and report data. The measures they produce inevitably highlight some things and not others. They structure decision making along those dimensions and in doing so encourage certain outcomes.

For example, virtually all user information regimes privilege popularity. Search and recommendation systems routinely rank their results in order of which had the most views, likes, or inbound links. As users follow those recommendations, the rich get richer. The very existence of the measure can affect the thing being measured and become a kind of self-fulfilling prophesy. If Amazon or Netflix reports that "people like you" are watching a particular movie, it's likely to get more attention. In that sense, recommendations don't just assess popularity, they help create it. Those who benefit from these metrics often understand their importance and sometimes try to manipulate the results. Making media measures, then, isn't only an exercise in data gathering; it's often a political process.

The role that media measures play in shaping the marketplace of attention will only grow. Most digital media are delivered by very large computers. They store the media we stream or download. They manage how we connect to broadband networks. They track our movements on the web and deliver tailored advertising. These computers, or servers, are capable of recording every comment or click we make, producing an incredibly detailed record of our actions, if not our full identities. This is the new world of "big data." It won't give us perfect vision, but will it change the lens we've used into a microscope. It will certainly change the way institutions see audiences, and perhaps how we see ourselves.

Audiences

The marketplace I have just described sets the stage for different kinds of audience behaviors to emerge. The audience behavior that has received the most comment is *fragmentation,* a term that means different things to different people. For some, it's simply a matter of media use being more widely distributed, even to the point where "hits" disappear from the culture. For others, fragmentation is a harbinger of social polarization as the former mass audience is balkanized into isolated groups. It's the prospect of balkanization that underlies some of the more dire predictions about digital media. In chapter 5, we'll look at the "hard evidence"[76] on audience behavior to assess the veracity these predictions.

We'll see that the growth in digital media outlets, each fighting for public attention, has indeed fragmented audiences across an ever-increasing number of outlets. But we'll also see that cultural consumption across all forms of media remains surprisingly concentrated, and it's likely to remain so. For a variety of reasons, older broadcast networks still have far larger audiences than most cable networks. And the top websites account for the overwhelming majority of user traffic. In fact, the more abundant the medium, the more concentrated audiences tend to be.[77]

These lopsided patterns of consumption have many labels—power laws, Pareto distributions, and the 80/20 rule just to name a few. Chris Anderson, the long-time editor of *Wired* magazine, dubbed them "long-tail" distributions in a well-known book by that name.[78] But do they signal balkanization or is something else happening beneath the veneer of fragmentation? Anderson predicted digital media would eventually move cultural consumption out into the niches of specialized content that populate the long tail, creating a "massively parallel culture," which for him was a positive development.

But others view the prospect of niches with more concern. A popular story line in many commentaries on audience behavior is that users will, for one reason or another, hunker down in enclaves of agreeable, like-minded media. Writers have called these audience formations *gated communities, sphericules, silos, echo chambers, cyber-Balkans, red media–blue media,* or *filter bubbles.*[79] All suggest the existence of highly segmented markets. In the extreme, they portend a society largely devoid of a common public sphere and polarized into isolated, even hostile, groups.

Although there are some reasons to be concerned, we'll see that for the most part people show very few signs of settling down into niches. Users typically move across many seemingly diverse outlets, producing high levels of audience overlap.[80] So, although audiences are fragmented in ways that would have been unimaginable in an earlier age of broadcasting, that doesn't appear to signal polarization. When we look at what people actually do, rather than what they say they do, we find a surprising, if rather messy, commonality to cultural consumption. So rather than facing the prospect of a massively parallel culture, the evidence suggests the emergence of what is more aptly labeled a massively overlapping culture.

In the Balance

A clear-eyed assessment of audience behavior provides a reality check on prophesies about digital media. No matter how intuitively appealing our theories might be, if they don't explain what's going on they need to be revised. Chapter 6, "Constructing the Marketplace of Attention," puts the pieces of theory and evidence in the earlier chapters together in a unique framework, one that describes how agents and structures work in concert to create audiences. Along the way, I'll identify a few theoretical blind spots in current approaches and explore the audience-making mechanisms that pose the greatest potential risks to society.

We'll see that although structures are often thought of as resources that people use to suit themselves, they also have the potential to steer audiences in one direction or another. My analysis identifies two dimensions of structure that seem to animate many of our hopes and fears about digital media: openness and obtrusiveness. Specifically, some structures seem open and likely to promote varied, serendipitous encounters. Other structures are closed and likely to encourage the formation of enclaves. Some structures are easy for people to see and use for good or ill. Other structures are unobtrusive and can influence people without their knowledge. If all structures worked in concert to accomplish a single purpose, they'd be a powerful determinant of what does and doesn't receive public attention. But oftentimes, the structural features of the digital media environment work at cross purposes, creating a delicate balance that audiences can tip in one direction or another.

In such a world, answering the question "where do preferences come from?" is of crucial importance. It goes to the heart of the relationship between structures and agents and clarifies the dynamics of the marketplace. Most social scientists believe that preexisting, "exogenous" preferences explain people's media choices. That is, we bring our wants and desires with us from outside the media system and these determine what media we encounter. If our likes and dislikes are immune from media influence, then the media will be brought to heel. But in a world where media constantly push things at us, it seems likely that our encounters with media might cause our tastes to change. If people's preferences are "endogenous," then media could cultivate our interests and shape public attention. Understanding the sources of our preferences will go a long way toward determining how the marketplace evolves.

In the chapter 7, "Public Attention in the Marketplace of Ideas," we'll consider how these mechanisms could affect the operation of the public sphere. The marketplace metaphor, which inspired the title of the book, provides the philosophical underpinnings of America's First Amendment freedoms of speech and press. It envisions spaces where people can freely express themselves, hear different points of view, and with any luck discover the truth. It provides a model for how media can inform citizens and support the practice of democracy. But with every new media regime, the marketplace of ideas is tested and realized in different ways. The dawning age of digital media is no exception.

In the world of old media, government regulators often required broadcasters to provide diversity.[81] Stations were compelled to offer different kinds of programming and contrasting points of view. Today, with so much available in the media environment, mandating diversity hardly seems necessary. But the wealth of blogs, affinity groups, specialized websites, and ideologically inflected television news channels doesn't guarantee that we'll have a marketplace of ideas where truth and falsehood confront one another.

If, as many fear, people successfully avoid everything they find distasteful, whether it's dissident voices or, for that matter, news of any kind, it could diminish the vitality of the marketplace. But if, as I argue, the marketplace of attention is concentrated and diverse, then people will encounter crosscutting ideas and preserve a healthy marketplace, albeit in a new form. Either way, the onus is largely on the audience and the future of the public sphere hangs in the balance. Understanding how public attention takes shape should shed some light on what's to come.

2   MEDIA USERS

Media users power the attention economy. Their decisions about what to read or watch or share, taken as a whole, create the audiences that sustain media and give them meaning. So our study of the marketplace of attention begins with them. The importance of figuring out what makes media users tick has been evident to researchers for a long time, which means there's a lot of material for us to digest. In this chapter we'll hear from economists, marketing researchers, sociologists, psychologists, political scientists, social network analysts, and people in communication and cultural studies. Each discipline has its own way of thinking about users. Most see them as purposeful, reasoning actors, or "agents," who are free do as they please. Some disciplines also emphasize how a person's place in larger social systems and networks can affect their actions. We'll cover all that territory, but to set the stage, it's useful to consider how our ideas of agency—or the power to act—affect how we study media users.

Ways of Seeing

The most popular and intuitively appealing way to see users is as individuals who employ media to serve their own purposes. With digital media at their beck and call, people can interact with friends and family via social networks, create and share content, or turn their attention to whatever suits their fancy. Depictions of knowledgeable, free-wheeling media users are everywhere. "After decades of vilifying the passive couch potato, the press now venerates the active participant in digital culture."[1] In industry, consumers are the newly empowered "kings" in the marketplace.[2] Among social commentators, they are the "people formerly known as the audience" who have now seized control.[3] In academic circles, they are "prosumers," who "are demanding the right to participate within the culture."[4]

But what powers do users actually have? Their agency can be roughly sorted into four categories. These are different expressions of agency that have emerged over time as new resources have become available. People have the power to make meaning, to choose, to share, and, in the aggregate, to affect industry practice.

In the very earliest days of television, only a few channels were available to viewers. Elihu Katz, a sociologist and pioneer in media research, recalled a time when Israeli viewers had only one TV channel, "Within two years of its inauguration, almost all households owned television sets, and almost everybody watched almost everything."[5] This had the benefit, in Katz's view, of providing a single forum that spanned ideological divides and promoted a sense of national identity and purpose.

Under those circumstances, it was difficult to be very choosy. But even when choices were limited, people were still free to interpret media messages in different ways. This power to make meaning has been studied by academics for several decades. Social scientists have long been intrigued by the ability of individuals to "selectively perceive" whatever media messages they encounter. For example, people with ethnic prejudices have been inclined to interpret anti-prejudicial messages as somehow reinforcing their beliefs.[6] In a more contemporary vein, viewers of the Fox News Channel seem able to deflect or reinterpret the messages of "mainstream media."[7]

Similarly, proponents of what came to be known as the "British cultural studies" were quick to observe that viewers of BBC news didn't always believe what they were being told, but were capable of "negotiated" or "oppositional" readings.[8] That is, they "read" media content in a way that matched their predispositions. They exercised their agency through interpretation.

Today, studying how people perceive or "decode" media texts remains an important academic pursuit. And it's not far removed from the focus group research that media producers use to understand how viewers respond to movies, TV shows, and commercials. Knowing what people make of the media they encounter can be extremely important. But because it happens after users are paying attention, it's of secondary importance here.

The era of one or two channel television is long gone. The growth of cable and satellite TV, along with an array of nonlinear, on-demand media, means that having too few choices is no longer a constraint. As digital media experts Lee Rainie and Barry Wellman put it, "Choice has exploded, putting control of what people watch—and where—in the hands of individuals. There are more—and more flexible—ways to watch.... Many shows are streamed on the internet and excerpted on YouTube or Hulu. Netflix and most cable TV providers deliver movies and TV shows on demand; podcasts and personal video recorders (such as TiVo) allow people to watch shows according to their schedules."[9]

For some time now, choice making has been the most studied form of agency. As we'll see in the pages to follow, legions of researchers in industry and academe have built an extensive literature on media choice. In almost all instances, researchers see people as being purposeful in their choices. As Herbert Simon noted, "Everyone agrees that people have reasons for what they do. They have motivations, and they use reason (well or badly) to respond to these motivations and reach their goals."[10] The work on media choice is relevant here because it helps us understand what's likely to attract public attention or sustain audience loyalties.

But newer media technologies don't just offer more choices, they now make it easy for people to create and share media. These newer expressions of agency are made possible by the "interoperability" of digital media. Researchers at Harvard argue, "the most fundamental shift made possible by interoperable technologies is the way they enable us to be not just passive consumers information but also active *creators* and reusers of content in a public networked environment. Digital technologies, rendered interoperable across platforms, empower consumers in unprecedented ways to express themselves through content creation and sharing."[11]

Creation and sharing are, of course, rather different activities. Most people who make media end up sharing it, whether it's uploading a video to YouTube, sending a picture to Instagram, or posting their thoughts on a blog. But we often share media we don't create, such as "retweeting" a message or passing along a link to something of particular interest. For the purposes of this book, I'll deal with media creation in chapter 3, "The Media." Sharing, however, is the province of all media users, whether they're creators on not.

As you might imagine, how and why people share is the subject of considerable interest in industry and academe, but it's a new enough phenomenon that we are only beginning to appreciate the ways in which people use the digital resources that make sharing possible. Social networks, powered by digital media, clearly play a role. But to fully understand how those networks operate, we need to move to a higher level of analysis and consider "mass" behavior. Aggregating users, in turn, creates another way of seeing users and constitutes a powerful new form of agency.

Broadly speaking, there are two ways to see users en masse. The older, more traditional approach is to conceive of people as members of a mass audience. That is, people are seen as a collection of individuals dispersed in space who have a common object of attention. Sometimes, those audiences are enormous. The 2013 Super Bowl, for example, attracted more than one hundred million viewers.[12] The term *mass* has a great many unflattering connotations, including visions of passive, undiscriminating couch potatoes or easily manipulated simpletons.[13] But none of these is inherent to its use as an analytical construct. A mass is simply a collection of people who are anonymous to one another and act independently.[14] The newer way to see users is as members of one or more networks who are aware of each other and may affect each other's behaviors.[15] Today's audiences are often a blend of the two.[16]

Either way, these can be large, complicated systems that have their own dynamics. Their constituent members and the structures that surround them interact in ways that aren't easily understood by looking at individual predispositions. Although media structures can certainly enable purposeful forms of social action,[17] they also can open the door for many unintended forms of mass behavior such as audience flows, herding, and information cascades. As a rule, users don't deliberately orchestrate these phenomena. But even if users are oblivious to mass behaviors, they can and do trigger institutional responses.

The agency users achieve through aggregation is a curious thing. It requires that many people act *and* that they be seen, usually through measurement and data gathering. And it operates even if the users themselves don't know it's happening. But it is a powerful expression of agency nonetheless. As a researcher at the University of Amsterdam pointed out, "the user's role as a data provider is infinitely more important than his role as a content provider."[18] This is so because data enable institutions to see users and calibrate their responses. Although data can help institutions to monetize or control users, it's also the mechanism through which audiences cause the media to change. As we'll see in chapter 3, the media track audience behaviors, often in real time, to adjust production practices, redesign websites, cancel unpopular offerings, and clone successes. In the marketplace of attention, this may be the most consequential form of agency.

Media Choice

As I noted, there's a large body of work on media choice done by people in industry and a variety of academic disciplines. As a rule, researchers have assumed that users will select what they like and avoid what they don't like. That approach to explaining choice has grown even more appealing now that users are empowered by an endless supply of anywhere anytime media.

Analysts often expect preferences to show up as an appetite for particular genres. Marketing researchers have spent years searching for "user-defined" program types that might signal audience loyalties. But other predispositions can be at work as well. People seem to prefer supportive, like-minded speech and dislike messages that challenge their beliefs. Psychologists and political scientists have a long tradition of studying the resulting patterns of "selective exposure." Or it might be that people choose media because they find it useful or gratifying or a marker of their social identity. The following sections provide brief summaries intended to give you a taste of the major research traditions that speak to media choice. Despite some differences, we'll see that each portrays users as making purposeful—often rational—media choices.

Rational Choice

Rational choice is a fundamental concept in conventional economics. But it has a very particular meaning that's not always clear to noneconomists. True rational choice is founded on three assumptions. First, each individual has settled preferences and knows how his or her choices will contribute to personal well-being or "utility." The pursuit of the pleasurable outcomes is sometimes called "hedonic utility."[19] Second, there is one objective reality that decision makers fully and accurately perceive. Third, decision makers have unlimited computational power to determine which of the available choices will best maximize their utility. Dan Ariely, a well-known behavioral economist, put it this way: "In conventional economics, the assumption that we are all rational implies that, in everyday life, we compute the value of all the options we face and then follow the best possible path of action."[20]

Economists have applied this model of choice making to audience behavior. In 1952, Peter Steiner published a classic piece on the workability of competition in radio. His purpose was to test whether monopoly or competition would maximize overall listener satisfaction. To do the analysis, Steiner made a number of assumptions about how program choices were made. Subsequent work of this sort has focused on television. All such efforts are broadly referred to as "traditional models of program choice"[21] and all adopt a rational choice model of behavior. They assume viewers have distinct program type preferences and that, in an advertiser-supported system, programs are a "free good." Therefore, program preferences determine program choices, at least among the available offerings. Although these models are often rather abstract, they're not idle academic exercises. During the 1970s and 1980s this way of thinking provided much of the intellectual justification US policy makers needed for deregulating broadcasting.[22]

Not all theories of media choice adhere to the strict assumptions of "rational choice," but all put a premium on the ability of psychological predispositions (e.g., preferences, tastes, needs, and attitudes) to explain our exposure to media. Basically, they assume that users have pre-existing preferences that drive their choices. And most assume that users can readily determine which media choices will achieve the desired outcomes.[23]

Unfortunately for social scientists, the link between preference and choice is not as tidy as most theorists assume. People's preferences are often "constructed" in response to various contingencies.[24] Their appetite for different types of media might vary with their moods, their social circumstances, or what they just consumed. After all, how much "binge viewing" can one person do? And even if users do have stable likes and dislikes, in a world of unlimited, on-demand options, people may simply be unaware that something they would really like is available and better than what they're currently using. As we'll see in the section on the "user's dilemma" people typically operate under conditions of "bounded rationality." They may try to realize their preferences, but will often fall short.

Genre Preferences

Users typically categorize media, whether it's music, films, or television programs, into genres. These categories help people make sense of their options and guide their choices.[25] Media producers and academics often assume that people have consistent likes and dislikes for genres, and that those preferences explain their choices. The question is which genres actually evoke systematic likes and dislikes. Knowing the answer could inform programming decisions, advertising campaigns, and theories of media choice.

Historically, most of the research on genre preferences has been done in advertising, marketing, and economics. And most of that has focused on television. Economic models of choice suggest that people who like one program of a type will watch other programs of that type. Conversely, viewers who dislike a program type will systematically avoid it. If that's true, it should be possible to reveal those preferences by analyzing program choices. Such loyalties would constitute "user-defined" genres.

Since the 1960s, researchers, employing very sophisticated statistical techniques, have tried to find which categories of programs systematically attracted—or repelled—different segments of the population.[26] But program type loyalties haven't been nearly as pronounced as the theory would have us believe. Indeed, one classic text on audiences concluded that "there is no special tendency across the population for people who watch one programme of a given type also to watch others of the same type."[27]

Of course, the media environment has changed since the 1970s. With abundant choice, people might do a better job of finding or avoiding certain types of content. In fact, news viewing now exhibits the double-edged nature of program type loyalty. In the digital media environment, where news and entertainment are constantly available, those with a preference for news can and sometimes do consume large amounts. Conversely, those with no appetite for news can avoid it in favor of entertainment. This kind of program type loyalty operates across media platforms and is evident in many countries.[28]

More finely tuned genre preferences, however, have been difficult to detect. Conventional, commonsense genres do bear some relationship to user loyalty. People who watch one crime drama tend to watch others. People who choose one situation comedy tend to choose others. Scheduling programs of the same type, back-to-back, on the same network does seem to increase audience flow.[29] But these aren't particularly powerful effects that suggest people have strong genre loyalties.

Social media users also show some evidence of genre preferences. For example, it appears that an interest in celebrity and entertainment news drives Twitter use among young adults.[30] Although that same study showed that an interest in other types of news—local, national, and international—was unrelated to Twitter adoption.

There are many reasons why genre preferences might not be evident in actual program choices,[31] but two are relevant here. First, rather than wanting a steady diet of a preferred type, people may actually like variety in their diets. Some time ago, marketing researchers speculated that people have "a need for a range of different program types...."[32] If that's true, people might choose the best representative from each of several genres. In which case, perceptions of quality could trump a mild affinity for a particular genre.

Second, it appears that people's likes aren't as strongly tied to genres as their dislikes. That is, although our likes might span many genres, we're apt to have certain genres we actively dislike and avoid. So, the appearance of loyalties results less from fans consistently seeking out a preferred type and more from a group of users who systematically avoid a genre.[33] You can test this on yourself. Think of the programs or the music you like. Chances are it's a varied collection. Now think of what you don't like. Most people conceptualize their dislikes in terms of genres. For example, my wife systematically avoids "scary movies," a genre she can spot almost instantly. If a subset of the population shares her aversion, they make everyone else look like tepid fans. Even in a media environment with something for everyone, avoidance still helps to explain patterns of choice.[34]

Tastes

Sociologists take a somewhat different tack on the consumption of culture, one that emphasizes the role of taste. The traditional view has been to think of cultural products arranged in a hierarchy from highbrow (e.g., opera, theater, classical music, etc.) to lowbrow (e.g., country music, heavy metal, soap operas, etc.). A person's taste for these products is associated with their social class, which is a result of their upbringing, education, and occupation. People with lots of "cultural capital" consume highbrow culture that, in turn, distinguishes them as a member of their class.[35] So, for example, a person might listen to Béla Bartók because she appreciates his skill as a composer and because it demonstrates her good taste and breeding.

The value judgments implied by this cultural hierarchy aren't really essential to explaining choice. In fact, many academics consider them passé and find merit in all forms of culture, including television. Nonetheless, they often see media falling into "taste cultures" that are consumed by the relevant "taste publics."[36] This way of thinking is not worlds apart from the expectation that people will consistently prefer some genres and not others.

Indeed, much of the research on how people express their tastes has examined their appetite for different genres of music. Because music spans so many taste cultures—from classical and opera to hip-hop and heavy metal—sociologists view it as a useful arena in which to analyze cultural consumption. The traditional expectation would be that people of a certain class will like genres only from "their" part of the cultural hierarchy. But another possibility, suggested by Richard Peterson, is that people who have lots of cultural capital are becoming "cultural omnivores," liking not only highbrow genres but also popular genres as well.[37] In the wake of Peterson's argument, many studies have tested or critiqued the omnivore hypothesis. Generally the findings suggest that, at least in Western nations, there are substantial numbers of omnivores who are more tolerant of cultural differences and inclined to like many genres.[38]

It's worth noting that these studies typically ask people how much they like standard music genres. In doing so, they often assume that people (1) will recognize each genre, (2) have clear, unequivocal judgments about each genre, and (3) actually listen to what they say they like. So these are not "user-defined" genres that are revealed by analyzing discrete song choices. Still, the findings bear two interesting similarities to those on genre preferences. First, the existence of cultural omnivores is consistent with the speculation that media users, rather than being devotees of a single genre, like having variety in their diets. Second, dislikes are more powerfully aligned with genres than are likes. That is, many people will consume across genres, but they're likely to have entire categories they avoid. One study found that even omnivores can have aversions to entire genres, such as "heavy metal."[39] So it seems that "people's musical tastes are somewhat less divided when they talk about particular musical works, whereas talking about musical genres encourages stereotyping."[40]

Uses and Gratifications

One of the most popular theories of media use in communications has been dubbed the "uses and gratifications" paradigm.[41] Instead of focusing on genre preferences or tastes to explain choice, this approach concentrates on people's needs. As described by its founders, uses and gratifications (U&G) is "concerned with (1) the social and psychological origins of (2) needs, which generate (3) expectations of (4) mass media or other sources, which lead to (5) differential patterns of media exposure (or engagement in other activities), resulting in (6) need gratifications and (7) other consequences, perhaps mostly unintended ones."[42] U&G assumes that users are aware of their needs, evaluate which media will best gratify those needs, and then choose accordingly. In that sense, U&G researchers make many of the same assumptions about choice that traditional economists do.

In practice, much of the empirical work on U&G has boiled down to cataloging the relevant needs or "gratifications sought" and assessing the extent to which media use succeeds in delivering "gratifications obtained." The number of gratifications sought varies from study to study and medium to medium. In television, one categorization scheme identified nine motives for watching: relaxation, companionship, habit, to pass time, entertainment, social interaction, information, arousal, and escape.[43] Simplifying things a bit, another frequently cited study described two basic motives: ritualistic and instrumental. Ritualistic uses included habitual, nonselective TV viewing, and instrumental uses included goal-directed choices of specific media content.[44] This way of explaining media use has been extended to online media, producing much the same insights.[45]

Two findings of U&G research are particularly germane to our discussion of media choice. First, no matter the number of motivations, there's general agreement that gratifications sought can vary from person to person and, within any individual user, they can vary over time. A person might seek entertainment and escape at one moment and information the next. Second, even if we assume people are clear about the gratifications they seek, they aren't always good about choosing the media that meet those needs. There's often a gap between gratifications sought and obtained. It could be that people aren't good at assessing which media choices (e.g.,

TV programs or websites) will deliver what they seek. In fact, they sometimes obtain "negative" gratifications. It could also be that, despite the
assumptions of the paradigm, people aren't completely clear about what
they want. As one study concluded, "we must call into question how active,
or in control, viewers are in the process of trying to fulfill various social
and psychological needs if they are unable to filter out unintended effects
of the programming."[46]

Selective Exposure

The idea of "selective exposure" embodies the conventional wisdom that,
given a choice, people will "see what they want to see." In the 1950s, with
the rise of theories such as "cognitive dissonance," this intuitively appealing notion gained academic credibility.[47] People were expected to select
media messages that supported their beliefs and, conversely, to avoid contradictory, dissonance-producing messages. Selective exposure has since
become something of a catch-all label that includes work on a variety of
psychological factors that might affect media choices, including perceived
utility, mood states, and hedonism. Although these theories see media use
as purposeful, most aren't wed to the assumptions of "rational choice."
For instance, people might selectively expose themselves to media without
being consciously aware of what motivates that behavior.

Theories of selective exposure have been a particularly popular way to
explain people's choice of information. By the 1960s, selective exposure
to information was "one of the most widely accepted principles in sociology and social psychology."[48] Although there are different reasons why
people might select like-minded messages, reducing cognitive dissonance
has been the most common explanation.[49] Nevertheless, in a well-known
critique of the research on selective exposure, Sears and Freedman found
little compelling evidence of a preference for supportive information. In
the wake of their analysis, academic interest in selective exposure briefly
waned. But by the 1980s, as new media began to empower users with more
choices, work on selective exposure enjoyed a renaissance.[50]

An area of research that's received considerable attention is the extent
to which political ideology drives the consumption of news. The question
is, do conservatives consume only conservative news outlets and liberals
consume only liberal news outlets? The theory of cognitive dissonance

suggests that they will. As well-known scholars at the University of Pennsylvania have described it,

> audiences enter the political arena with existing attitudes and preferences. Once there, they are more likely than not to seek out information that is compatible with these beliefs and to shun data that challenge them. When confronted with discomforting information, humans readily find ways to reject it. Among other moves, they (and we) apply tests of evidence to it that all but ensure rejection. By contrast, information that shores up existing attitudes is welcomed uncritically. In short, selective exposure, selective perception, and selective retention pervade the process by which we make sense of who we are as political creatures.[51]

If that's the case, selective exposure could help polarize the public along ideological lines. In the United States, that kind of phenomenon has been nicknamed the "red media–blue media" divide. But, as was the case with the research that Sears and Freedman reviewed, the evidence for ideologically motivated selective exposure is far from overwhelming. Many studies find that people are drawn to news that reinforces their political inclinations.[52] But that doesn't necessarily mean that they avoid news that challenges their beliefs.[53] Moreover, many studies that support the selective exposure hypothesis are based on experiments that force choices under unnatural circumstances or surveys that measure exposure with self-reports of media use.[54] The latter are problematic because people often misreport their exposure to news.[55] As we'll see in chapter 5, research using more accurate measures of media use (e.g., meters) finds surprisingly modest red-blue polarization in news consumption.[56] Nonetheless, the nature and consequences of selective exposure to news and political information are much debated in communications and political science.[57]

Selective exposure to information isn't driven exclusively by dissonance reduction. It's possible people simply choose media messages that are useful. Another strain of research on selective exposure finds that the perceived utility of information can affect choices and, in some instances, override dissonance reduction.[58] For example, patients might seek out troubling information about their disease or conservatives might choose to learn more about the views of a newly elected liberal.

Models of selective exposure have also been used to explain people's choices in entertainment. Some conceive of human beings as hedonistic creatures who seek pleasure and avoid pain.[59] One outgrowth of that approach is to understand media choices as an exercise in "mood management." That is, people choose media to alter or perpetuate their moods, even if they're unaware of those motivations. For instance, experiments demonstrate that subjects who are stressed tend to select calming programs or music.[60] Media choices can induce more pleasurable mood states in much the same way that selecting supportive messages can reduce cognitive dissonance.

Similar to U&G, research on selective exposure covers a wide range of psychological motives for media use. Some of these, such as political beliefs, might be relatively stable from one day to the next. Others, such as a need for escape or bad moods, could be more fleeting and difficult to harness as predictors of real-world media use.[61] And similar to U&G, it seems that people aren't good at matching their motives—conscious or not—with their choices. As one writer concluded, there's a "growing body of research suggesting that individuals are often not particularly adept at identifying their moods and the causes of their moods, nor are they particularly effective at managing their moods in ways that are desired."[62]

One area in which the findings on selective exposure differ somewhat from those on genre preferences and tastes is in the nature and power of avoidance. Although the theory of cognitive dissonance suggests that people will actively avoid unpleasant, dissonance-producing content, the evidence isn't compelling. When it comes to information at least, people do have some tolerance for hearing contradictory messages.[63] It may be that with this particular genre, there is some utility in knowing what the "other side" is saying, if for no other reason than it helps a person sharpen his or her own arguments or rebut his or her opponents. Although people probably recognize news outlets as conservative or liberal, most don't completely exclude a distasteful subgenre from their diet.[64]

The User's Dilemma

Thus far, we've seen that people have different motives for media use and that they act on these, consciously or not, to achieve different purposes. We've also learned that people aren't always very good at matching their motives with media choices. Songs or programs in a preferred genre are missed, gratifications sought aren't obtained, and moods go unmanaged.

The abundance of the digital media environment isn't making the user's job any easier. In this section, we'll consider how users cope with the dilemma of knowing what to choose. The strategies that they employ go a long way toward explaining what they actually consume. But to set the context, we return briefly to the idea of bounded rationality.

Bounded Rationality

Rational choice requires that people know all their options and are capable of calculating which choices will maximize their well-being. Although this is a common way to assess or explain behavior, when it comes to media use it's unrealistic. People rarely have complete knowledge of their options or the consequences of their actions. More typically, they assess a few salient factors, rely on a few rules of thumb, and make the best decision they can. These conditions of choice making are referred to as bounded rationality.[65] And they certainly characterize how people choose media.

The digital media environment complicates rational choice in two ways. The first is a function of its sheer abundance. In chapter 1, we noted the number of options that confront the typical user. No one could be expected to have complete knowledge of all of their choices. Although users do a number of things to inform themselves (e.g., using guides or recommender systems), these take time and never provide a complete, unbiased account of everything that's available. Second, media are typically "experience goods."[66] It's difficult to know whether any given offering will deliver the hoped-for gratifications until you've experienced it. Seeing a promo, reading a review, or getting a recommendation from a friend might help, but you can't be sure how you'll respond to something new until you've seen it. And even if you're familiar with a particular artist or news personality or television series, you never quite know how satisfying the next encounter will be. People might eagerly watch their favorite TV show only to realize that the new episode was a dud. In the face of these uncertainties, people use a variety of techniques to do the best they can. As Herbert Simon put it, they don't maximize, they "satisfice."[67]

Repertoires

One technique many people use to manage their choices is to limit the number of places they look for content. They watch a handful of TV channels, rely on a limited number of apps and follow a few friends or celebrities on social media. These are what researchers call media "repertoires."[68] They are small subsets of the available options that people use time and again. They simplify search and decision making. Presumably, outlets make their way into a person's repertoire because they've been fruitful in the past.

In the United States, television viewers typically watch fewer than twenty channels in a week, even if hundreds are available.[69] This pattern holds in other countries as well.[70] Repertoires also span different media platforms.[71] Some tilt more heavily toward news, others toward entertainment. Such repertoires are often associated with certain demographic traits, such as age and education. The most popular outlets will, by definition, be included in many repertoires, but beyond that each person's favorites can be rather idiosyncratic. If something falls outside a person's repertoire, it could have trouble gaining his or her attention.

Heuristics

People also use rules of thumb or "heuristics" when they choose media. These help them make judgments about the importance, credibility, quality, or type of media they're considering. Heuristics allow users to make quick, reasonably satisfactory choices. Many decision-making rules have been identified, and people may use more than one as they make choices. Two categories of heuristics are common.[72] One type depends on user expectations; the other depends on evidence of social confirmation.

People have certain expectations about the attributes different media products or services should have. These provide clues about quality, credibility, and genre. For example, Internet users quickly assess the quality of a newly encountered website. If it's poorly constructed (e.g., appearance, functionality, misspellings, etc.) or if it seems intent on manipulating its visitors (e.g., serving unwanted ads or requesting information), it's regarded with suspicion.[73] If a news outlet has a point of view or stories that rub users the wrong way, they'll often judge it to be less credible or "hostile."[74] People are also quick to judge genres. Most of us don't need to hear more than a bar or two of music to know if it's rap, country, or classical. People sort by genres and generally avoid ones they don't like or can't identify. Media that don't possess the attributes expected of a particular genre or that span genres often have trouble finding an audience.[75]

In addition to assessing the attributes of media, users rely on heuristics that connote popularity or social approval. The simplest is the "recognition heuristic." People typically assume that options they recognize are of higher quality than those they don't. The reasoning is that recognizability suggests popularity and popularity suggests quality.[76] This is similar to the "reputation heuristic" in which people assume recognizable names or brands have earned a reputation for quality and are motivated to maintain that reputation.[77] Small wonder that brands like Disney and Apple are so valuable and jealously protected.

An even stronger form of social approval is evident in the "endorsement heuristic."[78] As we'll see in the next section, other people's recommendations can be particularly powerful. Recommendations come in many forms. Traditionally people have turned to reviews and expert opinions. But they also rely on testimonials and ratings from fellow users, especially if no other indicators are available. Researchers have noted that "when there are no objective standards by which to evaluate their options and choices, people turn to others—especially those similar to them—to make sure they are on the right track."[79]

None of these heuristics is perfect. A seminal work on the subject cautioned that heuristics could result in seriously flawed or biased decisions.[80] Still people use them. They follow links, search program guides, or rely on repertoires to learn what's available. They make quick judgments about what they would like, what they should know, and what's to be believed. They satisfice. But the digital media environment is changing the old way of doing things. On the one hand, there's simply too much to cope with. On the other hand, people are relying on social networks and recommender systems as never before.

The Role of Social Networks

Social networks have long affected the media that people encounter. Media use is often a social activity. People go to movies together and, even when many TV sets are available, they often watch in groups. Increasingly, people extend those viewing groups to include virtual communities that "check in" when a program begins or tweet away as the action unfolds. If they're not in the audience themselves, they might still pass along links or recommend media to others. The social aspects of media use serve any number of purposes. They help regulate activities and interactions within homes.[81] They provide the grist for "water-cooler" conversations.[82] And they provide occasions for people to express their identities, manage friendships, and build social capital.[83]

Many of these functions characterized good old-fashioned, face-to-face networks and have been studied for some time.[84] Others, if not entirely new, have been changed or expanded with the advent of digital media.[85] Some operate at the level of interpersonal communication, but other social activities scale up in ways that dramatically affect how audiences take shape. It is the latter that are of concern here. Two features of social networks are particularly useful in understanding public attention: the presence of opinion leaders and the nature of social ties.

Opinion Leaders

We all belong to many groups. These include friends and families, religious and civic organizations, colleagues at school and work, and various "affinity groups" (e.g., fans or hobbyists). Some groups are enduring and well defined. Other groups can be more fleeting and permeable, particularly in a networked society.[86] Either way, they tend to be composed of people who are similar on at least one dimension, whether it's demographic similarities or shared interests and values. Groups generally demonstrate the old adage that "birds of a feather flock together," or what sociologists call "homophily."[87] And they often have "opinion leaders."

Opinion leaders, or "influentials," don't occupy an official position. Their identities vary from group to group and topic to topic. They tend to be in touch with the relevant media and stay relatively well informed about their supposed area of expertise—whether it's fashion or politics. Their opinions are respected, and so they're in a position to influence other group members.

In the 1940s, studies on voting and product preferences laid the ground work for an important book on media effects called *Personal Influence*.[88] It described what's called the "two-step flow" of mass communication. Rather than being directly affected by media messages, people often learned of things through opinion leaders in their social networks. These influentials would selectively share media within the group, sometimes with editorial comment. The two-step flow of communication shaped people's media diet, reinforced group norms, and made it difficult for media alone to change people's beliefs or actions. Even today, this model of opinion leadership seems to operate in social media.[89]

Social Ties

An opinion leader can be thought of as one point, or node, in a larger network of people who have social ties. In one of the most widely cited articles in the social sciences, Mark Granovetter argued that it was useful to draw a distinction among ties based on their strength.[90] Strong ties were characterized by frequent communication, intimacy, and reciprocity. These were typical of tightly knit "primary" groups, such as families and close friends, who are relatively homophilous. Weak ties involved more casual, often far-flung acquaintances. These individuals might well be more socially distant than primary group members.

Many network analysts believe that weak ties are particularly helpful in spreading novel information.[91] Because you have strong ties with your close friends, you tend to know what they know. Weak ties, which bridge disparate individuals and groups, can therefore be a valuable source of new information—such as finding out about a job. As a result, weak ties are important in spreading what some have called "simple contagions,"[92] where one exposure is enough to inform or create awareness.

Other analysts point out that tie strength is relevant to more than simply spreading new information. People sometimes pass along or "retweet" things that are familiar to group members. This seems to be an expression of solidarity or "social bonding." As Nicholas Harrigan and his colleagues have noted, "A classic case of social contagion as social bonding is 'liking' or 'sharing' on Facebook. Within Facebook, there is a hierarchy of positive responses to a wall post: a 'like,' and 'comment,' and a 'share.' Reposting a friend's post on one's wall ... is one of the highest compliments in Facebook etiquette and therefore a strong form of social bonding."[93] In this instance, strong ties might produce a kind of "echo chamber." Generally, strong ties seem to promote "complex contagions" that can affect people's beliefs and behaviors, not just what they know.[94] In any event, tie strength affects how information moves around social networks and the effect that information is likely to have.

Social Media

Face-to-face interactions among group members and opinion leaders still influence what media people encounter. But the growth of social media has changed the scope and quality of social interactions, and some of these activities have a profound effect on public attention. The most important media in this context are social networks, blogs, and search engines.

Facebook has roughly one billion users worldwide. Other social networks and micro-blogging sites, such as Twitter and Tumblr, have also gained traction. In the United States, the use of social networks and blogs accounted for almost a quarter of the time people spent on the Internet.[95] These platforms can and do support conventional groups. In fact, the overwhelming majority of social media use seems to be in support of maintaining relations with friends and family and is a type of interpersonal communication.[96] But these platforms also create far-flung networks that introduce new sources of influence.

Twitter users, for example, often pass along URLs that direct other users to media content. The vast majority of people on Twitter are "ordinary users," and among these only a small percentage of people actively direct others to media. But there is an even smaller group of tweeters, who constitute a new "elite" class of opinion leaders.[97] These include celebrities (e.g., Barack Obama, Lady Gaga), organizations (e.g., Amnesty International, Whole Foods), blogs (e.g., Mashable, Gizmodo), and the mainstream media themselves (CNN, *New York Times*). These elites constitute only 0.05 percent of Twitter users, but attract about half of all the attention. All in all, Twitter users get roughly half of their media referrals via intermediaries—elite or otherwise—and many are heavily dependent on two-step flows for the media they encounter.[98]

Search engines and other recommendation systems are another way for users to find media. Taken together, search engines and portals account for a little less than 10 percent of the time people spend on the Internet, although their total number of visitors often exceeds social networking sites.[99] This isn't surprising because search engines are designed to send people on their way, whereas social networking sites are often "sticky." As the *New York Times* reported, at Facebook the "goal is to draw more and more people to the site and keep them there longer."[100]

People search for all kinds of things. Often they know where they want to go and use search to find the right URL (e.g., the address for YouTube or Amazon). Sometimes they're looking for information. Sometimes they just want to pass time. But according to one study, almost a third of all Google searches were concentrated on popular culture (e.g., celebrities, TV shows, popular music) or contemporary events (e.g., news sites).[101]

Two features of social media distinguish them from more conventional social networks. First, they extend the notion of group membership far beyond the bounds of traditional, face-to-face acquaintances. The new digital groups are still homophilous, but they can now include thousands of people who have never met. Second, a user's ability to make sense of these groups often depends on reducing mountains of social data into a recommendation. Media outlets commonly direct users to the most-read story, the most-viewed video, or the most-downloaded song. Google deciphers the architecture of hyperlinks to rank recommendations. Amazon depends on matching a person's previous selections to other "people like you." Similarly, social TV guides, many of which are mobile apps, can filter by genre and suggest what's popular with your "friends."[102] All of these can be useful, even indispensable, "endorsement heuristics." They can certainly encourage herding and bandwagon effects.[103] And as we'll see in the chapter on media measures (chapter 4), none is without its own biases.

Going Viral

One of the more striking things about social networks is their ability to bring obscure stories or images to widespread public attention. These often spread through social media with great speed. The phenomenon is variously described as a cascade, contagion, burst, spread, or just "going viral."[104] If one person retweets a message or shares a link within his or her social network, and each of those individuals does the same, pretty soon almost everyone will get the message. Because the average Facebook user can reach 150,000 friends-of-friends,[105] this is a potentially powerful and inexpensive way to build public attention. But the fact is most things don't spread like a contagion. So why do some things go viral and can that process be controlled?

Those questions are the subject of ongoing research—and considerable debate.[106] We've seen that many factors can play some part in promoting contagions. These include the role of opinion leaders, the structure of social networks, the ability to see what other users are doing, and perhaps the nature of the media being shared. I'll briefly summarize what we know about these factors, leaving a discussion of recommender systems for chapter 4 on media measures.

The existence of opinion leaders has led some to suggest that a few "special people" could be identified and recruited to trigger social contagions.[107] As Duncan Watts has noted, that idea is "like catnip to marketers and businessmen and community organizers and just about anyone else in the business of shaping or manipulating people."[108] Elite influentials have some power to promote a message. A recommendation from Oprah or some other celebrity can certainly affect what people pay attention to. However, in these cases, it's difficult to disentangle effects of opinion leadership from the influencer's visibility in more traditional mass media. Overall, there is a weak correlation between a person's popularity and his or her ability to actually influence others.[109] Among ordinary people, opinion leaders are only slightly better at exercising influence and triggering cascades than anyone else.[110] But no one seems to do it with any regularity. Watts has reported that the vast majority of attempted cascades—over 98 percent—didn't spread.[111] In fact, Henry Jenkins and his colleagues flatly declare that "the influencer is one of the major myths of the Web 2.0 world."[112]

But focusing on opinion leaders and the structure of social networks doesn't tell us how the quality of the message itself affects the likelihood of a cascade. Perhaps some things are destined to spread. If we knew the recipe, we might be able to orchestrate cascades. There are many possible ingredients. The utility of a message or the credibility of its source could promote its popularity.[113] The openness or "producerly" quality of a text might encourage its spread.[114] Some think that novel items are more likely to go viral, although that's not always the case.[115] Or it could be that some things are just so bizarre or disgusting or endearing that they beg to be shared. To the extent that we have answers, it seems that affect-laden content, especially awe-inspiring, anxiety-producing, and anger-provoking stories, have a somewhat greater chance of spreading than others.[116] But in the end, social contagions remain a puzzle. Although it's certain that some things will go viral, our ability to predict what they will be, let alone manage the process, is limited.

The Structures of Everyday Life

Everything we've seen thus far portrays users as people possessed of considerable agency. They are free to act on their preferences and impulses, whether they are fully cognizant of them or not. They live in a world of anywhere, anytime media. And although bounded rationality might make it hard for them to achieve optimal results, their newly enhanced social networks make it easier than ever to exploit the resources that surround them. Academics commonly conclude that "today, we take it as given that people are purposive and active in their selection of media and content."[117] This vision of free-wheeling agents can sometimes cause us to forget just how deeply media use is embedded in the structures of everyday life.

These structures are often so mundane, so taken-for-granted, that we scarcely notice them. Yet they shape media consumption in profound and often predictable ways. Certainly no account of users would be complete without them. Sociologists have noted that structural factors, such as socio-economic status, can affect media use in a variety of ways.[118] For instance, even in an era when so many media are "free" for the taking,[119] having the resources to pay for subscriptions or services or having the skills to find what you want makes a difference.

Other structures are wed to the activities that fill people's lives. When people work or go to school affects how and when they use media. Still other structures are wed to culture. Where people live, the languages they speak, and the norms of their culture all shape their use media. As we've noted, people aren't prisoners of these structures, but they often reproduce them in their day-to-day actions. Habitual behavior—or what Anthony Giddens called the "recursive" organization of human activity—is a staple of social life and a powerful determinant of audience formation.[120]

When and where people are available to use media is one such habit. Audience availability is evident in seasonal patterns of media use. Television audiences typically peak during the coldest winter months when people are indoors and ebb during the summer when they're outside. In fact, television viewing has long been thought of as a residual category of leisure activity.[121] Moviegoing is highest during vacations. In the United States, attendance peaks during the winter holidays and again in summer. These are typically the times when studios release films that they hope will be blockbusters.[122]

Perhaps the most obvious impact of availability can be seen in the ebb and flow of audiences throughout the day. Radio listenership is highest when people commute to and from work. Television audiences build throughout the evening as people come home and turn on the set. These daily patterns aren't inviolable. Digital media are beginning to break down the barriers between work and play.[123] Still, predictable daily fluctuations happen everywhere in the modern world, with variations that reflect each society. Koreans, for example, tend to work late, delaying the peak of "prime time." As a rule, the media know what's coming and plan ahead.[124]

Stable patterns of use are evident across all media platforms, even those that are "on demand."[125] In 2008, the industry commissioned an unusual study in which researchers actually followed Americans throughout an entire day, noting in great detail which media they used and the circumstances that surrounded that use. The overall pattern of results is seen in figure 2.1. Television viewing accounted for over 60 percent of media use in the evening. Radio, the lion's share of "any audio," peaked during morning "drive time" and noon. Computer use, the so-called second screen, was highest during the work day. Overall, the various platforms that are represented here clustered nicely into user-defined "repertoires" that clearly reflected people at work, on the go, or at home engaged in leisure activities.[126]

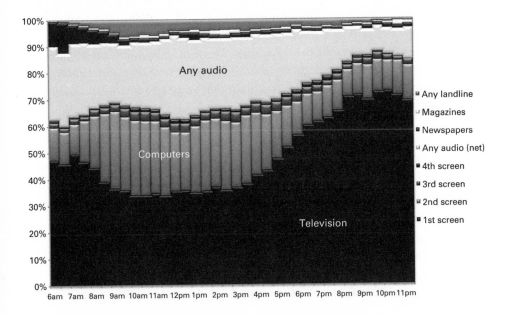

Figure 2.1
Hourly Variation in Media Use.
Source: Adapted from the Council for Research Excellence (CRE). Copyrighted information of The Nielsen Company, licensed for use herein.

The tightly knit relationship between television schedules and the rhythms of daily life caused one veteran BBC researcher to assess the prospects for on-demand media this way: "So, for all the ease time-shifting, the way our children (bless them) ignore schedules, and the rise of box-sets, the schedule is here to stay. It's television's killer app, which is ignored at its peril. The internet seems to struggle with time: apart from newness, and nowness, it lacks a temporal context."[127]

But patterns of work and play aren't the only structures that shape media use. Something as simple as where people live can affect what they attend to. Mark Zuckerberg, the billionaire founder of Facebook, said, "A squirrel dying in front of your house may be more relevant to your interests right now than people dying in Africa."[128] This rather blunt assessment is illustrative of a larger phenomenon called the "first law of geography," which stipulates that "everything is related to everything else, but near things are more related than distant things."[129]

Geographic proximity does seem to focus people's attention. Across nations, *Wikipedia* entries that have geographic tags are much more likely to be linked if they are in close proximity to one another, regardless of language.[130] Across large countries with distinct market areas (such as the United States and China), residents make use of local media outlets and are far more aware of what's going on in their hometown, even if the rest of the country is oblivious.[131] It seems likely that as mobile devices track and report user locations, a kind of hyperlocal targeting of messages will be possible. Perhaps a special at the corner restaurant or a home burglary—or a dead squirrel—will command the attention of a neighborhood.

Geographic proximity is often, though not always, confounded with "cultural proximity."[132] People who speak a particular language are quite likely to use and share media in that language. Such media often adhere to other cultural norms or expectations as well. Language, at any rate, has segregated audiences from the start.[133] Given the option, people will choose media in their preferred language and systematically avoid almost everything else. In a country such as the United States, where Spanish language media have become widely available, people who speak only Spanish choose mostly Spanish-language programming.[134] On a global scale, people turn to websites in their preferred language. The fact that other sites, in other languages, might offer new information or different perspectives on old information may never enter their minds.[135] These loyalties are unsurprising, but in a multicultural world they have the potential to create closely knit social networks and enclaves of media users.

The structures of everyday life have a profound effect on how people use media. They are durable and often unobtrusive. Unlike people's moods or the gratifications they seek, unlike their variable, not-so-well informed preferences, social structures persist. Where people live and work and the language they speak operate as constants. They create stable environments that encourage certain types of media use and discourage others. And yet, people scarcely think about how these environments affect what comes to their attention—and what does not.

The Puzzle of Preferences

There's no doubt that digital media offer a great many things that attract our attention. We have a seemingly endless supply from which to choose. Social media give us the tools to create and share ever more things with our friends and family. But not all of these activities scale up to meaningful patterns of public attention. Our challenge is to figure out what causes users to coalesce into audiences. Why do some media become popular, creating common knowledge and a shared cultural currency? What factors might contribute to enduring audience loyalties and will these enrich or divide us?

In many quarters, the answers are founded in user preferences. In a world of mostly free, anywhere, anytime media, it would seem that knowing people's predispositions would be a surefire way to explain what they see and hear. There's no doubt that understanding people's preferences can be helpful in explaining their media use—that's why we plowed through all those academic theories of media choice. But relying on preferences as the cornerstone of our strategy for explaining audience behavior only gets us so far. Preferences are a puzzle and offer a less stable foundation on which to build than is widely assumed.

First, from one moment to the next, our media preferences are often unclear and variable. A great many people are "omnivorous," although each person probably has a few aversions. For many people that includes an aversion to hard news. But among all the things we might like, it's difficult to know at any point in time what a person will choose. Our preferences vary in accordance with our moods and the social cues and requirements of the moment.

Second, even if people know the kind of media they want, they're not always able identify the best option. The great abundance that enables freedom of choice also presents users with a dilemma. To cope with the overwhelming number of things competing for our attention, we rely on an arsenal of tools and techniques. We restrict our choices to a relatively small repertoire of outlets and apps. We make quick judgments about the desirability of what we do encounter based a handful of heuristics. Unfortunately, these mechanisms are far from perfect, so the best possible choice can easily elude our notice. Increasingly, we rely on social networks and recommender systems to improve our odds. But these have their own limitations and can introduce new biases into the selection process that we'll discuss in the pages that follow.

Third, we don't have a very good understanding of where preferences come from. Some academic theories do take a stab at explaining their origins. Preferences undoubtedly reflect our upbringing and place in society. They surely serve to gratify some needs, confirm some prejudices, and tweak some mood states. But all of these approaches imagine people to have preexisting preferences that they bring to the media and that drive their choices. They allow very little room for the possibility that our encounters with media have other causes and that those encounters might actually shape our preferences, reversing the traditional direction of causation.

If the latter is the case, then our not-so-rigid preferences, operating under conditions of bounded rationality, could be affected by the media environment itself. That would be especially true if the media were actively engaged in cultivating our appetites and managing our exposure to their offerings. As we'll see in the next chapter, that's exactly what they're up to.

3 THE MEDIA

Media provide people with resources. Not so long ago, those resources were limited and controlled by large institutions. Today, digital technologies offer people a host of tools that were unimaginable just a few years ago. Users can tap into media whenever and wherever they want. They can create and share media with their friends or the entire world. In fact, the line between traditional media institutions and users gets blurrier every day. Yet, old or new, most media makers want public attention and will do what they can to attract an audience. In this chapter we'll consider the pervasive logic of the attention economy and how "the media" go about making audiences.

The Attention Economy

The abundant supply of digital media competing for a limited amount of human attention has created what some have dubbed the "attention economy."[1] In a world of limitless media, attention is a scarce and, therefore, valuable resource. It's essential if media makers are to promote their ideas, shape the culture, or just make a buck. Often the media are controlled by large institutions driven by commercial motives. But audiences are also vital to publicly funded media and a growing number of providers operating under the rules of a "sharing economy." No matter what their motives, they're all participants in the attention economy.

Commercial Economies

In the United States and increasingly around the world, the primary motivation of media institutions is making money. When parties exchange something of economic value, it's indicative of a "commercial economy."[2]

Broadly speaking, commercial media make money in one of two ways. First, they can sell media products and services directly to users. This is typical of movie studios, record companies, and retailers such as Amazon, Netflix, and iTunes. Second, the media can sell the attention of users to advertisers. In this case they have to acquire or produce media, with which they lure the audiences they then sell. The latter is called a "dual product" market, because it involves simultaneously providing media to people and people to advertisers.[3] This is typical of commercial broadcasting. Frequently, commercial media will make money both ways. Most cable networks, newspapers, and magazines have revenue streams that flow from subscribers and advertisers.

But old-fashioned mass media aren't the only ones intent on making money. Most major Internet platforms function very much like traditional media. Google, Facebook, and YouTube all provide products and services that lure audiences whose attention is then sold to advertisers. And many bloggers have joined in. Heather Armstrong, the "queen of mommy bloggers," attracts one hundred thousand daily visitors to her website. She's had advertisers since 2004, and now works with an agency that places more than a million dollars' worth of ads a year.[4] For all those operating within the commercial economy, public attention is the coin of the realm, so it's essential that they attract an audience. But the way to do that often depends on how much competition you face.

In a low-choice environment, where three or four networks compete, it makes sense for each of them to offer broadly appealing programs that "maximize" their audiences.[5] Economists argue this produces an "excessive sameness"[6] in the offerings, or what some would call "lowest common denominator" programs. As the competition increases, new entrants are inclined to offer something different, at least until the payoff in audiences doesn't justify the expense. This effectively increases the diversity of offerings available to the public. As Tewksbury and Rittenberg pointed out, "This economic explanation neatly describes the changes within the current media market. It is primarily the smaller, newer outlets that are willing to target niche audiences."[7] Of course, niche players are also interested in maximizing their audiences, but usually within a narrower universe defined by specific demographics or genre preferences.

Publicly funded media share many attributes with their purely commercial counterparts. They're often large institutions, such as the BBC, that spend lots of money to acquire or produce programming. But for them, funding comes from different sources such as state subsidies, license fees, and user donations. As a result, they have a rather different ethos. Historically, state broadcasters have been charged with offering citizens a steady supply of meritorious programming. In the late 1980s, one British government report noted the BBC was "expected to provide high quality programming across the full range of public tastes and interests, including both programmes of popular appeal and programmes of minority interest, and to offer education, information and cultural material as well as entertainment."[8]

At the time, Britain had only four TV networks, so attracting an audience wasn't much of a challenge. But just like commercial outlets, public media face increased competition, so audience behavior is now a concern of policy makers throughout Europe.[9] As one veteran audience researcher noted, even publicly funded media need to establish "their financial viability as well as their social, cultural and psychological impact [by collecting] evidence about the size and shape of media audiences and their patterns of media usage."[10] So all these media institutions find themselves in the business of attracting and documenting audiences.

That's not to say that everyone within those institutions, commercial or otherwise, marches in lockstep to build audiences. Individuals inside these organizations might be indifferent or resistant to "giving the audience what it wants." Within entertainment industries, some creators are more concerned about "art for art's sake" than pandering to an audience.[11] Within news organizations, editors and journalists have professional norms that encourage them to "give the audience what it needs." As a result they provide more hard news than most people seem to want. My colleagues at Northwestern have reported a persistent gap between the hard news that online outlets put on their websites and what visitors actually read—a gap that exists in many places around the world.[12] Whether these contrarian tendencies will survive the onslaught of competition remains to be seen. But the imperative to build audiences is here to stay, even among those who are happy to share media "for free."

Sharing Economies

Historians have long recognized that commercial economies aren't the only systems that govern human exchange.[13] The growth of social media and the appearance of users who don't seem to be motivated by financial gain have sparked renewed interest in the idea of a "gift" or "sharing" economy.[14] Unlike a commercial economy, money doesn't change hands. Instead people freely share or exchange things, including user-generated content, recommendations, or items of mutual interest. In a sharing economy, it's the users who create and spread media. In doing so, they become amateur members of "the media."

The emergence of this sharing economy has been a cause for celebration in many quarters. Addressing the traditional media on behalf of the audience, Jay Rosen, a well-known professor of journalism at NYU, blogged, "You don't own the eyeballs. You don't own the press, which is now divided into pro and amateur zones. You don't control production on the new platform, which isn't one-way. There's a new balance of power between you and us."[15]

In a similar refrain, Henry Jenkins and colleagues concluded, "The shape of our culture, thank goodness, is still under transition, and—as a consequence—it is still possible for us to collectively struggle to shape the terms of a spreadable media environment and to forge a media environment that is more inclusive, more dynamic, and more participatory than before."[16] There's no doubt that the media now include a great many providers who don't seem to be operating under the rules of the old system, but what are their motivations?

In sharing economies, motives are far more varied and less transparent than those that drive commercial economies.[17] Some people seem to be genuinely altruistic. The classic examples, cited by many authors, are *Wikipedia* and Linux software development.[18] These are services where anonymous contributors labor to create something for public benefit. Others seem intent on building communities around particular performers, genres, or political causes.[19] Still others use social media to promote social bonding within their networks, enhance their own social capital, craft their public identities, or achieve "micro-celebrity" status.[20]

Not infrequently, a person's motives for sharing appear selfless, but are actually self-serving. For example, Yochai Benkler noted a "Joe Einstein" phenomenon in which a person shared expertise for free. But this contributed to fame or "benefits to reputation" that could be valuable elsewhere.[21] Similarly, Chris Anderson, a well-known author and proponent of "free" media, explained that "the low-marginal cost digital book is really marketing for the high-marginal cost speech or consulting gig," which he conceded was his model for making money.[22] So many potentially beneficial forms of sharing have an ulterior motive that encourages the provider to seek public attention.

But for these forms of sharing to serve their purpose, an audience of some sort has to be paying attention. As a result, most media makers imagine an audience and try to curry its favor. As a study of Twitter users noted, "the strategies of micro-celebrity are not only used by people with large numbers of followers. Many users consciously use Twitter as a platform to obtain and maintain attention by targeting tweets toward their perceived audience's interest and balancing different topic areas."[23]

It's also the case that in a sharing economy, the audiences can materialize in unintended ways. Many people use social media for personal reasons.[24] They create media for its own sake or to share with family and friends. But there's no telling when media on a public website will "go viral." For example, at this writing, a home video called "Charlie bit my finger—again" is one of the most viewed clips on YouTube. Media objects can circulate in ways that were unimagined by their makers. So even if people have no interest in public attention, it may have it thrust on them—making the phenomenon relevant to this book.

In any event, a common objective in commercial and sharing economies is building an audience. That's clearly the mission of commercial media, whether it's selling products to people or people to advertisers. But it's also the goal of a great many providers who aren't trying to make a profit. As Henry Jenkins and colleagues conceded, "Users generating online content are often interested in expanding their own audience and reputation. They may measure their success by how many followers they attract on Twitter, just as television executives value the number of eyeballs their programs attract."[25] In that sense, the logic of the attention economy is pervasive. So the focus in the rest of this chapter is how institutional and interpersonal practices cultivate public attention.

That typically involves two activities. First, you have to produce media, such as programs or tweets, that are capable of sustaining the interest of users. Second, you have to devise some way for people to encounter what you've created. The first activity is about making media. The second is about making audiences. We'll deal with each in turn.

Making Media

Media making can include anything from a blogger's latest musings to a movie studio producing a multimillion-dollar film. These are obviously very different activities requiring different resources and presenting their creators with different challenges and rewards. At the risk of glossing over a great many details, it's possible to identify a few principles that guide the creation of media. These involve three interrelated decisions about how much to invest in making media, how to create media in an environment fraught with uncertainty, and how to take full advantage of media products that exist.

Deciding How Much to Invest

The first thing a media maker has to decide is what resources should be devoted to creating the object (e.g., a blog or a movie). In commercial enterprises, this calculation has two component parts. One is assessing the size of the prospective market; the larger and more affluent the potential audience, the greater the potential payoff. Hence, large markets may justify a larger upfront investment. This is one reason why Hollywood seems willing to spend millions of dollars making movies. They're accessible to a large, affluent population of English speakers and, depending on the genre, their high production values can attract audiences around the world.[26]

Different forms of media can have radically different production costs. Making a Hollywood blockbuster can require well over one hundred million dollars. A prime time television series can cost several million dollars an episode. Even less traditional on-demand services such as Netflix and Amazon are spending millions to produce series television.[27] All of these media have high "first copy costs."[28] That is, making the first copy of a movie or TV program is expensive. And all the money needed to produce that copy usually has to be spent, or "sunk," before you can realize any return.[29] So the risk of failure is enormous. Many Internet platforms, such as Google or Amazon, have their own version of high first copy costs. They have to invest heavily in software and server farms to provide competitive services, although they can often scale up to meet growing demand, hence not all their costs are sunk up front.[30]

Other forms of media making, such as blogging, writing a book, recording music, making a home video, or collaborating on software and wikis, have relatively low production costs.[31] In these instances, media makers don't risk much besides their time by jumping into the market.

This brings us to the second part of the investment decision: assessing the competition. If the audience you're after is desirable, you're likely to have competition. The high production and distribution costs of some media can impose barriers to entering the market. Let's face it: not everyone has the wherewithal to operate a TV network, although a quite a few companies have decided it's worth competing for the US television audience. When production costs are lower and the means of distribution are easily accessible, there are few barriers to entry. In these markets, such as the blogosphere or World Wide Web, the competition is essentially unlimited. In 2012, Nielsen was tracking over 180 million blogs—but who's counting?[32]

So the cold, economic logic of investing in media involves assessing the size of the potential audience and gauging the likelihood that others will enter the market. Although every media maker would probably like to have the entire "pie" to him- or herself, sometimes getting a tiny sliver of a very large pie is reward enough to justify the effort. Unfortunately for investors, this calculus is complicated by the unpredictability of audiences. Even holding the number of competitors constant, investments of a given size can yield very large or very small audiences.

Deciding What to Make

When it comes to creating media, the conventional wisdom is that "nobody knows" what will succeed in the marketplace.[33] The phrase "nobody knows anything" is attributed to the screenwriter William Goldman who observed that in Hollywood, no one seems to be able to predict which movies will be hits and which won't.[34] The industry is rife with examples of well-financed movies from major studios that failed in the box office (e.g., *John Carter*, *The Adventures of Pluto Nash*, *Heaven's Gate*, etc.) as well as low budget films that were hits (e.g., *Blair Witch Project*, *Paranormal Activity*, etc.).[35] Television isn't much different. Despite using the best talent and testing pilot programs, most new TV shows will fail. One network executive famously noted that "all hits are flukes."[36] Even the first Harry Potter book was rejected by eight publishers before seeing the light of day.[37] So it's difficult, even for experts, to know which freshly minted media will find an audience based on its attributes alone. There is no foolproof recipe for making a best seller. And that's true for big budget media or user-generated content.

But it's the institutional media makers have invested the most and so have the most to lose. The high-cost–high-risk nature of their business encourages them to hedge their bets. This involves creating media that are novel yet familiar and deciding whether to lead or follow the market.[38] Even in competitive markets, their decisions can produce a surprising level of sameness in cultural production.

Novelty versus Familiarity   Media makers who are intent on attracting an audience are faced with a puzzle. As Joseph Lampel and his colleagues explain it, "Competition in cultural industries is driven by a search for novelty. However, while consumers expect novelty in their cultural goods, they also want novelty to be accessible and familiar."[39] Striking this elusive balance to achieve what one professor called "reliable surprise," is a challenge for those making entertainment and the news.[40]

In television, creators try to manage this tension by developing new shows that aren't too dissimilar from past successes. They "pitch" new series by touting the reputation of the writers and producers for delivering hits or noting how the new show will be like—but a little different from—proven winners.[41] Creative industries have a tendency to use the same pool of "A-list" talent when they can afford it.[42] As Anita Elberse at Harvard Business School has pointed out, "Movie studios handsomely reward superstar actors such as Johnny Depp, Jennifer Lawrence, Will Smith, Kristen Stewart, and Robert Downey Jr. in hopes of converting fans of those stars into audiences for the studios' productions. The same goes for television networks.... The focus on star talent now extends into virtually all sectors of the entertainment industry."[43]

These strategies aren't a surefire way to eliminate risk, but they at least help creators rationalize their decisions in a world where "nobody knows." These impulses also help to explain the tendency of networks to commission spin-offs, such as the CSI and Law & Order franchises or movie studios to produce sequels, such as Star Wars or Pirates of the Caribbean.

In fact, many television show formats circulate around the globe.[44] America Idol began life as a British program called Pop Idol. The prototype for The Voice began in Holland and has been copied in more than fifty counties.[45] Other programs based on Survivor or Who Wants to be a Millionaire? have appeared in dozens of nations around the world. Usually, these "super formats" are adjusted to accommodate the sensibilities of local audiences.

As Jean Chalaby noted, "formats travel precisely because they adapt to local tastes, bringing together elements and languages from different cultures."[46] Whether these practices ultimately homogenize global culture or promote a healthy cultural exchange among nations is open to debate.[47]

Another factor that's important in managing the tension between novelty and familiarity is the genre of the offering. We noted in chapter 2 that people often use genres as a way to decide what they will and won't pay attention to. If they recognize something as belonging to a preferred genre, it might get past the front door. If its genre is unidentifiable, it may not get another look. Media makers can clarify what an offering is by adhering to the conventions of the genres. For example, film studios can "present the movie-going audience with core, easily recognizable features of genres (such as gunfights and horses for Western, bloody knives for Horror, or aliens for Science Fiction) designed to establish the film's genre identity and thus who its target audience is."[48]

Even innovative companies who aren't driven by the logic of advertiser-supported television are inclined to offer familiar products that don't violate genre boundaries. Netflix is now investing hundreds of millions in original programming. But as *Wired* magazine reported,

> All of Netflix's new shows are based on preexisting television and books: they are at least somewhat-known quantities, so the company has a better sense of how its customers will likely respond to them.... These shows match consumer tastes and can be slotted into existing genres—more precisely the categories on Netflix's site ("goofy comedies," "critically acclaimed cerebral foreign dramas," "quirky procedurals with a strong female lead"). The company is serious about making excellent content— but not thematically radical content, because it wouldn't know how to package that for its consumers.[49]

Spanning genres could offer more novelty and, perhaps, a refreshing change of pace. For instance, a 2011 film called *Cowboys & Aliens,* starring Daniel Craig and Harrison Ford, mashed together two genres and achieved some box office success. But "hybrid" genres often run into trouble, not because they lack merit, but because audiences don't know what to make of them.[50] In his review of *Cowboys & Aliens,* the late film critic Robert Ebert wrote, "I wish this had been a Western. You know, the old-fashioned kind, without spaceships. Daniel Craig, cold-eyed and lean, plays a character familiar in the genre."[51] So media makers span genre boundaries at their own peril.

Even news producers have to strike a balance between novelty and familiarity. Each day's news is by definition novel. But the way it's packaged provides a comforting familiarity that helps maintain the audience. As economist Richard Hamilton explained, "The uncertainty surrounding the content of a story prior to consumption ... leads news outlets to create expectations about the way they will organize and present information. Firms may stress the personalities of reporters since these can remain constant even as story topics change, so that readers and viewers can know what to expect from a media product even though they may not know the facts they are about to consume."[52]

Despite what economic theory predicts, increasing the competition doesn't do much to improve the diversity of news products. Quite the contrary, the 2006 edition of *State of the News Media* noted that "the new paradox of journalism is more outlets covering fewer stories. As the number of places delivering news proliferates, the audience for each tends to shrink and the number of journalists in each organization is reduced. At the national level, those organizations still have to cover the big events. Thus we tend to see more accounts of the same handful of stories each day."[53]

But there's another phenomenon that contributes to more outlets covering fewer stories. Journalists tend to imitate one another. Peter Vasterman at the University of Amsterdam noted that "journalism is a highly self-referential system: news is what other media consider newsworthy. This leads to a high degree of uniformity in the news selection and a pressure on every news desk to join the pack."[54] This pack mentality produces "self-reinforcing news waves" that sweep across the audience, effectively commandeering public attention. Sometimes the coverage seems warranted, such as reporting on natural disasters or inaugurations. At other times the frenzy is of questionable merit, such as coverage of celebrity weddings, divorces, and deaths. You might think that being able to deliver more stories via the web would increase variation in what's covered, but it doesn't.

Most newsrooms have an online presence, making it easy to monitor what their competition is doing. If one of them breaks a story, online distribution makes it possible to quickly replicate the story and make it available to readers. After all, you wouldn't want to lose readers interested in that news item, and the Internet doesn't impose any hard page limits. According Pablo Boczkowski, my colleague at Northwestern, this imitation leads to what he called a "spiral of sameness." He went on to note, "The rise of homogenization in the news has led to a state of affairs that neither journalisms nor consumers like but feel powerless to alter."[55]

Leading versus Following   This compulsion to keep one eye on the competition and another eye on the audience highlights a related tension that media makers have to manage. Do they follow the market by catering to existing preferences or do they lead the market by cultivating an appetite for something new? Either strategy can work: "cultural goods may become successful because they deliberately or accidentally tap preexisting consumer preferences, or cultural goods may become successful because they shape tastes to suit their own production."[56] The chance of the latter strategy working goes to the ability of media to change people's preferences, which I'll address in chapter 6. The former strategy is the more conservative of the two, and it's here that media measures play an especially important role.

Broadly speaking, firms in almost any business rely on "market information regimes" to make sense of what their customers and competitors are doing.[57] In commercial media, the most pervasive of these regimes have been the audience ratings services. Their numbers—the "ratings"—have long been used to monitor and effectively grade the success of media such as stations, networks, and individual programs.[58] Ratings, or for that matter box office receipts or sales figures, have traditionally taken some time make their way back to the people actually creating media, thus providing them with some insulation from the marketplace.[59]

But the ability of digital media to track and report the actions of users in near real time has moved market information to the center of many production processes. As the *New York Times* reported, "Forget zombies. The data crunchers are invading Hollywood. The same kind of numbers analysis that has reshaped areas like politics and online marketing is increasingly being used by the entertainment industry."[60]

These data affect the kinds of media that are made and how they're directed toward specific audiences. At one end of the continuum, audience information informs creative or editorial decisions much as it has in the past, except that it now looms larger as those decisions are made.[61] At the other end, it supports a cold-blooded process in which media content is tailored to audience demand then served to targeted users, often with an eye toward attracting specific advertisers and marketing specific products.[62]

C. W. Anderson, who has studied online newsrooms, notes that journalists and editors make growing, sometimes obsessive, use of web metrics such as "pages views" to decide what stories to run or where to place them. For instance, he quotes one web producer saying, "Usually I give a story at least an hour to prove itself. 500 page views is pretty good, and 1000 is great."[63] Anderson further observed that "a deliberate management emphasis on the widespread diffusion of metric data along with a fairly desperate need for greater traffic numbers that could boost online ad revenues were leading web producers ... to base more and more of their news judgments on raw, quantitative data."[64]

Anderson's research is instructive for two reasons. First, journalists, as well as other creators, have traditionally been indifferent if not hostile to user feedback.[65] But the idea of ordinary users actively creating and sharing news, coupled with increased competition and a steady stream of "*quantitative* feedback about what it is that audiences want,"[66] is changing the culture of news production, making it more inclined to follow the audience's lead. Second, the use of web metrics demonstrates how audiences cause media institutions to adapt. We noted in chapter 2, that when users are seen in the aggregate, they exercise a particularly potent form of agency. Here we have a demonstration of how commercial media makers see and respond to audiences.

Internet platforms, such as Netflix and Amazon, which are now making media and have their own data collection capabilities, will amplify these phenomena. *Wired* magazine noted that "Netflix has something that not even HBO's market researchers can compete with: years of near-perfect data on what its subscribers watch and like. Netflix has already tapped into that information to pick new projects."[67] Similarly, Amazon tracks reactions to pilot programming, creating "a giant decentralized TV focus group. The viewing data and feedback will be used to select—and tweak—the most promising projects, so that when the series launch, they'll already be optimized for both quality and buzz."[68]

Whether these uses of data usher in what *Wired* calls a new "platinum age of TV" or just produce marginally different media products remains to be seen. Many writers and producers aren't particularly happy with the growing reliance on research. One film writer argued that "it's the enemy of creativity, nothing more than attempt to mimic that which has worked before. It can only result in an increasingly bland homogenization, a pell-mell rush for the middle of the road."[69] Still, it seems the use of audience metrics in media making will only grow. One reporter for the *New York Times* concluded that "as the stakes of movie making become ever higher, Hollywood leans ever harder on research to minimize guesswork."[70]

And Now, for Something Completely Different   Most of the media I've described thus far are commercial ventures, backed by lots of money. But it could be that grassroots, user-generated content, less burdened by high production costs and the need to satisfy investors, will offer something completely different. It does appear that music making, book writing, and, to a lesser extent, independent film and video making are showing signs of increased diversity and originality.[71]

But nothing has produced as much optimism as the prospect of grassroots, citizen journalism. Observers such as Dan Gillmor and Yochai Benkler see the digital media unleashing ordinary people to gather and report information outside the channels of traditional mainstream media. Those people, who Gillmor has referred to as the "former audience," are "learning how to join the process of journalism, helping to create a massive conversation and, in some cases, doing a better job than the professionals."[72]

For some, this change seems inevitable. Eric Schmidt, the long-time CEO of Google, and his coauthor have argued that "it is manifestly clear that mainstream media outlets will increasingly find themselves a step behind in reporting of news worldwide. These organizations simply cannot move quickly enough in a connected age, no matter how talented their reporters and stringers are, and how many sources they have. Instead, the world's breaking news will continually come from platforms like Twitter: open networks that facilitate information-sharing instantly, widely and in accessible packages."[73]

In fact, ordinary citizens do sometimes break news, post images, or unearth stories that elude professional journalists. And sharing this information on digital networks can promote new forms of collective action.[74] But it turns out the overwhelming majority of items that are reported in social media or dissected on blogs originate from traditional outlets.

The Project for Excellence in Journalism studied all the major news stories circulating in Baltimore, including those presented on blogs and websites. They found that "fully 83% of stories were essentially repetitive, conveying no new information. Of the 17% that did contain new information, nearly all came from traditional media either in their legacy platforms or in new digital ones."[75] Additionally, the purloined stories were often reported without attribution, leading audiences to believe they were getting something original when they weren't.

In a similar vein, *Advertising Age* noted that Reddit, the social news site where users "upvote" stories to the front page, is like a mainstream outlet from which blogs regularly draw their stories.

> Reddit has become, simply put, mainstream media.... [It] closed out 2012 with more than 37 billion page views and 400 million unique visitors. Even people who don't check the so-called social-news site regularly— or at all—constantly experience the Reddit Effect because ... the mainstream blog media is almost ridiculously (even pathetically) dependent on Reddit.... Reddit's longtime tagline is "The front page of the internet," but it could just as easily be "The crib sheet for weary bloggers who need to hit page-view quotas."[76]

More generally, much of what passes as original user-generated content is derived from existing mass media. Users appropriate images or story lines or music to "remix" it into something else.[77] Not infrequently, their efforts echo and reinforce mass culture. As Jenkins and colleagues conceded, "In actuality ... audiences often use the commodified and monetized content of commercial producers as raw material for their social interactions with each other."[78]

But attributing media content to either old or new media misses a larger point. Social media and mainstream outlets often collaborate in bringing news and popular culture to public attention.[79] Researchers at Stanford and Cornell have studied how "memes," or little bits of text, circulate between mainstream media and blogs. For example, at the 2008 Republican National Convention, vice presidential nominee Sarah Palin joked that the only difference between a hockey mom and a pit bull was lipstick. Not long after, then-candidate Obama used the expression "lipstick on a pig," which greatly offended the McCain campaign.[80] The meme trackers noted a spike in the use of "lipstick on a pig" across media platforms. This event created something of a "news wave" sloshing back and forth between old and new media. For a brief period of time, it seemed like everyone was talking about it. According to their research, stories generally moved from major news outlets to blogs, usually with a two-and-a-half hour lag, while "in only 3.5% of the cases stories first appear dominantly in the blogosphere and subsequently percolate to the mainstream media."[81] In subsequent work, Stanford researchers reported that the incidence of hashtags in Twitter follow a similar pattern.[82] So new media rarely offer something that's completely new; rather, they selectively amplify what's already out there.

Making the Most of What You've Got

Once media are created, makers will generally try to get all they can from their investment. They try to find new audiences for what they have "in the can." One strategy is to sort out audiences by their willingness to pay. For example, some people will stand in line to buy tickets for Harry Potter or Twilight movies as soon as they come out. Others are perfectly willing to wait until it's available on Netflix, HBO, or "free" television. Hollywood has long used this method of price discrimination, called "windowing," to wring every last dollar out of their films.[83] Another strategy is to use some or all of the product over and over again in different contexts. The audience-making potential of media can vary dramatically by genre. The old movies owned by studios can be enormously valuable. Films such as *The Wizard of Oz* or *The Godfather* accumulate audiences across generations. Yesterday's news, however, doesn't have much of a shelf life. The ability of media to be rereleased, repackaged, and repurposed, in turn, weighs into calculations about how much to invest in the first place.

Digital media present particularly interesting possibilities for reuse because they can be reproduced at almost no cost. They're what economists call "public goods."[84] That is, once they've been created, any number of people can consume them without diminishing the quantity available for others. Digital media are very different from "private goods," such as loaves of bread or printed books, in which one person's purchase reduces the inventory.

The public good nature of digital media has profound effects that ripple through commercial and sharing economies. For profit-making enterprises, making low-cost copies gives them considerable flexibility in pricing their products—assuming they can protect themselves from piracy. It also allows them to dismember content and reuse it, such as distributing news or video clips across multiple platforms. For social media, it enables people to effortlessly share what they've created or found with others. As proponents of "spreadable media" have noted, "digital goods can be shared under a variety of contexts simultaneously, and access to the item can be sold or offered as a gift without content ever leaving one's possession." So even those operating under the rules of a sharing economy can exploit digital media to make the most of what they've got.

Making Audiences

None of these activities in media making does much to deliver an audience. And that, after all, is the name of the game. Investing a lot on money to create something with high production values might help, but "nobody knows." Striking the right balance between novelty and familiarity is difficult at best, and feeding research into the process offers no guarantees. Still, there are things that the media can do to encourage public attention.

Broadly speaking, audience-making strategies can be sorted out along two dimensions. The first has to do with the technology that's used to deliver media. Linear media, such as TV networks, present content using a kind of flow that opens up certain audience-making possibilities. Nonlinear media, such as video on demand (VOD) or most Internet platforms, present different challenges and opportunities. The second dimension has to do with whether the media actively "push" things out to users or help users to "pull" media on their own. As we'll see, these tools and techniques are used in various combinations to try to manage public attention.

Linear versus Nonlinear

Electronic media began as linear delivery systems. Radio, and then television, offered audiences a stream of programming designed to keep people tuned in. Even in today's world with hundreds of channels delivered by cable and satellite, users may have to accommodate themselves to the schedule of linear delivery. By the early 1980s, low-cost video cassette recorders (VCRs) began to break the strangle hold of scheduled programming.[85] Although VCRs made "time shifting" a possibility, they were cumbersome and not the game-changing technology some had imagined. By the early twenty-first century, however, a host of user-friendly nonlinear systems were available. They included DVRs; VOD; web-based platforms such as iTunes, YouTube, Netflix; blogs; and the online outlets of mainstream media. All of these let users fetch what they want at almost any time.

The convenience of nonlinear media, allowing people to get what they want when they want it, has led to widespread speculation that linear media are on their death bed. In an interview with the *New York Times Magazine,* one advertising executive explained that

> most media, like television, used to be a kind of flow. You'd sit down, you'd turn it on and you'd watch. The reason advertising is completely broken is that the flow doesn't exist anymore. There's no prime time. There's no such thing as must-see TV. Everyone's composing their own flow. And once you start becoming the composer of your own flow, you can't go back. You're like, Why would I have somebody dictate to me what I watch when I'm used to programming for myself?[86]

In a similar vein, an extensive report on Britain's digital future anticipated that "users will cross over from an environment in which content is consumed passively through the linear schedule to one where content is consumed actively through search and on-demand."[87]

These proclamations bring to mind Mark Twain's famous quip that "the reports of my death are greatly exaggerated." Perhaps in the fullness of time linear media will disappear, but it's not imminent. For one thing, people refuse to abandon linear media. Although some media use has shifted to nonlinear delivery, Americans still spend roughly 90 percent of their viewing time watching live TV.[88] That dogged persistence in linear media use is evident around the world.[89] And newer services, such as Pandora, are perpetuating linear delivery.

The widespread use of social media also bolsters linear media. A great many people now "tweet" about programs or media events as they are aired. By one count, "a full 40 percent of Twitter's traffic during peak usage is about television."[90] Marlene King, the executive producer of "Ravenswood" and "Pretty Little Liars," assessed the phenomenon this way:

> It feels like social media is creating "must-see TV" again. Where, because our fans want to have a massive Twitter party together on Tuesday night when we air, they all sit down and watch. They don't want to come to the party late. They don't want to see the clues later. They want to experience it together. So, we're feeling like it is bringing fans to watch the show live again. As opposed to DVRing it and not being up-to-date with your friends.[91]

Many media outlets are also partial to linear delivery. Although there is some willingness on the part of commercial media to release entire series, such as *House of Cards,* that can be cherry-picked or consumed in one sitting, the public's appetite for "binge viewing" appears to be limited.[92] As Jeff Bewkes, the CEO of Time Warner, put it, "It's hard if you envision a world five years from now with all on-demand: How are you going to find everything? You have to use your network to launch things in a way people can understand what it is."[93] Of course, Time Warner, the owner of several linear TV networks, isn't a disinterested party, but it does appear that most commercial outlets are going to create "ancillary material related to their viewers' favorite programs and [make] it available for web viewing and mobile use, while keeping the program itself in its original boob-tube environs."[94] So it would seem that linear is here to stay, unless users demand everything in nonlinear form, which they show little sign of doing.

The audience building potential of linear media comes from the "flow" that it creates. That's the basis for many of the strategies I note here. People watch or listen to one thing and they encounter something else they hadn't anticipated. Flow is created in a couple of ways. Linear media can do it by stringing together one program or song after another, leading audiences into something new or unexpected. That's how most advertising works. But linear and nonlinear media share a second kind of flow. Once you come across a media object, it has the ability to introduce you to things you haven't chosen in advance. A variety show might induce you to listen to a band that you've never heard of. A website might feature a story you weren't looking for. All of these things can build audiences if they're skillfully done and users play along.

This brings us to a subtle distinction worth noting. What exactly is flowing? Is it media or audiences? Since the 1970s, cultural critics have noted how linear media orchestrate flow by creating "viewing strips" or "flow texts."[95] Their focus on texts was understandable. In a media environment with a handful of channels and no remotes, it probably was scheduling that determined audience flow. But even the recent work on "spreadable media" asks "how might we better understand the ways in which material travels within a networked culture?"[96] What's most important for our purposes is how people deal with this juxtaposition or passing around of texts. It's how *audiences* flow from one media encounter to the next that's of central interest. Flow texts don't matter much unless people "go with the flow."

Push versus Pull

The second dimension of audience making involves what are sometimes called "push" media and "pull" media. Although these terms appear with some regularity in trade and academe publications, their definitions vary. In essence, they represent two very different approaches to making an audience. With a push strategy, the media seek out the users. The most heavy-handed example is advertising, in which messages are delivered to members of a target audience, sometimes with great precision. With a pull strategy the users seek out media. For example, people might plan their day around watching the Super Bowl or a World Cup match. Although these might seem like diametrically opposed strategies, they often work hand in hand.

Push and pull carry with them a number of connotations. Push media are generally associated with linear delivery systems that exploit "passive" audience members by serving up a diet of whatever the media order. Pull media are often associated with nonlinear media in which "active" audience members pick and choose whatever they have a taste for.

But greater choice and user empowerment provide an ironic twist. As digital media present people with more and more options, they encounter the "user's dilemma" (see chapter 2). They rely more heavily on repertoires, heuristics, and various forms of recommendation. Many of these reinstate the features that push media. For example, as we'll see in the following chapter, most recommender systems effectively steer people in the direction of popular and personalized options. That is, they push certain kinds of content.

The fact is that linear and nonlinear media will use push and pull in their in their attempts to make audiences. Radio and television have, for a long time, used every trick in the book to cultivate audience loyalties. They sequence programming to enhance audience flow and monitor the results with ratings data. But many websites are playing the same game by doing what they can to increase their "stickiness." As Jenkins et al. argue, "The key to stickiness is putting material in a centralized location, drawing people to it, and keeping them there indefinitely in ways that best benefit the site's analytics. (The process is not that unlike a corral; audiences are pushed along predefined routes matching a publisher's measurement needs and are then poked and prodded for analytics data)."[97]

A Map of Audience-Making Strategies

So, the distinctions between linear and nonlinear or push and pull media are often murky. Nonetheless, these dimensions still provide a useful way to map the various audience-building strategies the media use, as depicted in figure 3.1.

The upper left-hand quadrant includes many of the most familiar ways to make an audience. Traditionally, broadcast advertising has pushed messages out to audiences by dropping commercials into the flow of a program. Advertisers choose those programs or stations based on the size and composition of their audiences, although they sometimes pay a premium to be associated with a particularly popular or prestigious outlet. Across radio, television, and cable, advertisers spend close to $100 billion in the United States alone in order to construct an audience for their messages.[98] Increasingly, buying public attention is informed by data and decoupled from the content of the programming that's actually delivering audiences to the ad. This kind of media buying was done by the Obama campaign in the 2012 election. As described in a report by the *Washington Post*, "The team

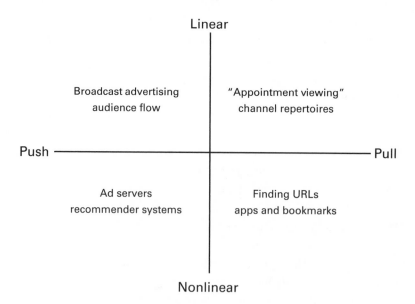

Figure 3.1
Audience-making Strategies.

bought detailed data on TV viewing by millions of cable subscribers, show-ing which channels they were watching, sometimes on a second-by-second basis. The information—which was collected from set-top cable boxes and sold by a company called Rentrak—doesn't show who was watching, but the campaign used a third-party company to match viewing data to its own internal list of voters and poll responses."[99]

Even though it's now easier for viewers to avoid the commercials embedded in the flow of programming, advertising still represents a pow-erful way to build audiences and command public attention. Whether that power is used for good or evil is, I suppose, in the eye of the beholder.

But linear flows do more than just deliver audiences to advertising. Exploiting the existence of flows is one of the most effective tools a pro-grammer has for managing audiences. For example, one of the tried-and-true ways to introduce a new show is to schedule it after a successful program or, better yet, in between two hits. These strategies are referred to as "lead-in effects" or "hammocking."[100] Within-program flow can be an effective way to introduce audiences to something new. How many comedians or bands have achieved their first widespread public attention by appearing on late-night talk shows? Although some people think the days of audience flow are over,[101] there's little evidence to support that belief. Audience flow is still very much in evidence in the United States and around the world.[102]

The tendency of linear program audiences to flow from one item of content to the next obviously can be used for commercial purposes, but this method of audience building isn't used exclusively for making money. State broadcasters, like established networks everywhere, have seen news audiences erode in the face of increased competition. Some, such as Dutch networks, have taken to scheduling short news bulletins at various times throughout the day in an effort to "trap" viewers,[103] which they have done with some success. As Anke Wonneberger and her colleagues note, "Simul-taneous scheduling of these bulletins on commercial and public service channels during daytime made it simply more likely to encounter news when watching TV. These bulletins might also just be short enough so that viewers do not find it necessary to change channels even if they were not initially interested in watching news."[104]

All these audience-building techniques take advantage of structural fea-tures in the media environment to introduce some certainty into audience formation. Although it's extremely difficult to predict the audience for a new movie or book *based on its attributes alone,* you can do a number of things to increase its chances of being a hit with aggressive distribution and marketing.[105]

Linear media offer an important tool for delivering an audience with a degree of predictability. New programs get a leg up on the competition if they're introduced at the right time on the right network. In fact, broadcast advertising depends on the stability of linear audiences to predict the future. In the United States, audiences are brought in well in advance of when commercials air. In television much of this buying occurs during the "upfront" market, which happens months before shows premier in the fall. Media buyers rely heavily on the rhythms of everyday life and the stability of linear audience flows to predict program ratings.[106] So although "nobody knows," fortunately for the media, making an audience doesn't depend exclusively on the media object alone.

The quadrant in the lower-left corner of the map identifies the ways in which nonlinear systems push media out to audiences. These include the use of ad servers, recommender systems, and, more broadly, any number of social media.

Most forms of digital media are delivered to us by large computers called "servers." They store the endless pages and videos that websites send to us whenever we request them. They manage how traffic is directed around digital networks such as the Internet. And they can target advertising to us whenever we are within reach of an "ad server." This is a species of advertising that in some ways is like its linear cousin and in other ways quite different.

Similar to broadcast advertising, it takes advantage of people who are attracted to particular service or bit of content, a story on your favorite blog or online news outlet, or even the e-mail service you frequent. Once the ad server notices you're there, it sends you an ad—often it's one tailored to the kind of person it assumes you to be. If you've ever had the sense that a particular kind of ad was following you around the Internet, it was probably an ad server at work.

Although this tactic is broadly similar to advertising in linear media, it differs in some important ways. First, it permits a much higher degree of targeting. Whereas broadcast advertising can reach enormous numbers of people, many of those in the audience are, in the parlance of advertising, "wasted exposures." Ad servers have the potential to direct specific messages to specific individuals. Second, these systems are even more data driven than broadcast advertising. Servers record every action a visitor takes, which are then analyzed on the fly. The *New York Times* explains the result: "On the Web, powerful algorithms are sizing you up, based on myriad data points: what you Google, the sites you visit, the ads you click. Then in real time, the chance to show you an ad is auctioned to the highest bidder."[107] Third, buying attention in this way effectively divorces the ad from the surrounding content, turning human eyeballs into even more of a commodity than they were under the broadcast model.

These powerful audience-making tools have potentially troubling consequences that go beyond simply managing attention. Joe Turow, a professor at the University of Pennsylvania, believes they will create "reputation silos: automated packaging of commercial messages and editorial matter that present individuals with content—advertising, information, entertainment, and news—that has been customized to reflect the data mining's profiles of them."[108] The end result can threaten the production of independent, high-quality media and make publishers evermore beholden to advertisers.

The recommender systems, on which we all depend, also build audiences. Many people see these as benign services that simply allow people to pull content more effectively. As big data enthusiasts point out, "After all, Amazon can recommend the ideal book, Google can rank the most relevant website, Facebook knows our likes, and LinkedIn divines whom we know."[109] But as we'll see in the next chapter on media measures, these systems are never completely neutral. Obviously Amazon and other retailers have an ulterior motive for recommending media. Even search engines have biases. For example, they tend to direct attention to the most popular websites, promoting a rich-get-richer phenomenon.[110]

In fact, search engines are an essential tool for those wanting to attract public attention on the web. As one expert noted, "anyone who wants their message heard by a large audience must find a way onto the results pages of various search engines. If there is an emerging attention economy, the search engine is the trading floor."[111] This realization drives providers, from big institutions to bloggers, to figure out a way to improve their ranking. For those who can afford it, there are even firms specializing in "search engine optimization." These companies will, for a fee, devise ways to improve a site's visibility. So, most recommender systems are actually pushing things in our direction.

Even our social networks push things at us. Sometimes it's welcomed, sometimes it's annoying—like one too many baby pictures appearing in our newsfeed from Facebook. Sometimes, it's designed to sway our opinions or appeal to our prejudices—such as people retweeting messages for political effect.[112] Nor are the intentions of the sender always transparent. We've seen just how varied the motives for sharing can be. Oftentimes, these interpersonal communications don't scale up to significant levels of public attention. But they all push things our way, and if they go "viral," there's almost no escaping them.

The right-hand side of the map locates audiences that are made by the media exerting a pull on people. Frankly, the instances of genuine pull audience building are few and far between. Yes, there are many times when people seek out media. But you have to wonder where their preference for whatever it is they're choosing came from in the first place. The origin of preferences is something we'll explore in chapter 6. For now, we'll assume that people have well-established preferences that motivate their choices.

The most obvious example of pull audience building in linear media is "appointment viewing." People know when a media event or their favorite program is scheduled and they plan to be in the audience when it airs. Many hit or cult programs achieve this level of dedication. Genres such as sports or major events such as the Oscars, which have a limited shelf life, seem to encourage appointment viewing.

You might think that the widespread availability of nonlinear platforms, such as DVRs, VOD, or Hulu, would do away with appointment viewing. But that's not the case. Many people like the sense of occasion that the first broadcast of their favorite program brings. As we've seen the growing use of Twitter and other social media platforms seems to reinforce that sense of occasion and encourage live viewing. Popular programs such as *American Idol* or *Dancing with the Stars* generate real-time buzz that doesn't work well with time shifting.

I noted in chapter 2 that when users are confronted with an overabundance of choice, one of the ways they cope is to use channel repertoires. Almost everyone has a small subset of channels, usually fewer than twenty, which they use repeatedly, even when hundreds of options are available.[113] These are outlets with which they are familiar, usually including major networks, and have a track record of providing the kinds of media they're apt to like.

With the exception of a handful of broadcast networks, which still try to offer something for everyone, most small networks behave as economic theory would predict. They identify a niche and try to control that market. As a practical matter, that means channels become content specialists with readily identifiable brands. ESPN specializes in sports, CNN specializes in news, The Food Network—well you get the point. People know what these outlets offer and turn to them when they want a particular kind of content. In that sense, they support a pull model of audience making.

Of course, most channels would like you to stay as long as possible, so just like websites they can be sticky. They certainly exploit all their opportunities to manage audience flow. And just like all linear media they can introduce you to things you hadn't chosen in advance. You might tune to MTV to see one reality show and get sucked into another. You might choose Fox News to get "fair and balanced" coverage and hear a commentator that gives new meaning to that phrase. So even here, the techniques of push media are very much in operation.

The last quadrant in our map, pull strategies enabled by nonlinear media, is where you might expect to find the richest array of new audience-making possibilities. People use on-demand platforms like DVRs and Hulu to grab specific content, although these often build the audiences for "live" TV. People certainly use search engines to find specific URLs. For example, they want to see the menu at a particular restaurant and they just need a web address. Or they may use apps on their smartphone much as they use channel repertoires. But here again, instances in which users truly pull media are surprisingly rare. As Eli Pariser explained, "Internet enthusiasts were excited about the shift from push to pull for reasons that are now pretty obvious: Rather than wash the masses in waves of watered-down, lowest-common-denominator content, pull media put users in control. The problem is that pull is actually a lot of work."[114] People rely on shortcuts to simplify choice making and often, when they do, they open the door for push media to reappear.

Desperately Seeking Attention

Commercial media, public broadcasters, and a great many people who share media "for free" are desperately seeking attention. Audiences are necessary whether you want to wield influence, enlighten people, build a public identity or brand, or make money. Unless you can attract public attention, media making has very little point. But in the digital media marketplace, getting attention isn't easy.

Your success in doing so depends, in part, on the media you make. All media makers must walk a fine line between offering something that's new and providing media that are familiar to users. Some media, such as movies, television, and even many web-based services, are expensive to create. As the cost of making media increases, the stakes for getting it right go up. To mitigate their risk, media often imitate what's already successful. Even user-generated content often feeds off popular culture. Outlets that have the resources, make extensive use of audience data to give people what they seem to want. The result of these practices is a surprising sameness across the digital media environment that its sheer numerical abundance would seem to belie. And still "nobody knows" just what will attract public attention.

But the fate of any media offering rarely depends just on the thing itself. The *Field of Dreams* principle, "build it and they will come," doesn't apply to the marketplace of attention. The media, big or small, must have some way to construct an audience. It might be as simple as word of mouth that happens to spread through social networks. But once again, nobody knows what will gain traction and what won't. Quite often, audience building involves a more calculated effort to optimize search engine rankings, exploit the flow characteristics of existing media, target specific messages to specific audiences, or marshal the publicity machines of major studios and publishers. Anita Elberse summarized the audience-making strategies of commercial media this way:

> The highest-performing entertainment businesses take their chances on a small group of titles and turn those choices into successes by investing heavily in their development, supporting them with a high level of promotional spending, often well in advance of their release into the marketplace ("coming soon to a theater near you") and distributing them as widely as possible. It may not look anything like the way products in other sectors of the economy are introduced, but it works.[115]

Most of the media we encounter are pushed at us, even if we don't notice that it's happening. In all of these efforts to make, manage, or monetize audiences, data and analytics play an increasingly important role. Media measures are becoming the ties that bind users and the media together.

4   MEDIA MEASURES

Each of us uses just a tiny portion of the media available to us. Our actions typically reflect a blend of habits and preferences, but our appetites vary and our knowledge of the offerings is far from perfect. So getting exactly what we want, when we want it, can be difficult. In the aggregate, the choices we make create something of value to the media—public attention. As a result, the media do all they can to create and sustain that attention, including everything from heavy-handed campaigns designed to enforce exposure to more subtle attempts at currying our favor. Users and the media are in constant contact. Each party assesses its options, looks for advantage, and accommodates itself to what seems possible. But how are those assessments made? These days, both parties are increasingly dependent on media measures to manage their affairs.

Measurement has been an essential part of media industries for a century. But in an age of abundant digital media, even ordinary users have become dependent on media metrics. These exercises in collecting and reporting data can have profound, if underappreciated, consequences. As one *New York Times Magazine* story concluded, "Change the way you measure America's cultural consumption ... and you change America's culture business. And maybe even the culture itself."[1]

In this chapter we'll consider the rise of media measurement and how different "information regimes" have come into existence. We'll note the methods they use to create metrics and recommendations, the biases that are built into those measures, how such practices can affect audience formation, and "maybe even the culture itself."

The Rise of Media Measures

Media measurement began in the early twentieth century as a way for advertisers to assess the value of media outlets. Newspapers and magazines could simply certify how many copies they printed to establish the size of their audiences. But radio presented a different problem. Listeners left no traces. Dispersed across vast distances, tucked away in private places, the radio audience seemed as immaterial as the airwaves that carried the broadcast signal. For radio to succeed as an advertising medium, it needed a way to authenticate who was listening. By the 1930s, the affected industries found their solution in a new kind of company that specialized in audience measurement. These "ratings" services, as they came to be known, used the newly developed tools of sampling and statistical inference to estimate listenership. With that information, the business of radio prospered. When television came along, it simply adopted the measurement practices of radio.

By the 1980s, most Western nations, which were initially less wedded to advertiser support than the United States, had regular audience measurement as well. In all these instances, the basic recipe for measurement was the same. The ratings service drew a representative sample; measured people's choices with questionnaires, diaries, or meters; and inferred the size and composition of the larger audience.[2]

Ratings services are an example of what sociologists call *market information regimes.* These regimes become "the prime source by which producers in competitive fields make sense of their actions and those of consumers, rivals, and suppliers that make up the field."[3] Many institutions, such as the media, need a steady supply of data to function. Without it, they're blind. But the information they depend on is never completely neutral. It's constructed, and the way it's made can affect the very thing it's supposed to measure.

For example, the recording industry once determined a song's popularity using *Billboard* charts. In the 1980s, it shifted to a more accurate "SoundScan" system based on sales that were measured with bar-code scanners. But changing methods had the effect of fragmenting the industry and elevating the importance of some genres such as country music.[4] Similar cases of measurement changing an industry have been documented in television and book publishing.[5]

Ratings services have continued to evolve, adapting to new media and exploiting new sources of data such as Twitter and Facebook.[6] In an age when people and advertising messages move easily across different media, there's also been a push to assess "cross-platform" audiences.[7] Worldwide, media measures now guide the allocation of roughly a half trillion dollars in advertising.[8] And because they are a common measure of success or failure, they're often the bane or the salvation of media makers.

But by the 1990s, a new kind of information regime began to emerge. Spurred by the growth of the World Wide Web and the bewildering number of choices it offered, media users now needed information to make the most of those resources. Search engines, portals, and social-sharing platforms all began offering users tools to help users make sense of their options. These "user information regimes" were available to ordinary people.

Market information regimes that provide institutions with surveillance and user information regimes that give people tools to navigate cyberspace might seem like very different enterprises, but they're actually alike in many ways. Both aggregate data, often by recording the behaviors or declarations of media users. In doing so, they take actions that are ordinarily dispersed through time and space and make them visible. The data are then reduced to create rankings, recommendations, or statistical summaries that users can act on. Further, because these metrics are built by aggregating what ordinary people say or do, they seem trustworthy.[9]

To further blur distinctions, many institutions now use data from companies such as Google as market information. So Google—and Facebook and Twitter—serve different masters and the data they collect serve different purposes. As media critic and activist Eli Pariser explained it, "The masses of data Facebook and Google accumulate have two uses. For users, the data provides a key to providing personally relevant news and results. For advertisers, the data is the key to finding likely buyers. The company that has the most data and can put it to best use gets the advertising dollars."[10] Given the power of data to affect the media environment, it's important to know something about how media measures are made.

Making Measures

You might imagine—if you think about it at all—that the measures provided by ratings services and search engines are the impartial result of applying the best scientific methods to the problem at hand. And as such, they present a complete, unbiased picture of the media environment. Although good measurement takes full advantage of the best scientific methods, the finished products never capture media use in a comprehensive, completely objective way.[11] Rather, they are the result of business considerations that reflect the economic and political realities of the marketplace. Within those constraints, measurement companies make choices among research methods and how the resulting data will be reported. These decisions inevitably create metrics and services that are biased in particular ways.

The Business of Measurement

In the United States, ratings services are operated as profit-making companies that compete for the business of advertisers and the media. In many other places around the world, the users of ratings data form nonprofit coalitions called *joint industry committees (JIC)* to commission and pay for measurement services.[12] Although the new recommender systems play by a somewhat different set of rules, all enterprises engaged in measurement have clients to satisfy and budgets that limit what they can do. This introduces a combination of political and financial considerations into the creation of media measures that seems far removed from scientific methods.

Those considerations were very much in evidence in 2002 when Nielsen began making a change in how it produced local TV ratings. For decades, US markets, from New York to North Platte, had been measured with a combination of household meters and paper diaries, although in most markets it was just the latter. Nielsen wanted to introduce people meters in the largest markets, a technology they had been using to produce national TV ratings for well over a decade. Doing so would improve the accuracy of the diary-based ratings, which were known to overstate the audience for popular offerings and understate the audience for most cable networks. It would also enable Nielsen to fold the newly people-metered households into the national panel, increasing the accuracy of national estimates.[13]

Although these might seem like uncontroversial improvements, any change can produce winners and losers. Advertisers and cable networks, which stood to gain, were generally supportive. Established broadcasters, who expected people meters to produce higher costs and lower ratings, were unhappy. Rupert Murdoch, the owner of Fox television stations, was particularly displeased. But it would be impolitic to argue against people meters simply because Fox benefited from flaws in the old system. So Murdoch orchestrated what at first appeared to be a spontaneous public uprising against Nielsen. He funded a coalition of minority groups called "Don't Count Us Out," who claimed that by undercounting minority viewers—a claim that was shaky at best—Nielsen threatened the existence of minority programming.[14] By one account, Murdoch spent nearly two million dollars behind the scenes, organizing news conferences, running inflammatory ads, and operating telephone banks.[15] The firestorm, in turn, triggered congressional hearings and threats of regulation.

Although Nielsen avoided new legislation and eventually made the changes it had planned, the episode demonstrates the political and economic dimensions of measurement. Not all disputes are quite so ugly. More often, the affected parties weigh in through trade associations, self-regulatory bodies such as the Media Rating Council, entities such as JICs, or ad hoc industry organizations such as the Coalition for Innovative Media Measurement. But it is a political process, and it's not unique to traditional ratings services.

Enterprises such as Google and Facebook began as attempts to build a better search engine or a more robust social network. These, and other "Web 2.0" platforms, provide users with a variety of services, which they hope will make money. Many, such as search engines, social networks, and high-profile bloggers, are analogous to traditional mass media. That is, they offer people a service—usually free of charge—and then sell the resulting user attention to advertisers. Others, such as Amazon, Netflix, and iTunes, guide people through vast inventories to sell them a particular media product. Either way, they all live and breathe data.

Tim O'Reilly, the man credited with coining the term *Web 2.0,* has noted that "every significant Internet application to date has been backed by a specialized database."[16] Google "crawls" the web to track how web pages are linked. Amazon and iTunes maintain a detailed record of every customer's product purchases. Facebook gathers enormous amounts of information including users' self-declared attributes, their likes, their network of friends, and the extent of their interactions. Increasingly, mobile devices are gathering information on people's geographic location or taking pictures that enable image recognition.[17]

These data power the services that attract users in the first place. The more that people use any given platform, the more data they provide.

And the more data that are collected, the more powerful and valuable the database becomes. As O'Reilly and his coauthor John Battelle explained, "if a company has control over a unique source of data that is required for applications to function, they will be able to extract monopoly rents from the use of that data. In particular, if a database is generated by user contribution, market leaders will see increasing returns as the size and value of their database grows more quickly than that of any new entrants."[18]

But using these data to guide or manage users has its own economic and political implications. We've noted that Google not only measures popularity but also creates it. That power hasn't gone unnoticed by institutions and individuals desperate to climb to the top of Google's rankings. There is, in fact, a cottage industry devoted to "search engine optimization" that tries to exploit Google's method of ranking for the benefit of clients. Google monitors the situation. It constantly tweaks it's algorithm to improve the quality of search results,[19] and occasionally lowers the boom on cheaters. In 2011, JCPenney was caught creating thousands of bogus links that artificially boosted its rankings. As punishment, Google buried JCPenney's search results.[20] Similar to TV ratings, search rankings have financial consequences, so that penalty had teeth.

Unlike traditional ratings services, however, Web 2.0 services often gather information surreptitiously, without people actively agreeing to be studied. In a forward-looking and generally upbeat book on *The New Digital Age,* two top Google executives characterized the issue this way: "Today, many online platforms will relay data back to companies and third parties about user activity without their express knowledge. People will share more than they're even aware of. For governments and companies, this thriving data set is a gift, enabling them to better respond to citizen and customer concerns, to precisely target specific demographics of the population, and, with the emergent field of predictive analytics, to predict what the future will hold."[21]

The web's ability to gather personal information whether you like it or not creates a tension between the benefits derived from these data—by institutions and users alike—and people's expectations about privacy. Those tensions won't disappear anytime soon, and they are more the province of politics than research methods. In the United States, there's an effort to mandate a "do not track" feature in browsers.[22] In Europe, where fears about "big brother" watching are even more pronounced, there's serious talk of a "right to be forgotten."[23] So the business of measurement can face political constraints in how information is gathered and reported.

What Information Gets Collected?

Within those constraints, all efforts at data gathering require decisions about what information to collect. Generally, these involve two considerations: who are we going to study and what about them are we going to measure? Sometimes, researchers have considerable latitude in deciding how to answer those questions. Sometimes, the answers are largely given.

As I noted in the introduction to this chapter, for a long time the basic recipe for collecting audience information was to draw a representative sample, ask questions or record behaviors, and make inferences about the larger population. Although that strategy gives researchers a lot of flexibility, and is still very much in use, it has trouble coping with the sheer abundance of digital media.[24] To make a long story short, the behaviors of highly fragmented populations are difficult to estimate with anything less than massive samples. And massive samples can be expensive. Large markets, such as the entire United States or the World Wide Web, are sometimes worth the expense. But smaller markets are not, so new recipes have to be found.

The most important innovation involves using servers. These are the machines that provide most Web 2.0 services. In fact, virtually all digital media are managed by computers called servers. When you watch television on a cable or satellite system, it's usually delivered to a digital "set-top box." When you request a page or a video from a website, it served from a computer. When you keep seeing that annoying ad that seems to follow you around the Internet, it's being directed by an ad server. When you interact with your friends on Facebook or Twitter the process is managed by servers. All of these machines keep a record of what was done and when it happened. As Eli Pariser has noted, "Gmail and Facebook may be helpful, free tools, they are also extremely effective and voracious extraction engines into which we pour the intimate details of our lives."[25]

The good news, from a measurement perspective, is that servers produce a massive amount of data on a huge number of users. And their observations are generally unobtrusive. Whether this constitutes a true census is doubtful, but there's certainly enough to overcome the issue of fragmentation that plagues samples.[26] The bad news is that this strategy comes at the cost of limiting whom you can study and, more important, what about them you are able to measure—which are pretty fundamental limitations.

To illustrate, consider using the data from set-top boxes (STB) to produce television ratings. These boxes, which are in millions of homes, assemble digital signals into TV channels, on-demand movies, or whatever else has been requested. A properly programmed box can record what's being sent to the screen and when a set changes channels. It would seem that all that a would-be ratings service has to do is harvest the information that is sent back upstream. Proponents of this method sometimes claim it offers a census of all television viewing, so there's no need to make statistical inferences about the audience. But those claims are misleading.

First, not all homes have cable or satellite service, and even in those that do, some TVs get a signal "over the air." Any device that isn't attached to a box—that extra set in the kitchen or bedroom, that iPad using a wireless network, and so on—avoids detection, so you almost never have a census of all TV viewing. To make matters worse, you can't measure exactly who is using these devices—or if anyone is watching at all. There are ways to estimate the size and composition of audiences you can't directly measure but, once again, these rely on statistical inference.

Most server-centric data suffer in varying degrees from these kinds of limitations. Websites try to discern the identity of visitors by making sense of IP addresses, or planting "cookies" on the visitor's browser, or making inferences about age and gender from fragmentary information.[27] Although these techniques are useful, they're far from perfect.[28] In the end, no measurement service, search engine, or social network collects all the information it would like from all the relevant people.

What Information Gets Reported?

Still, an awful lot of data are collected. But in their raw form, they're not of much use. They have to be reduced into summaries or recommendations that people can understand and act on. In fact, the practice of analyzing and interpreting data is sometimes called "data reduction."[29] This book isn't the place to wade into the statistical intricacies of data reduction. But two broad approaches are so common, and so consequential, that they deserve comment. The first, aggregating data to provide summaries, happens across all manner of media. The second, crafting algorithms to make recommendations, is the stock and trade of many Web 2.0 services.

The simplest way to make sense of a mountain of data is to count heads. How many people visited that website, viewed that page, or downloaded that video? Of the people who watched that TV program, how many were women and how old were they? In all of these instances, you're describing the size and, often, the composition of the audience. These are basic measures of popularity, made by aggregating data into categories and summarizing the results with numbers. When those numbers are expressed as percentages of the population (e.g., 10 percent of households watched that program), they're called *ratings*. And as we've seen, ratings can be worth a lot.

Of course, the counting isn't quite that simple. Ratings services are trying to accurately describe entire populations. But because no measurement service can collect information from all the relevant people, statistical adjustments are made. Ratings services routinely apply mathematical weights to people in over- or underrepresented categories to "balance" the sample. Doing so isn't a perfect solution, but it has the effect of making different kinds of people count proportionately in the final estimates. More important, it's a practice that's transparent to ratings users and usually authenticated by an outside party.[30]

Newer forms of digital media are rife with head-counting exercises. Topics "trending" on Twitter are immediately apparent to users and often reported in the press. The same social chatter is harvested by "social listening" firms and translated into metrics that rate engagement.[31] YouTube makes it easy to see how many times a video has been viewed. iTunes reports on the popularity of songs. Online versions of older media, such as the *New York Times*, routinely let readers know which articles were the most read, e-mailed, and commented on. And the increasingly ubiquitous "like" button is providing the raw material for even more exercises in head counting.

These new measures obviously appeal to people. Perhaps they offer a more democratic assessment of what's worthwhile than the judgment of a few experts. Perhaps in a world of endless choice, they're a more timely and comprehensive way to sort through the options. And, unlike traditional ratings, they're readily available to the general public. As O'Reilly and Battelle noted, "this is just the beginning. With services like Twitter and Facebook's status updates, a new data source has been added to the Web—real-time indications of what is on our collective mind."[32] These metrics are clearly a force in shaping public attention.[33]

But these measures often aren't as transparent as traditional ratings. The problem is generally one of not knowing who or what is represented in the aggregated number. As Tarleton Gillespie of Cornell noted, "a casual visit to Twitter's home page may present Trends as an unproblematic list of terms that might appear a simple calculation. But a cursory look at Twitter's explanation of how Trends works—in its policies and help pages, in its company blog, in tweets, in response to press queries, even in the comment threads of the censorship discussions—Twitter lays bare the variety of weighted factors Trends takes into account."[34]

Using social media to assess the state of public attention, then, can be deceptive. Not all people use social media and not all social media users are equally active. As a rule, contributions to social-sharing platforms, such as YouTube or Digg, are dominated by a relatively small number of people who seem to relish the attention they get.[35] We know, for example, that a few "power users" on Facebook are far more likely to comment or use their like button than the average user.[36] If something trends on Twitter, does that mean it's of broad public interest, that a few power users have latched on to it, or that the way in which data are weighted have affected the result? In principle, these are answerable questions. In practice, it's often hard to tell. The companies that gather and report the data, many of whom hope to sell advertising, are somewhat secretive and may or may not make their methods known.

Algorithms offer another way to reduce mountains of data into actionable recommendations. With the growth of server-generated data and high-speed computers their use is commonplace. In fact, one book claims algorithms now "rule our world."[37] Basically, an *algorithm* is a computer program that runs data through a series of instructions or decision points to reach some ideal result. The goal is usually to make a prediction. For instance, algorithms predict which websites are most likely to give us the information we want or recommend which books and movies will appeal to us.

There are a number of ways to build an algorithm. But two approaches to recommendation are common enough to describe here: search and collaborative filtering. Any discussion of these, however, should begin with a caveat—there's a lot we don't know. Most algorithms are proprietary. And although we have a general idea of how Google or Amazon makes a recommendation, the specifics are secret. Furthermore, popular algorithms aren't static. They're being tweaked all the time. Google, for instance, changes its search algorithms more than five hundred times a year.[38]

Search engines offer recommendations in response to a query. Once you enter a search term, the recommendations you get are generally a function of hyperlinks.[39] Websites often point to other sites by providing a link. With big enough computers, it's possible to "crawl" the web and see how pages are linked. Google, for example, indexes twenty million web pages a day.[40] Although links reveal the existence of pathways rather than actual traffic, they are routinely used to indicate circulation, affiliation, and just plain importance.[41]

Google's algorithm, called PageRank, uses links to score the importance of web pages.[42] It's built on the proposition that the importance of a page is revealed by the importance of other pages that point to it. As one computer scientist explained it, "There are in fact three distinct factors that determine the PageRank of a page: the number of links it receives; the link propensity, that is, the number of outgoing links, of the linking pages; and the PageRank of the linking pages."[43]

This approach can create a circular system in which the rich get richer, so there are ways to adjust the algorithm and introduce some fresh blood.[44] Today, modern search engines

> use complex algorithms and hundreds of different ranking criteria to produce their results. Among the data sources is the feedback loop generated by the frequency of search terms, the number of user clicks on search results, and our own personal search and browsing history. For example, if a majority of users start clicking on the fifth item on a particular search results page more often than the first, Google's algorithms take this as a signal that the fifth result may well be better than the first, and eventually adjust the results accordingly.[45]

Facebook has also entered the fray with a "graph search" function. Rather than links, it uses "likes" to find people, places, or things. The shift from links to likes has the potential to produce rather different results.[46] But as Clara Shih, a marketing expert noted, using likes will still "create a virtuous cycle in which popular pages show up in Graph Search, making users more likely to engage with those pages, making those pages more likely to show up in future search results, and so on."[47] So either way, masses of information are distilled into a rank-ordered list with the most important or popular items at the top.

Another way to generate recommendations is with collaborative filtering. Amazon and Netflix are well known for using this approach. In a nutshell, these systems develop a profile of each user by tracking their purchases, rentals, downloads, evaluations, and so on. The algorithm then compares them with other users who have similar profiles.[48] The objective is to recommend things a "person like you" might enjoy. For example, if most people with your profile have bought the book *Fifty Shades of Grey* and you haven't, you're likely to get a recommendation. Collaborative filtering has been used to recommend movies, music, news items, television programs, and just about everything else. The latest generation of recommender systems takes a variety of contextual information into account, such as where you're located or what's on your calendar, to predict what you'll want next—even if you haven't asked for it.[49]

In addition to helping people find things, these automated recommendations are often intended to sell another book or deliver a highly targeted message. Although most users probably recognize those motives, the recommendations still seem to be welcomed. The ability of recommending institutions to suggest just the right thing at just the right time is critically dependent on the scale and scope of their data-gathering operation. They need large volumes of server-generated information to refine behavioral and contextual recommendations. If these data can be wed to additional information describing the users (purchases, preferences, affiliations, activities, etc.), targeting and appeals can be honed even further.[50]

Bias in Measurement

All media measures are biased. That doesn't mean that they're deliberately skewed to achieve some nefarious purpose—although that could be the case. It means they can never offer a completely objective picture of reality. Bias is inherent in the process of collecting and reducing data. There are an endless number of things that could be observed. There are different ways to record those things. And there are, as we've just seen, many different methods for boiling all that data down into metrics that can be used. In the process, some things will go unexplored and some things will end up on "the cutting room floor."

Human beings orchestrate that process. They decide what's useful, feasible, or marketable. Such judgments are baked into any media measure and they produce bias. What's important is identifying the most prevalent forms of bias and understanding how those affect the operation of the marketplace. There are three biases worth noting: the behavior bias, the personalization bias, and the popularity bias.

The Behavior Bias

The vast majority of digital media measures are constructed from records of people's behaviors. That's been true since the earliest days of radio and it remains true today. The very first ratings service decided to measure exposure to radio by recording listeners' tuning behavior. That wasn't the only way to conceive of media use—it could have been defined as listener attention or engagement—but exposure achieved a quick industry consensus. As historian Mark Balnaves and his colleagues explained, "for the purposes of buying and selling radio airtime, or programmes, a metric that showed the fact of tuning in to a programme and the amount of time listening to a programme had a simplicity that was essential for bargaining in highly competitive environments."[51] Modern techniques for measuring digital television do essentially the same thing. People meters and STBs record the content or channel that's been selected and infer exposure from those choices.[52]

Web 2.0 services are no less dependent on behavioral data. Although some gain insights from user comments, most of the information being collected is fairly construed as behavioral data. Servers track what people buy, the websites they visit, the information they request, the materials they download, the pages they link to, and the things they share. In fact, a sea of behavioral data is being produced every second of every day. It has the virtue of being cheap and abundant, which makes it a tempting resource. But behaviors, even if they're accurately measured, can be difficult to interpret.

The biggest temptation is to think of choices as a stand-in for preferences. In fact, in economics there's a formal assumption that choices are a measure of "revealed preferences."[53] That kind of thinking is common in recommender systems. Even critics of those systems seem to confound the two. "The new generation of Internet filters looks at the things you seem to like—the actual things you've done—or the things people like you like—and tries to extrapolate."[54] But as we saw in chapter 2, there's reason to doubt that choices are a simple reflection of preexisting preferences. Media use isn't always a well-informed expression of our personal preferences. It's shaped by the nature of our social networks, the tools we use to find content, and the structures of everyday life.[55]

Inferences based on behaviors must, therefore, be made with caution. Does watching a video mean you like it? Should every purchase on Amazon be construed as a tacit recommendation to other "people like you"? Does linking to a web page or sharing a link represent approval or condemnation? Is retweeting a message a judgment on its novelty or an expression of identity and "social bonding"? Does hitting the "like" button mean you really liked it or is it just a way to get some benefit? The meaning of behaviors isn't always straightforward. Yet when we reduce them to simple headcounts or recommendations, we often treat them as if it they were. Behavioral data may give us a fair approximation of what's commanding public attention, but they can rarely tell us why.

The Personalization Bias

With so much to choose from and so little time, an important function of media measures is to guide people's selections. Personalized recommendations, which somehow anticipate what we would find useful or interesting, mean we don't have to waste time searching and considering every option. Skill at providing those recommendations has been a recipe for success on the web. But commercial platforms aren't the only ones with a personalization bias. As I'll argue in the following, the very nature of our social networks contributes to metrics that personalize our encounters with digital media.

For profit-making websites, the drive toward personalization is easy to understand. What Pariser calls the "race for relevance" has motivated most Silicon Valley firms because they recognized the best way create loyal customers "was to provide content that really spoke to each person's idiosyncratic interests, desires, and needs."[56] As we've seen, this is the raison d'être of collaborative filtering. Google has been tailoring its search results since 2009.[57] And Facebook's graph search provides yet another method of personalization. According to the *New York Times,* "Its algorithms vet who among a user's Facebook friends the user is closest to and whose answers the user would like to see at the top of search results."[58]

Social networks and affinity groups also contribute to a personalization bias in a somewhat less calculated manner. As noted in chapter 2, virtually all social networks are homophilous.[59] Their members tend to have similar backgrounds, interests, and predispositions. Within those networks, media that address the relevant group interests, norms, and prejudices will tend to circulate more readily. Social news sites such as Reddit or Digg encourage this selectivity by eliciting, aggregating, and ranking recommendations about what merits attention.

In fact, the recommendations that come to us through our own social networks can be more automated than we imagine. Facebook personalizes what will go into each user's newsfeed with an algorithm called "EdgeRank."[60] EdgeRank is proprietary, but similar to a graph search it clearly prioritizes updates from the people with whom we have strong ties. In other words, among all our Facebook friends, we're likely to hear more from people just like us. This sort of tailoring contributes to a personalization bias that's widespread among social media.

The biggest concern about personalization is that it will cause users to retreat into comfortable enclaves, which will have the effect of narrowing their horizons and confirming their biases.[61] Personalization might, for instance, encourage conservatives to see "red media" and liberals to see "blue media." Pariser calls these enclaves "filter bubbles" and argues that users are often unaware that the filters even exist.[62]

But the social effects of recommendations from friends are difficult to pin down. It's a challenge to differentiate the impact of social contagions from homophily.[63] People may see and do the same things, not because of recommendations but just because they're alike. Still, there's some evidence that prodding from friends encourages people to vote, which might affect close elections.[64] And it appears that recommendations from people you know can override tendencies toward selective exposure.[65] Mutz and Young have speculated that fully automated "impersonal" recommendations—such as collaborative filtering—might be less potent sources of influence than "personal" recommendations.[66] But in a world where Facebook and Twitter filter personal messages and recommendations through algorithms, those distinctions are getting fuzzier every day.

The Popularity Bias

Almost all the methods described produce a rank-ordered list of recommendations. Search engines sort web pages by the number and importance of their inbound links. Social networks and content providers point users to the most-read story, the most-viewed video, or the thing most "people like you" have bought, or rented, or liked. The methods that user information regimes employ routinely privilege popularity. As Carl Bialik, the *Wall Street Journal*'s "numbers guy," quipped, "The Internet has facilitated an outbreak of popularity contests."[67]

Although critics of popular culture have, historically, viewed popularity as a dubious indicator of quality, recommender systems have been largely immune from this skepticism. Rather, users and social commentators alike often celebrate these systems because they embody the "wisdom of crowds"—the notion that many ordinary decision makers can produce collective judgments superior to those of experts. This popular concept offers an appealing corrective to self-serving institutions and self-appointed authorities telling people what's best. But even if one accepts that premise, user-information regimes often fail to meet the prerequisites for producing good decisions.

According to James Surowiecki,[68] the writer who helped popularize the concept, wisdom is realized when large numbers of diverse individuals make decisions or predictions independently. Aggregating these autonomous judgments often produces a result demonstrably better than expert opinion. Unfortunately, most user-information regimes violate these precepts, something that Surowiecki himself recognized.

First, recommendations are often made on the basis of relatively small, homogeneous groups of people. As we've seen, members of social networks or affinity groups are homophilous. In most groups, the number of members is limited. Anthropologist Robin Dunbar argued that humans are incapable of maintaining more than about 150 meaningful interpersonal relationships, thus limiting the size of networks.[69] Although some find evidence of that ceiling in social media use,[70] other network analysts argue "Dunbar's number" is too low.[71] In any event, social networks, which function as recommending bodies, typically don't have the size and diversity essential for producing wise judgments. Nor does collaborative filtering correct the problem. Although the best systems sit astride vast stores of data, they are required to do so because relatively few people are ultimately useful in making a recommendation. That is, filtering algorithms search for and preferentially weight your "closest peers" or "nearest neighbors."[72] These often constitute just a tiny sliver of the people in the database.

Second, none of the described user information regimes promote the kind of independent decision making required for optimal recommendations. Search engines offer users information about what others have done, effectively guiding subsequent decision making. Aggregating and reporting what visitors to a website have chosen or what members of a social network recommend introduces powerful signals about social desirability for those who follow. Humans are prone toward herding,[73] and seeing what other people are doing can trigger stampedes.

Sociologists at Columbia University, for example, conducted a large-scale Internet-based experiment in which people were allowed to download music from any one of several obscure bands.[74] Within these experimental conditions, the more information people could see about what other people had downloaded, the more they were inclined to follow the leader. The quality of the songs made relatively little difference. Across conditions, user information produced "winner-take-all" results. But you couldn't tell in advance who the winner would be.

If autonomous decisions produce the best outcomes, contagions and herding seem anathema to extracting wisdom from crowds. But these kinds of popularity-based rankings are everywhere. As Nate Silver, an expert on prediction, warned, "This is another of those Information Age risks: we share so much information that our independence is reduced. Instead we seek out others who think just like us and brag about how many 'friends' and 'followers' we have."[75] So, we should be circumspect about the popularity bias in measurement. Such metrics can tell us what's attracting attention—and in doing so promote popularity—but they aren't a failsafe guide to what's truly worthwhile.

Seeing the World through "Big Data"

We've noted the ability of servers to track millions of users engaged in trillions of transactions through every second of every day. Google handles more than three billion search requests daily.[76] Facebook users "like" something 2.7 billion times a day, not to mention all the other activities that are being recorded.[77] In fact, most sectors of the economy are experiencing the same explosive growth in the volumes of information being collected.[78] This deluge is commonly referred to as "big data."

A great many commentators and consultants have argued that the emergence of big data will cause us to reinvent everything from manufacturing to marketing to medicine to weather forecasting to stock trading to the very practice of science itself.[79] Although I've alluded to the impact of server-generated data on media measurement, it's worth considering whether big data will fundamentally change the way we see the marketplace of attention, and in doing so alter its operation.

The term *big data* is delightfully ambiguous. For some, it's anything too big to manage on a spreadsheet, for others it's a dataset that requires nothing less than a supercomputer. It usually covers two different topics that are often lumped together: data and analytics. To get a handle on the contributions and limitations of big data, it's useful to treat these separately.

Proponents of big data often imply that bigger must be better. I noted that most media measures have a behavioral bias that can make their interpretation problematic. But for Chris Anderson, the longtime editor of *Wired* magazine, more data somehow obviate that problem. "Who knows why people do what they do? The point is they do it, and we can track and measure it with unprecedented fidelity. With enough data, the numbers speak for themselves."[80] However, most people who know what the data do and do not contain come to a different conclusion. Researchers at Microsoft Research have cataloged the real world shortcomings of big data, from representativeness to just plain error and concluded that "just because Big Data presents us with large quantities of data does not mean that methodological issues are no longer relevant. Understanding sample, for example, is more important now than ever."[81]

The numbers never speak for themselves. In order to make sense of them, they have to be analyzed. Data must be cleaned, weighted, and reduced. Quite often, big data are fed into algorithms to create actionable metrics. And as author Chris Steiner noted, "At the heart of all these algorithm-enabled revolutions on Wall Street and elsewhere, there exists one persistent goal: prediction—to be more exact, prediction of what other humans will do."[82]

But forecasting what people will do, want, or find rewarding is trickier than making predictions about the physical world. Consider using big data to predict the weather. A forecast doesn't change the weather. Predicting we're going to get an inch of rain doesn't make it so. And if it does rain, you can measure the accuracy of your prediction. All you have to do is go to the rain gauge to know whether you got it right. The social world doesn't always play by the same rules.

Predictions about social activity can affect the thing they're predicting. If Google predicts a website will be useful, that encourages traffic, which seems to further justify the recommendation. If the nytimes.com touts an article as the most read, it tempts people to read it. If we follow that implied recommendation, it adds to the temptation of others. If Amazon predicts we'll enjoy a book because "people like us" have bought it, we might add it to our shopping cart creating sales that wouldn't otherwise exist. These measures don't stand apart from the reality they purport to measure; they reshape it.

The same can be true of measurement in the hands of media professionals. For instance, the media would love to identify new talent before they attract widespread attention. *Advertising Age* described the challenge. "Brands have been working with YouTube stars—iJustine, Shay Carl, Michelle Phan and the like—for years, but what if you could identify a not-yet star before they got big?"[83] To do that, one agency tracks fifty thousand channels and twenty-five million videos on YouTube to predict who is on the verge of stardom. Those with good scores can be signed to a contract. It's possible the talent identified in this way would hit it big without intervention. But using metrics to identify winners can create winners. Unlike the weather, social predictions can change outcomes.

The distinction predicting the physical world and predicting the social world seems lost on many proponents of big data. In the social world, algorithms powered by big data have the potential to create "self-fulfilling prophesies." As the great sociologist Robert K. Merton explained, "public definitions of a situation (prophecies or predictions) become an integral part of the situation and thus affect subsequent developments. This is peculiar to human affairs. It is not found in the world of nature."[84] Self-fulfilling prophesies create two problems, one for the analysts and one for the rest of us.

The quality of algorithmic predictions ought to be judged by the accuracy of the prediction. But any assessment depends on how well we can measure the thing we're predicting. In the world of big data, some things are more knowable than others. We might be able judge how well a model explains TV program ratings or how manipulating a sales pitch affects purchases.[85] But when Google predicts that we'll find a website useful or

Netflix predicts that we'll like a film, how do we know these predictions have truly identified what is most useful or enjoyable? We may find the recommendations helpful, but we can't be sure if they are optimal. Taking people's acceptance of a recommendation as evidence of its quality might simply perpetuate a self-fulfilling prophecy. Judging predictions in the social world isn't as simple as looking at the rain gauge.

The larger consequence of self-fulfilling prophecies is that they can shape the very nature of cultural consumption. Public measures can "react" with the world they measure, altering social reality.[86] This would most likely happen as the result of some systematic bias built into the metrics that increasingly guide our choices. Two biases, personalization and popularity, may well have that ability.

Personalized recommendations steer us in the direction of media that resonate with our interests and prejudices. Recommenders are usually left to guess who we are and what we'd like by making inferences from our past behaviors. Eli Pariser calls this a "you loop" and explains the mechanism this way: "You click on a link, which signals an interest in something, which means you're more likely to see articles about that topic in the future, which in turn prime the topic for you. You become trapped in a you loop, and if your identity is misrepresented, strange patterns begin to emerge, like the reverb from an amplifier."[87] It's possible that by priming certain things and not others, we could develop a taste for what is recommended. As we've seen, many social commentators fear personalization could polarize society, but if those systems cater to and create preferences, the effects could be far more pronounced. We'll explore that possibility in greater depth in chapter 6.

The popularity bias, however, might mitigate these affects. Rather than pulling us apart, it tends to concentrate public attention. Although popularity is hardly a foolproof guide to what is of greatest importance or highest quality, it seems clear that recommending things that are popular drives traffic and further enhances popularity. Reducing oceans of data to a simple head count and reporting it can inflate the final tally.

None of these tendencies is mitigated by the sheer bigness of big data. Similar to all other media measures, the new metrics are human creations and as such are just as subject to bias and abuse. But their sheer pervasiveness is new, and that makes them an increasingly important force to be reckoned with. They can offer enormously useful tools for institutions and individual media users.[88] But these are not neutral players in the market-place of attention. Media measures enter into that world in powerful ways that are insufficiently appreciated and often difficult for ordinary users to detect. It's certainly possible that the social world will come to resemble what the data encourage us to see.

5 AUDIENCE FORMATIONS

We've waded through a lot of material that suggests how audiences ought to behave. Users, the media, and the measures on which they both depend all play a role in how public attention takes shape. But there's no consensus on what kind of audience formations will emerge from that combination of factors. Perhaps users, empowered with on-demand media platforms, will demonstrate clear-cut loyalties that effectively narrow their diet of media to a few favored offerings. But it could also be that the variable nature of our preferences leads to equally varied patterns of consumption. Perhaps digital media will encourage endless audience fragmentation, the demise of blockbusters, and the formation of many tightly knit enclaves. But it could also be that our social nature and the popularity bias of our filters will continue to concentrate public attention.

The best way to sort through these possibilities is to look at hard evidence about how audiences actually behave. Because I've just finished explaining the imperfect and biased nature of all media measures, I should probably say something about my own biases when it comes to "hard evidence." The audience formations that are reported in the pages that follow are all based on measures of behavior. In an age of great abundance, when users can access most things with the click of a mouse or a remote control, people's self-reports of their behaviors are especially prone to error.[1] So, whenever possible, the audience formations I describe are based on meters or server-generated data. These data can't tell us everything we'd like to know, but they can measure exposure with considerable accuracy. As such, they provide a basis on which to evaluate what people are doing with all the media resources at their disposal.

The studies that I report include my own work and that of colleagues in academe and industry. Most of the research is quite recent. Some of it is proprietary or has been presented only at conferences or professional meetings. The point of this review is to focus on those studies that help us judge various predictions about what the future holds and shed light on the differences of opinion that confront us. The first section reviews research on audience fragmentation and the causes of popularity. We then consider the factors that drive audience loyalties. I'll present evidence on the audience for local news and information, an overlooked but potentially important topic. And finally, I'll make a case for the existence of a "massively overlapping culture" in media use.

Audience Fragmentation

One of the most widely observed consequences of the growth in digital media is audience fragmentation. As more offerings are delivered on broadband networks and more choices are available on demand, patterns of use become more widely distributed. From the perspective of traditional broadcasters and other "mainstream media," the newcomers are unwelcomed competition that "erodes" their audiences. Social commentators, however, are divided on whether fragmentation is good or bad. Some celebrate these changes as signaling a more responsive marketplace and robust public sphere.[2] Others see cause for concern. For them, fragmentation spells the end of a common cultural forum or, worse, the birth of media enclaves and "sphericules" that scarcely interact.[3] So it's important to assess the state of audience fragmentation and the factors that control it.

Although there are different ways to conceptualize fragmentation,[4] by far the most common is a "media-centric" approach that focuses on the size of the audience for discrete media outlets (e.g., channels, websites, etc.) or products (e.g., movies, music, videos, etc.). Those units are sometimes grouped into larger categories or brands. The total size of each unit's audience can be reported at a point in time[5] or in a series of cross-sectional "snapshots" over time.[6] The latter is often used to illustrate long-term trends in fragmentation and is a staple of many industry reports and forecasts.

For example, figure 5.1 depicts the decline in the combined prime time audiences of the oldest US television networks—ABC, CBS, and NBC—as a series of vertical bars. In 1985, the "big three" accounted for almost 70 percent of all the time people spent watching television. Over the next two decades, their combined share of audience dropped steadily to under

30 percent. The cause was an equally dramatic increase in the number of channels competing for the audience, as indicated by the ascending dark line punctuated by triangles. In 2008, the last year Nielsen reported such numbers, the average US television household received roughly 130 channels. This kind of audience erosion has also happened to state broadcasters in Europe and Asia.[7]

A popular way to represent media-centric data is to show them in the form of a "long tail."[8] Here units are arranged from most popular to least with the total audience for each (e.g., monthly reach, unique visitors, total sales, etc.) shown vertically above the unit. Long-tail distributions go by different names including *power laws* and *Pareto distributions*. A related phenomenon, in which people rather than things are the units of analysis,

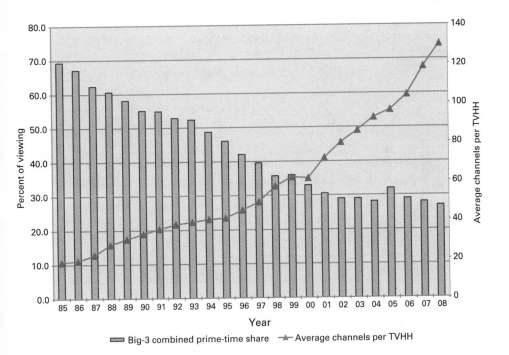

Figure 5.1

Television Audience Fragmentation over Time.

Source: Adapted from Webster, James G. "Beneath the Veneer of Fragmentation: Television Audience Polarization in a Multichannel World." *Journal of Communication* 55, no. 2 (2005): 366–382.

is what marketers call the *80/20 rule.* That is, in most consumer markets you can expect that 20 percent of your customers account for 80 percent of your sales. All of these distributions depict lopsided patterns of use in which a few dominant players account for most of the consumption. Such winner-take-all markets are routinely observed in cultural consumption.[9]

Figures 5.2 and 5.3 are long-tail distributions based on Nielsen data from March 2009. Figure 5.2 shows the audience for US television channels. Figure 5.3 shows the same thing for major Internet brands.

Figure 5.2 indicates that, in the United States, the major broadcast networks (shown in white bars) reach a greater percentage of the population (i.e., monthly cumulative rating) than the cable networks with which they compete. So, even though broadcast networks have seen their audiences decline over the years, they are still in a class by themselves when it comes

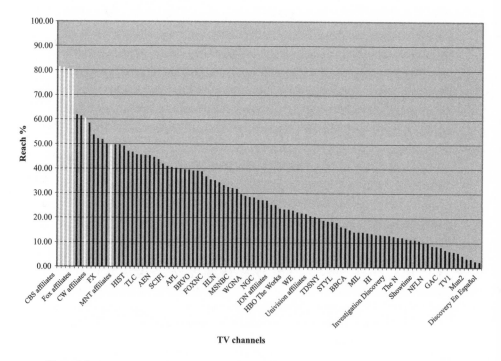

Figure 5.2

A Long-Tail Distribution of TV Channels.

Source: Webster, James G., and Thomas B. Ksiazek. "The Dynamics of Audience Fragmentation: Public Attention in an Age of Digital Media." *Journal of Communication* 62 (2012): 39–56.

to commanding public attention. The gradual downward slope of the graph suggests a moderate degree of market concentration.

Figure 5.3 shows the long-tail distribution of Internet brands, ordered by their monthly reach (i.e., unique visitors as a percentage of the total audience). Here the market leader was Google (58.92%), followed by Yahoo! (51.19%), MSN/Windows Live (39.40%), YouTube (35.77%), AOL Media Network (32.51%), and Facebook (29.35%). In these data, however, we see a relatively sharp drop in attendance as we move down the tail. That indicates a much more concentrated market than the one we saw in television. Considering that this example includes only the top 138 brands, you can imagine how long and skinny the tail would be if we were to include all Internet outlets. So concentration and fragmentation coexist in long-tail distributions, although the balance seems to vary by medium.

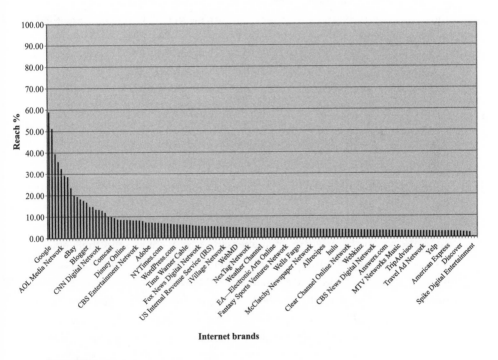

Figure 5.3

A Long-Tail Distribution of Internet Brands.

Source: Webster, James G., and Thomas B. Ksiazek. "The Dynamics of Audience Fragmentation: Public Attention in an Age of Digital Media." *Journal of Communication* 62 (2012): 39–56.

Typically, audiences in less abundant media, such as radio and television, are more evenly distributed across outlets (i.e., more fragmented) than in media with many choices, such as the Internet.[10] So although increased competition enables fragmentation, the sheer number of competitors alone does not determine the extent of that fragmentation.

In any medium, the real question for most professionals and theorists is just how far the process of fragmentation can go. Will future audiences distribute themselves evenly across all the choices at their disposal or will a few popular offerings continue to dominate the marketplace? Chris Anderson expects that in a world of infinite choice "hit-driven culture" will give way to "ultimate fragmentation."[11] Others are convinced that winner-take-all markets will continue to characterize cultural consumption.[12] I suspect the latter outcome—continued concentration—is far more likely. There are four factors that lead me to that conclusion.

First, media structures—such as distribution networks and the architecture of the web—offer mundane, almost mechanical, explanations for what gets public attention. Although these structures evolve in response to how people use them, that process can take time. One such structure is television network coverage (i.e., how many people can receive the signal). The signals of older broadcast networks still reach more households than cable networks. And the newest cable networks have to fight to be carried on cable systems. With larger potential audiences, it makes sense for incumbents to invest more in programming. It's hardly surprising, therefore, that major broadcast networks continue to attract the largest audiences. Of course, digital delivery across platforms may level the playing field, but increased reliance on the web is likely to introduce other kinds of favoritism.

Digital networks privilege incumbents (i.e., older nodes) in their own way. It's a phenomenon that network analysts call "preferential attachment."[13] That is, as new players join the network, they tend to preferentially link to more prominent, heavily trafficked sites. Although there are many examples of newer outlets quickly becoming popular (e.g., Pinterest, Twitter), in general, the web tends to help the rich get richer. This phenomenon occurs without making any assumptions about the quality of the sites. As one expert noted, "It appears that the natural tendency of the web (and many similar networks) is to link heavily to a small number of sites: the web picks winners."[14]

Second, quality undoubtedly does play a role in concentrating public attention. Although it's notoriously difficult to assess, quality certainly varies across media offerings. As long as prices aren't prohibitive, attendance should gravitate to higher-quality choices. Digital media make it especially easy for users to consume quality products. On the one hand, the pure "public good" nature of digital media means they're easily reproduced and, often, "free."[15] As economists Robert Frank and Philip Cook noted, "If the best performers' efforts can be cloned at low marginal cost, there is less room in the market for lower ranked talents."[16] Further, the increased availability of on-demand media allows people to be choosy. Older linear systems sometimes force-fed users content. But as Chris Anderson himself pointed out, the change from CDs to iTunes coupled with personalized recommendations has enabled users to select the "best individual songs" from albums and skip the "crap" in between.[17] Consuming only the best the digital marketplace has to offer is easier than ever before. To the extent that there is a consensus on the quality of offerings, it effectively reduces the number of choices and concentrates public attention on those options.

Third, the social nature of media consumption will continue to concentrate attention. Media have long served as a "coin of exchange" in social situations.[18] A few programs, sporting events, or clips on YouTube are the stuff of water-cooler conversations, which encourages those who want to join the discussion to see what everyone else is talking about. The advent of social media, such as Facebook and Twitter, extend these conversations to virtual spaces and focus the attention of those networks on what members find noteworthy.[19] Often this will focus attention on high-profile outlets, hit shows, or live, event-driven programming such as the Super Bowl, Olympics, Oscars, and Grammys.

Fourth, the pursuit of quality and the social aspects of media now come together in media measures. We've seen that people use recommender systems to assess their options and guide their choices. In a world of bounded rationality, these measures signal what seem to be a consensus on quality and an indication of what "people like you" are choosing. They're also biased in favor of things that are popular. The more salient these recommendations are, the more they herd people to what's popular.[20] Although quantifying the "wisdom of crowds"[21] in this way may not be a reliable indicator of quality, it focuses public attention nonetheless.

The forces that concentrate audiences—along with the inclination of the media to themselves imitate what's popular—suggest that audiences will not spin off in all directions. The never-ending production of media by professionals and amateurs alike will necessarily grow the long tail even longer. But the endless supply of media won't produce endless audience fragmentation. A relative handful of movies, blogs, and videos gone viral will continue to command a disproportionate share of public attention, whereas most other things will be doomed to obscurity.[22] If anything, we should expect that the head of the long tail to remain and its tail to get much, much skinnier.[23]

But even more important than the shape of long-tail distributions is what they hide. With long tails it's easy to see what's popular and what is not. They don't, however, tell us how people move across media offerings. It could be that most people are loyalists who have a taste for specialized genres and effectively camp out in their preferred niches. Alternatively, it could be that people range widely across all the offerings at their disposal. Either possibility might lurk "beneath the veneer" of audience fragmentation.[24] Knowing what's going on has implications for how media providers build audiences and how users organize into communities or networks. So our next concern is to understand the nature of audience loyalties.

Preference-Driven Loyalties

By far, the most widely held expectation is that audience loyalties will be driven by user preferences. As noted in chapter 2, each academic discipline seems to have its own variation on this theme. Economists and marketing researchers assume that people have clear program type loyalties and that these will explain their patterns of choice. The only trick is to discover what those program types actually are. Sociologists also assume that people's tastes will translate into preferences for established musical genres (e.g., classical versus rock). Psychologists and political scientists expect people to have a confirmation bias, especially when it comes to news and information. That bias encourages "selective exposure" to like-minded speech and an avoidance of anything to the contrary. Communications researchers put stock in people's needs and their drive to gratify those needs.

As we've seen, each of these traditions offers research in support of its hypotheses, but surprisingly little meets my earlier definition of "hard evidence." In the following, we'll consider studies that use data on expo-sure to assess program type loyalties—including an aversion to news—and evidence of the so-called red media–blue media divide.

In 2011, Turner Broadcasting began a research project to help identify viewer-defined program types. Turner, a part of Time Warner, operates a number of television networks including TBS, TNT, and truTV. Each net-work specializes in a particular type of programming and each wanted to hone its "brand." TBS has emphasized comedy programming, TNT drama, and truTV has offered what it called "actuality" programming. The last two networks were particularly dependent on scheduling reality programs. The problem was that there were a great many reality programs and they weren't necessarily alike. They included everything from *American Idol* to *The Iron Chef* to *Cops* to *Survivor*. It seemed unlikely that people who liked one reality program would necessarily like all other reality programs. Turner wanted to better organize reality TV into subgenres that would be consistent with viewer preferences. They could then use that information to refine how they programmed their networks.

To do so, they worked with Nielsen to sort programs into categories defined by patterns of viewing. If certain programs tended to be viewed by the same people, the inference was they were programs of the "same type." To do this, they employed a data-reduction technique called *factor analysis,* which audience researchers have been using since the 1960s.[25] The exercise produced eighteen reality program groups or subgenres.[26]

Among the insights, Turner discovered that two similar-sounding pro-grams, *Pawn Stars* and *Hardcore Pawn,* appealed to different sets of view-ers. The former emphasized characters and their back stories, the latter emphasized physical conflict. *Pawn Stars* was a better fit for the TNT brand, whereas *Hardcore Pawn* worked on truTV.

The first lesson to take from this exercise is that identifying audi-ence-defined program types is of practical value to the media, although the way programs group together isn't always obvious. Genre preferences, so defined, have a modest power to describe and cultivate patterns of audi-ence loyalty.

The larger lesson is two-fold. The media, at least those with the resources to do so, use media measures to see *and* adjust to what users are doing.[27] Theoretically, this is illustrative of how "duality" works in the media mar-ketplace. Measurement makes people's actions visible, which informs the mechanisms that reproduce and change the structural features of the environment. Analytically, duality makes it difficult to disentangle the effects of agency and structure. For example, are people loyal to a channel or website because it offers the kind of material they prefer or do they encounter media because it is delivered by an outlet to which they are loyal? The two are confounded and, in all likelihood, both are responsible for the patterns we observe.

One genre that's been of particular interest is the news. Watching or reading the news seems essential if citizens are to operate effectively in a modern democracy. In 2007, Markus Prior, a political scientist at Princeton, published a provocative book that argued that structural changes in the media environment were reshaping the audience for news.[28] According to Prior, many people have an aversion to news and prefer entertainment. This has always been true, but in the early days of television viewers couldn't escape the news. That's because only a few US networks were on the air and they all scheduled news at the same time. If you wanted to watch television—and most people did—you ended up watching the news, learning about current events despite yourself. However, as cable made more and more channels available, people who had never liked the news stopped watching. The opposite was also true. People who liked the news now had twenty-four-hour news networks to watch. As a result, although average news consumption remained relatively constant, it was increasingly polarized. That is, we went from everyone watching a little news to some people watching a lot and others avoiding it altogether. Prior went on to argue that this change led to differential levels of political knowledge and inclinations to vote.

It now appears that news avoidance operates across media platforms[29] and, to varying degrees, across different cultures.[30] At the risk of greatly oversimplifying this literature—which has different ways of defining and measuring what constitutes exposure to news—the general pattern looks like the graphs in figure 5.4.

Graph (a) is based on metered measures of television news viewing and radio news listening in the New York and Chicago media markets in 2006. Graph (b) is based on people-meter measures of television news viewing in Seoul Korea in 2001 and 2007. The average news consumption in graph (a) is higher, in part, because it includes a more expansive definition of news. But both suggest about a third of the population avoids news programs

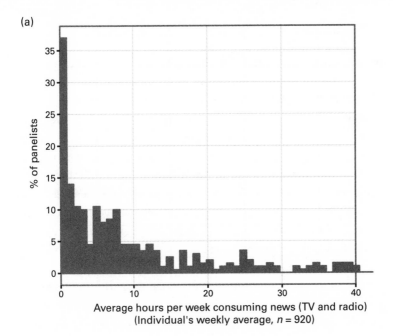

(a)

% of panelists

Average hours per week consuming news (TV and radio)
(Individual's weekly average, *n* = 920)

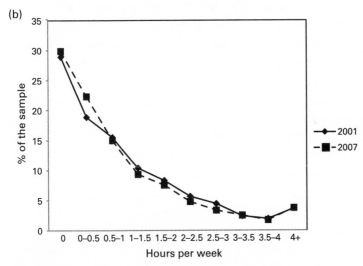

(b)

% of the sample

Hours per week

◆—2001
■–2007

Figure 5.4

Exposure to News in the United States and Korea.

Sources: (a) LaCour, Michael J. "A Balanced News Diet, Not Selective Exposure: Evidence from a Real World Measure of Media Exposure." Presented at the Annual Midwest Political Science Association, Chicago, April 2012. Reproduced with permission of the author. (b) Adapted from Kim, Su Jung, and James G. Webster. "The Impact of a Multichannel Environment on Television News Viewing: A Longitudinal Study of News Audience Polarization in South Korea." *International Journal of Communication* (2012): 838–856.

altogether and only a small percentage are news "junkies." These patterns are generally consistent with an 80/20 rule in which a relatively small percent of the population accounts for the lion's share of consumption.

The news preferences that seem to get the most attention, however, are those driven by people's political ideologies.[31] Do politically conservative and liberal users attend only to like-minded media? If so, it would show up in audience loyalties that could potentially polarize the electorate. In the United States this is often called the red media–blue media divide, and it's a specific instance of the larger phenomenon of selective exposure. But here again reliable measures of exposure to partisan news are surprisingly scarce. In the following I'll summarize select studies of a red-blue divide in television, online news outlets, and social media.

LaCour obtained data from Integrated Media Measurement Incorporated (IMMI), which in 2006 hoped to become a ratings service.[32] IMMI gathered data with smartphones that panelists in the New York and Chicago media markets carried with them throughout the day over a period of months. These phones were programmed to detect the audible portion of radio and television programs at thirty-second intervals, which were taken as evidence of exposure. With those data, LaCour was able to construct very precise measures of exposure to conservative and liberal television news programs including *The O'Reilly Factor* and *Fox News Live*, on the one hand, and *MSNBC News Live* and *The Daily Show* on the other. He was also able to construct a "net selectivity" score that measured each person's exposure to "like-minded" or "crosscutting" news. So, for example, if a Republican watched *The O'Reilly Factor,* she was exposed to like-minded news. If she watched liberal news like *The Daily Show,* that exposure was crosscutting. The reverse was true for Democrats. LaCour's results are shown in figure 5.5.

What's striking about this figure is that it's not particularly polarized. Although Democrats are somewhat more inclined to watch like-minded news than Republicans, both groups are exposed to a fair amount of crosscutting news. The only notable exception is a small group of Republicans who, consistent with the selective exposure hypothesis, tune out liberal news.

But perhaps television is still too much of a mass medium to truly support ideological loyalties. Online media outlets, however, are available on demand and can be far more extreme than anything you're likely to encounter on television. Gentzkow and Shapiro, professors at the

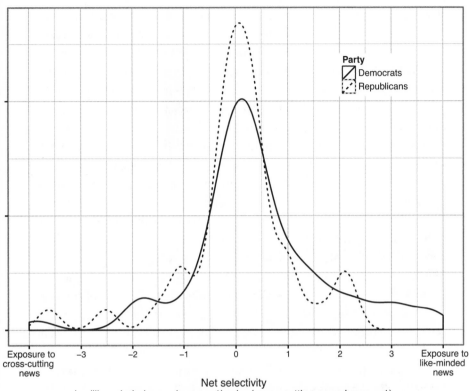

Figure 5.5

Partisan Exposure to Like-Minded and Crosscutting News.

Source: LaCour, Michael J. "A Balanced News Diet, Not Selective Exposure: Evidence from a Real World Measure of Media Exposure." Presented at the Annual Midwest Political Science Association, Chicago, April 2012. Reproduced with permission of the author.

University of Chicago's Booth School of Management, decided to test for evidence of ideological segregation on the Internet.[33] To do so, they used 2009 data from comScore, which provides audience ratings on websites in dozens of countries around the world.

With those data, they were able to measure the conservativeness of 1,379 national news and opinion websites by looking at the percentage of self-identified conservatives who visited the site. Their analysis showed that the audience for news websites is highly concentrated—like the long-tail distribution of all websites: "The top 4 sites—Yahoo! News, AOL News, msnbc.com, and cnn.com—account for more than 50% of all visits, the top 10 sites account for more than 60%, and the top 20 sites account for nearly 80%."[34] This pattern is consistent with other, server-generated data on traffic to news and opinion websites.[35] The biggest outlets tend to be politically centrist. So although there are, indeed, many politically extreme sites online, they get very little traffic.

Gentzkow and Shapiro also noted that users often visit many ideologically diverse sites. "Visitors of extreme conservative sites such as rushlimbaugh.com and glennbeck.com are more likely than a typical online news reader to have visited nytimes.com. Visitors of extreme liberal sites such as thinkprogress.org and moveon.org are more likely than a typical online news reader to have visited foxnews.com."[36]

So, much like television news, there was a good deal of crosscutting exposure to online news. Overall, ideological loyalties on the Internet are only slightly more pronounced than those in television. By way of comparison, ideological segmentation is far more pronounced in the face-to-face encounters people have in their neighborhoods or workplaces than it is in their use of online media.[37]

Of course, those "face-to-face" interactions increasingly take place on social media platforms such as Facebook and Twitter. Could it be that these social networks, perhaps in combination with various forms of user-generated content, are more inclined toward ideological extremes? The evidence is mixed. Researchers at Indiana University have found that "political retweets" are highly segmented. That is, partisans retweet political messages to those with whom they are ideologically aligned. But their "mentions" tell a different story, leading to the following conclusion: "While we know for certain that ideologically opposed users interact with one another, either through mentions or content injection, they very rarely share information from across the divide with other members of their community."[38] Similarly, the ways in which ideologically slanted blogs link to videos or other blogs show evidence of preaching to the choir and crosscutting engagement.[39]

But, the existence of links, like-minded or otherwise, doesn't tell us the purpose behind those links, whether readers follow them or how people make sense of the material they encounter. Given the rapidly evolving nature of social media, the following conclusion from researchers at

Harvard's Berkman Center for Internet and Society seems broadly applicable to the partisan loyalties evident in social media: "Further nuanced and 'high-resolution' research into patterns of posting, commenting, and discussion; participation; and the capacity of the blogosphere to drive levels of engagement along various dimensions will be necessary to understand the implications of these findings more fully."[40]

Overall, there is very little evidence that people's political ideologies segregate them into tightly knit "echo chambers" offering nothing but like-minded speech. On the contrary, although people who pay attention to the news can and do encounter a healthy dose of information from ideologically agreeable sources, they also come into regular contact with crosscutting stories, images, and commentaries. These patterns of audience behavior should allay our worst fears of an impermeable red-blue divide.[41] But there is a limit to what we can infer from data on people's exposure to media.

Just because users have been exposed to something doesn't tell us what it means to them. As noted in chapter 2, people selectively perceive media messages. In the case of ideologically charged news, researchers at the University of Pennsylvania have argued that conservative media, especially Fox News, Rush Limbaugh, and the opinion pages of the Wall Street Journal, present their audiences with a coherent picture of the political world—one that frames "mainstream media" as having a liberal bias and a double standard. If their audiences adopt those frames, it can insulate them from their exposure to crosscutting media. That is, although conservatives might well see mainstream media, they "don't buy it." In fact, these frames "encourage the audience to reinterpret mainstream media in ways that reinforce the messages of the echo chamber."[42]

Political scientists are also concerned that focusing on people's ideological or policy differences may cause us to miss a more insidious form of polarization. There's evidence, at least in the United States, of a growing antipathy between liberals and conservatives.[43] Republican partisans seem to loath Democrats as never before and vice versa. This kind of "affective polarization" extends to rank-and-file voters and can make it difficult for people to find common ground. Just why this is happening isn't entirely clear, although nasty campaign advertising and partisan media seem to be implicated. So although the patterns of exposure we've reviewed can tell us the shape of public attention, they can't necessarily reveal the consequences of those encounters.

Structure-Driven Loyalties

In an age when digital media are available anywhere, at any time, it's tempting to assume that preferences alone would be enough to explain audience loyalties. Structures such as channels or program schedules seem less important than ever. But the growth of on-demand media doesn't mean that older structures are unimportant or that newer, less visible structures such as filtering algorithms aren't emerging. Nor are structures a characteristic of the media alone. Users operate within social structures that encourage audience loyalties that can have little to do with a preference for genres or politically like-minded speech. In the following we'll see how media structures, as well as the structures of everyday life, can shape audience loyalties.

There's a tradition in marketing research, going back to the 1960s, that explains audience loyalties as a function of media structures.[44] This includes work on "audience flow" and "channel loyalty," which documents that audience duplication[45] is better explained by how programs are scheduled than by genre loyalties. In fact, at the time researchers confidently claimed that "there is no special tendency across the population for people who watch one programme of a given type to watch others of the same type."[46] So much for preference-driven loyalties! The problem, of course, is that this finding came from a three-channel world with relatively little program differentiation and even fewer opportunities for viewers to reveal their true preferences.

Even so, more recent research in this tradition has produced only slightly different results. Audiences still tend to flow between back-to-back programs, although lining up programs of the same type enhances that flow.[47] That's one reason why you see "spinoffs" scheduled immediately after their popular parent (think *NCIS*). And channels still seem to matter. In fact, channel loyalties are more pronounced now than before,[48] which seems to result from channels specializing in a type of content such as the networks at Turner Broadcasting. Hence, we're again reminded of the how channels and preferences are confounded in a multichannel environment.

Rather than deciphering patterns of audience duplication, another way to think about loyalty is to identify the heaviest users of a channel or website. In other words, who are the loyalists? In summer 2012, PBS presented a study defining its loyalists as the top 20 percent of all public television viewers.[49] They found that their loyalists accounted for 83 percent of all PBS viewing. That is, just 20 percent of the viewers who watched anything on PBS accounted for 83 percent of the "people hours" devoted to that network. By way of comparison, the top 20 percent of Fox News viewers accounted for 95 percent of all Fox's viewing, whereas Comedy Central's loyalists accounted for 77 percent of all their viewing.[50] These patterns are very much in keeping with the 80/20 rule.

You might think that these loyalists were devoting most of their lives— or at least most of their media usage—to watching their favorite channel. Certainly many people expect specialized channels and niche offerings to have small-but-loyal audiences. This way of thinking conjures up an image of choosy users who are attracted to specialized offerings but not much else. But that's almost never the case.

There is a well-established phenomenon in marketing and audience behavior called the "law of double jeopardy."[51] In a nutshell, it stipulates that unpopular offerings have two problems. Not only are their audiences small but also the people who do partake aren't that fond of the offering and don't spend much time with it. This happens because niche products, such as obscure films or books, attract heavy users of those media who can be hard to please. As a rule, it's heavy users who are in the audience for unpopular offerings. Popular offerings attract light users. That's what makes them popular.

Consistent with the law of double jeopardy, PBS found that, as a group, their loyalists devoted only 6 percent of their total viewing time to public television. That pattern is typical of most TV channel audiences.[52] Channel loyalists, at least by this definition, are generally just heavy users of *the medium*. In this case, a few people end up watching a lot of PBS because they watch a lot of television. But watching a lot of TV is more a function of your leisure time than anything else. So what appears to be loyalty to a particular outlet or genre can actually be driven by the structures of everyday life.

I noted many of these day-to-day structures in chapter 2. It's no secret how patterns of work and play explain variation in the total audience for different media platforms.[53] That's why prime time programs have the largest television audiences. Less frequently considered are the audience loyalties that can result from language and geography.

Within any given market, language seems to engender loyalties. In fact, the only small-but-loyal audience those early marketing researchers could find was attributable to "minority" language broadcasts.[54] In other words, those stations didn't attract many viewers, but those who did view spent a lot of time there. In 2008, my colleague Tom Ksiazek and I used "portable people-meter" (PPM)[55] data to see how language affected radio and television use in Houston, Texas.[56] Houston has a large Hispanic population, some of whom are bilingual and some of whom speak only Spanish. As you might imagine, Spanish speakers relied heavily on Spanish language outlets, and English speakers used English language outlets almost exclusively. Language segregated those audiences much more effectively than any ideological loyalties. Only bilingual users moved comfortably between those worlds.

Across markets, such as the World Wide Web, language is confounded with geography, complicating the picture. To oversimplify things, there are two different schools of thought about what explains audience formation on this global platform. One argues that economic structures such as market power and trade will enable core nations, especially English language sites, to remain dominant.[57] Another school of thought asserts that cultural structures such as language and proximity will trump economic advantages and reveal more balkanized geographic loyalties.[58] The former usually supports its case with evidence of how websites link to one another, which reveals a centralized network with English at its core.[59] But as I've noted, hyperlinks don't show actual traffic, so true audience loyalties can only be inferred.

To provide a clearer picture, my colleague Harsh Taneja constructed a network based not on hyperlinks but on patterns of audience flow between sites. If the audience duplication between any pair of sites exceeded chance, they were linked.[60] This was done across the top one thousand sites, which accounted for 99 percent of all the traffic on the web. The audience-based network is rather different than one built from hyperlinks. Figure 5.6 shows a hyperlink network on the left (a) and an audience network (b) of the same websites on the right.

As others have found, the network constructed from hyperlinks (a) is rather centralized but the network built from audience behavior (b) is

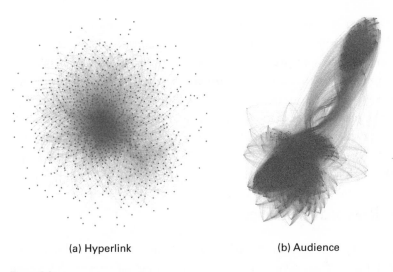

(a) Hyperlink   (b) Audience

Figure 5.6

Hyperlink and Audience Networks.

Source: Adapted from Taneja, Harsh. "Mapping an Audience Centric World Wide Web: A Departure from Hyperlink Analysis." Presented at the Association for Education in Journalism and Mass Communication, Washington, DC, August 2013. Used with permission.

more segmented. The cluster in the upper right of the audience network, which is somewhat separated from the rest, is composed of Chinese websites. The larger cluster in the lower left is centered on United States and "global" websites. Those global sites typically offer multiple languages and have no discernible geographic home. They include many corporate sites as well as networking platforms such as Facebook and Twitter. The bigger cluster also contains several smaller groupings that are hard to pick out in this black-and-white figure. They include Russian, Japanese, and Korean sites that cluster tightly together. All in all, geography, followed by language, does the best job of explaining patterns of audience duplication, whereas hyperlinks do a poor job of explaining audience flow.[61] It's the combination of language and geography that drives audience loyalties on the World Wide Web, although more work needs to do be done to sort out the contributions of each.

Geography surely has effects quite apart from language. The United States, for example, is divided into 210 market areas (e.g., Chicago, Las Vegas, Nashville, New York, Miami, etc.). Each of these is served by local news outlets. It stands to reason that people in each market will know a good deal more about developments in their hometowns than what goes on in other markets. This would produce a "geography of local knowledge,"[62] driven more by structure than genre preferences. Yet our preoccupation with national news means we know very little about those variations.[63] With the proliferation of mobile devices and the ability of platforms such as Google and Foursquare to track our whereabouts, it seems likely that "hyper-local" affinities will be identified and cultivated to produce yet another wrinkle in these structure-driven loyalties.

Local News and Information

Although we know relatively little about the audience for local news and information, it deserves a closer look. Not only might it help us understand the geography of local knowledge but it may also well serve as a corrective to at least some of the social ills ascribed to preference-driven loyalties. In the following, we'll consider the content of local news, its place in the diet of media users, and how it might mitigate partisan divides and the polarization of political knowledge.

As I noted, the United States has 210 television markets each with its own local news programming. Other large countries, such as China and most European nations, have local media serving cities or regions.[64] US markets typically have three or four broadcast affiliates that dominate the local TV news market. Bigger markets support more hours of programming, but most markets schedule their shows in the early and late evening, before and after prime time.

LaCour's study of partisan news polarization—or the lack thereof—also provided an opportunity to measure just how big a contribution local news makes to an average viewer's diet of news. The results are summarized in figure 5.7.

Local news accounted for almost 60 percent of the time people spent watching TV news. Although the balance between liberal and conservative news varied somewhat with a viewer's political party, all consumed a substantial diet of local news.[65] Moreover, it appears that local news is in the diet of people who otherwise avoid national news. In a study of cross-platform news use, almost 80 percent of "news avoiders" reported some exposure to local TV news.[66] Although there is evidence that local

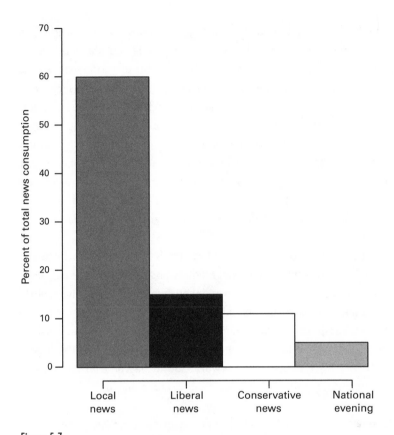

Figure 5.7

News Diet.

Source: LaCour, Michael J. "A Balanced News Diet, Not Selective Exposure: Evidence from a Real World Measure of Media Exposure." Presented at the Annual Midwest Political Science Association, Chicago, April 2012. Reproduced with permission of the author.

news audiences are eroding, especially among younger viewers, broadcast news continues to be an important source of local information.[67] But what do people see?

Although there is variation from market to market and from early to late news broadcasts, the single biggest block of content is devoted to weather and sports.[68] These segments are traditionally scheduled in the second fifteen minutes of a half-hour program because they seem to draw viewers who will queue up in the first fifteen minutes. The remainder of local news is devoted to stories on politics, crime, health, and topics of local interest.

We don't know much about the ideological slant of local TV news, so we're left to speculate. Although it would make sense for stations in very conservative or very liberal markets to be mindful of those sentiments, they would also be loath to alienate any more viewers than necessary. With three or four stations competing for a local—and therefore smaller—audience, taking an extreme editorial stance just doesn't make sense. The strategy that works for Fox News in a national market of three hundred million viewers isn't appropriate when you're trying to capture a third of a market with one million viewers, which means that even if local news items are susceptible to an ideological slant, they shouldn't have much of a red or blue tint. I suspect most of what passes for local news is in the political mainstream.

If that's the case, a substantial diet of local news might mitigate the polarizing effects of more partisan national media. Consumers of extremely conservative news outlets, who have been encouraged to distrust the reports of the national "mainstream media," may be less apt to apply that frame to local news. Familiar local faces reporting on bank robberies, car crashes, or the machinations of local government seem less alien than the highly paid anchors of New York–based networks. So it may be that many news items commanding public attention don't trigger an "us versus them" interpretation.

Local news might also mitigate the polarization of political knowledge that results from people avoiding news. Those concerns have emerged from an analysis of national media. But local news still seems to draw people who otherwise avoid national news. Perhaps, they really tune in to see the weather or sports. But in the process of queuing up for those segments, they may catch stories about crime or politics, producing the kind of "by-product learning" that characterized the early days of national broadcast television.[69] Even a little exposure to news among these viewers seems to encourage their civic engagement.[70] If linear media continues to gently enforce exposure to things not chosen in advance, it should promote a stock of common political knowledge.

Massively Overlapping Culture

A recurring prophesy about digital media is that public attention will become increasingly balkanized. These are usually motivated by a belief that preference-driven loyalties will polarize the audience into distinct niches. Sometimes the preferences in question are political ideologies that create enclaves of like-minded users who are at odds with the rest of society. Sometimes the focus is on genre preferences that encourage discrete taste cultures that scarcely interact.

Chris Anderson, author of the popular and provocative book *The Long Tail,* expressed this general line of thought as follows. "The same Long Tail forces and technologies that are leading to an explosion of variety and abundant choice in the content we consume are also tending to lead us into tribal eddies. When mass culture breaks apart, it doesn't re-form in a different mass. Instead, it turns into millions of microcultures."[71] Although Anderson acknowledged that these microcultures might somehow interact, he predicted the end result would be a "massively parallel culture." In a similar vein, technology columnist Farhad Manjoo argued that digital media supported the existence of "parallel realities,"[72] each operating with its own set of facts.

Whereas many would agree with these predictions, the notion of parallel cultures or realities can be misleading. Parallel lines don't intersect. They suggest an unflinching devotion to whatever cultural content defines each line. This is an expectation based more on theory and anecdote than a judgment based on what media users are actually doing. In chapter 2 I noted the fickle nature of preferences and the inclination of many to be "omnivores." In this chapter we've seen considerable evidence of crosscutting exposure to news. An alternative vision of the future, then, might be that we're headed for a massively *overlapping* culture. So which is a more apt representation?

Anderson and a great many prophets of balkanization buttress their predictions by pointing to audience fragmentation. As we've seen, long-tail distributions tell us about the relative popularity of media offerings and little else. Nonetheless, some interpret the proliferation of unpopular content on the long tail as evidence of niches that play to powerful audience loyalties. And that's where they get on thin ice.

To illustrate the problem, consider figure 5.8. It combines data from figures 5.2 and 5.3 to give us a sense of how audiences are distributed across the principle outlets of TV and the web. It tells us something about popularity and the extent to which the digital marketplace is concentrated. But it tells us nothing about loyalty to any one outlet. It could be that people

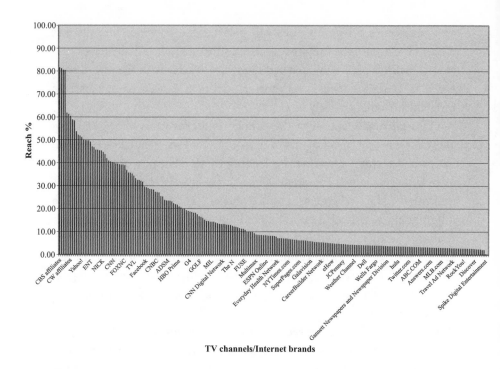

TV channels/Internet brands

Figure 5.8

A Long-Tail Distribution of TV and Internet.

Source: Webster, James G., and Thomas B. Ksiazek. "The Dynamics of Audience Fragmentation: Public Attention in an Age of Digital Media." *Journal of Communication* 62 (2012): 39–56.

who watch CBS affiliates stick with their favorite channel and have no encounters with material further out on the long tail. Similarly, it could be that the few devotees of Spike Digital Entertainment, which is out on the long tail, spend lots of their time there. Alternatively, users might range widely across many outlets, from Fox News to ESPN to Twitter.com. Looking at a long tail can't tell us. What we really need to answer this question is media exposure measured across multiple platforms. Using anything less invites analysts to make a huge inferential leap.

To get beneath the veneer of the popularity data, my colleague and I created an audience network across outlets, much like the one we saw in figure 5.6. We were able to do this because the data we used to create figure 5.8 came from Nielsen's "Convergence Panel," which tracked each person's use of television *and* the Internet. Each outlet was conceived of as a node in a network. The nodes were linked if they shared an audience above the level of overlap that would occur just by chance.[73] Figure 5.9 shows just a portion of that 236-node network to give you a sense of what the network looked like. You can see, for example, that almost half the people in the sample used NBC *and* Yahoo in the course of a month, which is well above a random level of duplication.

Using this approach, it's possible to count how many outlets any one channel or website is linked to—which is something network analysts call a *degree score*. So if CBS viewers watch little else besides CBS, it will have a low degree score. But if they tend to spend time with many different outlets, CBS will have many links and a high degree score.

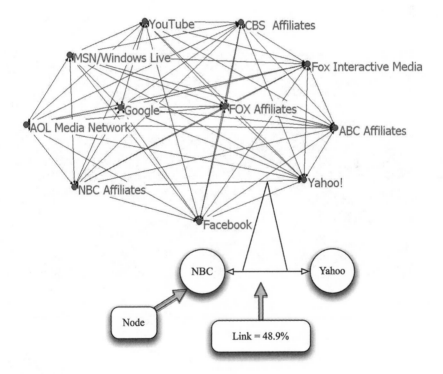

Figure 5.9

An Audience of Network TV and Internet Outlets.

Source: Webster, James G., and Thomas B. Ksiazek. "The Dynamics of Audience Fragmentation: Public Attention in an Age of Digital Media." *Journal of Communication* 62 (2012): 39–56.

Interpreting unpopular outlets as niches with small-but-loyal audiences would suggest that they will have low degree scores. But if people move among many outlets, those nodes will have high degree scores. To boil all of this information down, we converted degree scores for each outlet into percentages (i.e., what percent of the other 235 outlets did it link with?) and arranged them in the form of a long tail from highest to lowest. Figure 5.10 shows the result.

This figure is remarkable for how little variation there is. Almost every outlet shares an audience with every other outlet, above and beyond the level of duplication that would be expected by chance alone. For example, the audience for Spike Digital, which had the lowest degree score, still uses almost 70 percent of the other outlets depicted in this graph. Far from being the massively parallel culture that Anderson envisions, these outlets

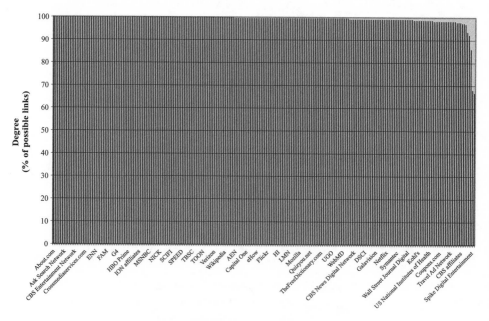

TV channels/Internet brands

Figure 5.10

Distribution of Degree Scores among Outlets.

Source: Webster, James G., and Thomas B. Ksiazek. "The Dynamics of Audience Fragmentation: Public Attention in an Age of Digital Media." *Journal of Communication* 62 (2012): 39–56.

suggest a massively overlapping culture. No outlet lays exclusive claim to an enclave of loyalists.

In fairness, our sample in this study of audience overlap didn't extend very far out on the long tail, and so it may not settle the question. It might be that farther out on the tail there are niches of bona fide loyalists. But other evidence makes that seem doubtful. Gentzkow and Shapiro, who looked at many smaller, more extreme sites, still found overlap and concluded that "if we were to sample readers from conservative sites like drudgereport.com, we would find that most of their readers get most of their news from sites that are substantially less conservative. Similarly, if we were to sample readers from liberal sites like huffingtonpost.com, we would find that most of their readers get most of their news from sites that are substantially less liberal."[74]

It could also be that outlets are too broad to reveal what items of content are being selected within a channel or website. Conservatives, for example, might cherry-pick only certain things from a network, such as CBS, and avoid anything with a tint of "blue." Liberals and conservatives who watch CBS might end up seeing very different things. To begin to peel back the layers of the onion, so to speak, we'll look at an analysis of television viewing done by Turner Broadcasting. First, we'll see how the audience for the three major US news networks overlaps with others channels. Then we'll see what programs each of those audiences is viewing.

Tables 5.1 and 5.2 are based on Nielsen data collected from February 18–24, 2013. That was a week when viewing levels were high and reruns were few and far between. It ended with a Sunday night telecast of the Oscars on ABC. The tables sort people into four audience groups. The first includes all viewers ages eighteen and older. The next three are the eighteen and older audiences for CNN, Fox News, and MSNBC. Fox News and MSNBC are often characterized as appealing to conservative and liberal viewers, respectively. CNN is more middle-of-the-road. In each case, anyone who watched at least six minutes of a network was included in that audience group—which is an industry standard for determining a network's "cumulative" audience.[75] As you'll see, a viewer could show up in more than one column if he or she watched more than one network.

In table 5.1, you'll note that each of the three older broadcast networks reached about half of adult viewers in the course of a week. So, for example, 51 percent watched ABC and 48 percent watched CBS. These numbers are a

Table 5.1

Network Reach within Audience Groups

Percentage of Each Group Who Viewed Selected Networks				
Network	*All viewers*	*CNN viewers*	*Fox News viewers*	*MSNBC viewers*
ABC	51	75	65	68
CBS	48	68	66	63
NBC	41	62	56	57
FOX	35	45	48	43
Turner Network Television	21	31	30	35
History Channel	21	33	37	35
Comedy Central	15	23	16	32
PBS	14	23	18	24
Fox News Channel	11	30	100	23
MTV: Music Television	10	11	7	15
Cable News Network	10	100	27	38
Black Entertainment Television	7	12	6	16
MSNBC	7	28	16	100
Telemundo	5	2	1	2
CNBC	4	17	14	19

Source: Adapted from an analysis by Turner Broadcasting. Copyrighted information © 2013 of The Nielsen Company, licensed for use herein.

measure of their unduplicated audience, or "reach." Among news viewers, who tend to be older and watch more TV, each broadcast network's reach is closer to two-thirds of the audience. Even popular cable networks don't have nearly as many viewers. So as we noted with the monthly data in figure 5.2, broadcast networks are still a major presence in TV viewing.

It's worth noting that the vast majority of adults don't watch cable news networks in any given week. The reach of Fox News and MSNBC is 11 and 7 percent of the adult population, respectively. This observation is consistent with the argument that the audiences for partisan news broadcasts are relatively small, attract those who are already believers, and are essentially "preaching to the choir." As a result, partisan media have relatively little room to affect a change in attitudes. In an environment of abundant choice, those who are less politically committed simply tune out the partisan news, often in favor of entertainment.[76]

It's also worth noting what other networks the supposedly liberal and conservative viewers of MSNBC and Fox News actually watch. First, similar to CNN viewers, they watch other news networks. Thirty-eight percent of MSNBC viewers watch CNN, and 23 percent watch Fox News.

Similarly, 27 percent of Fox News viewers watch CNN and 16 percent watch MSNBC. So, consistent with the other research we've seen, there seem to be many occasions for exposure to crosscutting news and information. In fact, Fox News viewers watch many channels, including some that might surprise you. They are, for example, slightly more likely than all adults to watch PBS (18%) and Comedy Central (16%). These finding are consistent with what's been reported elsewhere. The audience for any given channel almost always distributes its viewing pretty much like other channel audiences.[77]

Still, using many different channels doesn't tell us what specific programs are watched by liberals and conservatives. It could be that Republicans have a very different media diet than Democrats. A few studies have tried to assess whether partisans have differing tastes in entertainment programming.[78] Generally, the findings suggest that conservatives are overrepresented in the audiences for detective shows such as *NCIS* and sporting events such as NASCAR and golf, whereas liberals are more likely to watch comedies such as *30 Rock, Modern Family,* or, of course, the *Daily Show* or *Colbert Report.* Some of those reports leave readers with the clear impression that the red-blue divide extends even to entertainment. As a writer for the *New York Times* concluded, non-news viewing "is every bit as polarized as the political culture."[79]

But these claims should be taken with a grain of salt. Even when they are based on "hard evidence" of viewing, two qualifications are in order. Programs are identified as being liberal or conservative by creating an index. For example, if Democrats are overrepresented in a program audience by

13 percent, then the program would have an index value of 113, suggesting it's a "blue" program. But that still means that an awful lot of Republicans are in the audience. Second, programs with high index values are almost always watched by small audiences. One program with a very high conservative index was *The American Bible Challenge,* one with a high liberal index was *Chappelle's Show.*[80] The middle-of-the-road programs with indices near 100 usually have the largest audiences.

Another way to look at this question is to simply ask, "what are the most popular programs among liberals and conservatives?" Nielsen doesn't report viewer's political affiliations or ideologies but, as a stand-in, we can at least compare the most popular programs among Fox News and MSNBC audiences. You can see the results in table 5.2. It reports program rankings based on the reach of all programs telecast during that week in February 2013.[81]

The most popular program, by a very wide margin, was the broadcast of the Oscars. It reached 28 percent of the US adult population, or more than sixty-two million people. In 2013, the nominated films included *Lincoln, Zero Dark Thirty, Les Miserables,* and the winner *Argo.* All of these movies were heavily laden with "political" ideas that audiences would be hard-pressed to miss. This broadcast was easily the most popular program among news network audiences, reaching a third of Fox News viewers and 40 percent of the MSNBC audience.

Aside from this programming event, the second most popular program among all viewing groups, including MSNBC viewers, was the Sunday afternoon coverage of the Daytona 500. The third most popular was *NCIS*—except for Fox News viewers, who had it fourth. Beyond that there is some divergence, although, everyone's list is dominated by evening programs on broadcast networks. *The Big Bang Theory, American Idol,* and *Person of Interest* were popular with everyone. Even *Modern Family,* which ranks 153rd among Fox News viewers reached 6 percent of that audience—or about 1.4 million viewers. Overall, there's a high correlation ($r = 0.7$)[82] between the programs popular with Fox News viewers and the ones watched by MSNBC viewers.

There are, however, a few deviations from that norm. The third most popular show among Fox News audiences was *The O'Reilly Factor;* it reached 19 percent of Fox viewers. The fourth most popular among MSNBC viewers was *Hubris: Selling the Iraq War.* It reached 11 percent of that audience. But even at that, *O'Reilly* was seen by over a half million MSNBC viewers, and *Hubris* was seen by 370,000 Fox viewers.

Table 5.2

Top-Ranked Programs among News Network Viewers

Rank among Adults 18+						
Network	Program	All viewers	CNN viewers	Fox News viewers	MSNBC viewers
ABC	The Oscars	1	1	1	1
FOX	NASCAR: Daytona 500	2	2	2	2
CBS	NCIS	3	3	4	3
CBS	The Big Bang Theory	4	7	43	10
FOX	American Idol (2/20)	5	4	15	5
CBS	Person of Interest	7	6	18	7
CBS	CSI	12	37	75	75
ABC	Modern Family	15	53	153	34
CBS	60 Minutes	26	5	41	6
NBC	NBC Nightly News (2/18)	31	11	108	12
CBS	CBS Evening News (2/21)	73	39	166	91
FNC	The O'Reilly Factor (2/20)	168	154	3	262
MSNBC	Hubris: Selling the Iraq War	756	134	658	4

Source: Adapted from an analysis by Turner Broadcasting. Copyrighted information © 2013 of The Nielsen Company, licensed for use herein.

Well, enough with all these numbers. The bottom line is there's very little evidence of a massively parallel culture in the media choices of users. People demonstrate only modest loyalties to genres and political ideologies. They certainly don't spend their lives barricaded in enclaves of like-minded speech or any other single type of media. There is, however, considerable evidence of a massively overlapping culture in which people move freely among a great many cultural offerings. Although it's hard to say just what people make of all those encounters, at least they're having them.

6   CONSTRUCTING THE MARKETPLACE OF ATTENTION

The first chapters of this book provided the pieces of a puzzle we have yet to solve. They described the predispositions of media users, the strategies and constraints of media providers, and the role of media measures—all of which influence public attention. But these strains of argument and evidence rarely come together in one complete picture of how audiences take shape. Rather, we confront a variety of theories about how people and systems are supposed to behave. The audience formations we just reviewed offer a rough empirical test of how well those theories work. Unfortunately, our expectations of audience behavior don't always square with what people actually do so our purpose in this chapter is to draw on all that material to develop a more comprehensive and dynamic model of how the marketplace of attention is constructed.

Structuration

In the first chapter, I described a structurational theory of society that could be used to explain the operation of the digital media environment. It argued that purposeful, reasoning agents used structures, such as language or social institutions, to achieve their own ends. And in doing so, they reproduced and altered those very structures. Although it's an "unlovely term at best,"[1] structuration provides a useful way to organize the material we've encountered into a unified framework.

Within that framework, it is the nature of the interaction between structure and agency that's of central concern. Since Anthony Giddens's pioneering work, there have been many attempts to clarify that relationship.[2] Historically, structure and agency have often been pitted against one another. William Sewell noted an unfortunate tendency to conceive of structures as rigid elements, "like the girders of a building," which constrain and determine what agents can and cannot do.[3]

The consensus now seems to be that structures are more malleable. They provide people with a way to exercise their agency, which has the effect of perpetuating and modifying those very structures. The constitution of the society, then, is a collaborative effort, or "duality," between agency and structure. Further, although agents may anticipate the consequences of their actions, oftentimes the results of the process are unintended. As Giddens noted, even people who reflect on what they do may not "know all there is to know about the consequences of what they do, ... nor do they know all there is to know about the conditions of their actions."[4]

We've seen many examples of these structurational processes in the preceding chapters. Individuals choose whatever TV shows they please. Networks monitor those choices, analyze them to judge audience loyalties, and adapt their programming accordingly. Recommender systems take data on what media people select, link to, or "like" in order to assess and organize those offerings. Their metrics guide other users and so reshape or reify media structures. In all of these instances, people use structures to exercise their "free will." Those actions affect the structural features of the environment, sometimes in ways that people neither recognize nor intend. Further, it is almost always media measures that connect agents and structures, fueling the structurational process. Hence, we have a framework that organizes users, the media, and measurement into one system.

The Dimensions of Structure

Researchers in media industries and the academy have had an on again, off again relationship with structures. Traditionally, they've been seen as rigid constraints that herd "passive" audiences in one direction or another.[5] With the advent of ubiquitous digital media, however, our interest in structures has gone in two different directions. Some seem to believe that structures are less relevant to user behavior than ever before. For example, Joe Turow reports a growing sense among those in the industry that "consumers no longer typically confront media products as unified branded products or programming flows. Many read individual newspaper articles, listen to individual songs, and view individual program episodes unmoored from the 'channel' that has been constructed by the content-creating firms."[6]

For many, these changes seem to free agents from structures and empower them to do as they wish. For others, structures remain potent, sometimes hidden forces that shape our encounters with media. These forces can operate to the detriment of individuals and society, even if that result is unintended.

As you can probably tell by now, I think structures are still a force to be reckoned with. But our conceptualization of structures is not particularly well developed. For audience analysts, the relevant structures are of two sorts: media structures and social structures. Media structures, which have undergone dramatic changes with the advent of digital technology, have attracted the most comment. They include the architecture of distribution systems (e.g., channels, websites, hyperlinks, etc.) and the information regimes that monitor and direct media use (e.g., ratings services, recommender systems, etc.).

Less carefully considered are the social structures that organize everyday life (e.g., leisure time, socioeconomic status, language and geographic proximity, etc.). These are less susceptible to manipulation, although media will often exploit them in some way (e.g., programming to proximate or available audiences). They are also deeply engrained in the fabric of society and so have the potential to exercise an enduring influence on how people act. As we saw in the last chapter, all of these structures seem to drive patterns of audience behavior.

Media and social structures can be organized along two dimensions, which show up as recurring themes in much of the literature on digital media—a literature that usually highlights the media structures. The first dimension considers the openness of structures. That is, do the structures encourage or at least allow crosscutting exposure to popular culture or do they promote a closed environment more characteristic of an echo chamber? The second dimension reflects the extent to which structures are obtrusive or unobtrusive. That is, can users see the structures in operation or not?

Open versus Closed Structures

I've noted a divide among books and academic theories that forecast how digital media will affect society. Some have a positive, almost utopian outlook. But a great many envision a gloomier future. Either way, these arguments seem to gather much of their force by characterizing the media environment as relatively open or closed. Openness is a function of many things, including technology, institutional practices, and how people use those resources.[7] Whereas the optimists see open structures allowing people to consume, create, and share a varied diet of media, the pessimists see closed structures filtering out discordant media encounters and balkanizing people into groups that are prone to various forms of social polarization.

In theory, a perfectly closed system has the potential to create positive feedback loops that cause users to "spin out of control."[8] For example, people who are politically conservative might succeed in encountering only like-minded content, which, in turn, would move them to ever-more extreme positions. This is exactly the kind of mechanism that would fuel "echo chambers" [9]and "group polarization."[10]

Conversely, open systems, which encourage crosscutting encounters, have the potential to limit these sorts of spirals and might actually promote a more robust public sphere. Palfrey and Gasser call these "interoperable" systems and argue they "afford consumers more choice by limiting the effects of being locked in to any one system. They can promote cross-cultural understanding, by the free movement of ideas, and the flow of trade."[11]

Either way, commentators who highlight this dimension of structure assign considerable importance to its ability to determine social outcomes. Although some present "hard evidence," many depend on anecdotes or a theoretical model of how people are expected to behave to buttress their conclusions. Terms such as *enclaves*,[12] *gated communities*,[13] *sphericules*,[14] *cyberbalkans*,[15] *filter bubbles*,[16] and *massively parallel culture*[17] all conjure up closed systems. Whether people actually settle down in those niches is another matter. Certainly our evidence of a massively overlapping culture suggests that they don't. Audiences, it seems, are rarely confined to a closed system of news or entertainment—at least for now.

Obtrusive versus Unobtrusive Structures

A somewhat less obvious conceptualization of structures organizes them by their obtrusiveness. Obtrusive structures are apparent to users. As such, people can actively choose to use them or not. For example, most users know which channels and websites specialize in different kinds of content (e.g., news versus entertainment) and act accordingly. They construct channel repertoires or rely on a handful of their favorite apps. Their use of these structures is purposeful. Unobtrusive structures, however, work behind the scenes. Users may have no idea that they are operating within a structured environment. For example, it might not occur to them that their search results or news feeds are tailored by an algorithm.

Gauging the obtrusiveness of media structures is further complicated by the sophistication of each user. What is apparent to some is invisible to others. There is a growing body of research on a second generation "digital divide" that finds some people are quite knowledgeable about the digital resources at their disposal and others are barely literate.[18] A computer programmer might understand how search algorithms work and take their advice with a grain of salt. But many people are more naive or completely oblivious.[19]

Obtrusiveness is typically used to describe media structures. But it can also help us conceptualize social structures. We saw in the last chapter how language and geographic proximity shape public attention. It seems to me that these might be fairly characterized as unobtrusive social structures. Yes, we know that we speak a particular language and live in a particular place, but it's easy to take that for granted. These structures hide in plain sight. As one sociologist noted, "we might think of the different layers of social structures as more or less hidden from everyday consciousness, more or less powerful in guiding human thought and action, and more or less durable in their resistance to change."[20] Many social structures, such as religion or socioeconomic status, could also contribute to enduring predispositions that shape the public's encounters with media.

A Map of Media Structures

These two dimensions can be used to create a map that helps us see how media structures organize media use. It concentrates on media structures because they are less durable than social structures, more subject to manipulation, and have received far more attention from social commentators. For simplicity, I show obtrusiveness and openness as "orthogonal," or uncorrelated, factors. Whether that's actually the case remains to be seen. Some arguments, for example, imply that unobtrusive structures beget closed systems. The four quadrants of the map identify four very different media environments within which users operate.

The map also organizes at least some of the literature on the social impact of media. I've taken the liberty of locating a few influential books within a 2 × 2 grid, shown in figure 6.1. My point is not to reduce any of these carefully crafted arguments into two-dimensional caricatures, but to illustrate how our understanding of structures seems to underlie our hopes and fears about the effects of digital media.

The upper left-hand quadrant supports some of the more optimistic assessments of digital media. Both Yochai Benkler[21] and Henry Jenkins[22] take comfort in the ability of users to engage in all manner of social production. In this world, people make purposeful use of digital resources to create and share media across social networks. They organize and interact with others in ways that are the essence of a structurally open environment. According to Benkler, "Individuals are using their newly expanded practical freedom to act and cooperate with others in ways that improve the practiced experience of democracy, justice and development, a critical culture, and community."[23]

The upper right-hand quadrant describes a more problematic world. Here, people use the resources at their disposal to create relatively closed

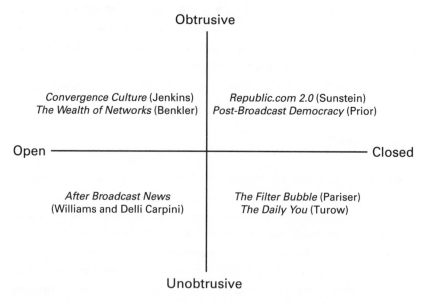

Figure 6.1
Organizing Media Structures

structures. The irony is that this self-segregation depends on the existence of a larger, more open, environment, which users refashion by exploiting obtrusive structures. At a minimum, they will select only preferred outlets or genres. Markus Prior, for example, argues that political involvement becomes polarized because "some people take advantage of greater media choice to become more knowledgeable, while others take advantage by avoiding politics altogether."[24] Among those paying attention to news, a more extreme ideological polarization seems possible. For instance, Cass Sunstein believes people will actively use filters to "sort themselves into echo chambers of their own design."[25] In either event, it's the users who are in charge.

The lower right-hand quadrant paints an even more chilling picture. Eli Pariser[26] describes a world in which ubiquitous recommender systems serve us a personalized diet of things we're predisposed to like. Likewise, Turow documents a system of commercial media that effectively targets and divides consumers into precisely defined niches.[27] Both envision closed structures that exploit and manipulate our social identities. And both identify unobtrusive, data-driven systems as the instrument of this social balkanization. As Pariser concludes, "what's troubling about this shift towards personalization is that it's largely invisible to users and, as a result, out of our control."[28]

The media environment suggested by the lower left-hand quadrant is an odder mix. It posits the existence of unobtrusive structures, about which we are generally suspicious, coupled with an open environment, about which we are generally approving. But this combination isn't that uncommon. In *After Broadcast News* Williams and Delli Carpini argued that throughout history, technological and cultural changes have produced different "media regimes." Each regime has had its own norms about what constitutes the news and who produces it. Yet, "At most points in time, the structure of this gatekeeping process is largely invisible, with elites and citizens alike at least tacitly accepting the rules by which information is disseminated as natural and unproblematic."[29] Much like Prior, they note that the days in which a few broadcast networks dominated the news are over, supplanted by an era of digital abundance. But unlike Prior, they see this as the harbinger of newer, more open structures that break down the silos of the old media regime, "the Internet and related communication technologies dramatically highlight the inadequacy of late-twentieth-century distinctions between types of media and genres, producers and consumers, mass and interpersonal communication, and public affairs and popular culture."[30] Hence, structures may be unobtrusive and yet support an environment in which boundaries seem to dissolve.

These are the structures that animate many of the claims made by social theorists. But as I noted, it's the nature of the interaction between structure and agency that's of central concern in structuration. How is it that they *mutually* constitute the media environment? Unfortunately, most of the preceding material tells us very little about how people shape structures or vice versa. Instead we learn either how people exploit whatever structures are made available or how structures, "like the girders of a building," constrain their encounters with media. The best way to illuminate this theoretical blind spot is to consider how agents operate within a structured environment.

The Interaction of Structure and Agency

To understand how structures and agents interact we have to come to grips with the question "where do preferences come from?" The literature on media use puts a premium on preferences. They are what most theorists use to explain how agents engage media structures. People's needs, wants, and prejudices are typically the first thing we turn to when explaining audience behavior. Even theorists who differ on whether media structures are open or closed often assume that users will be active participants in managing their encounters with media and that these encounters are the result of preexisting preferences.

Such preferences are sometimes called "exogenous."[31] That is, they come from outside the system. As economist Samuel Bowles noted, "the axiom of exogenous preferences is as old as liberal political philosophy itself."[32] But there's another possibility. "Endogenous" preferences are produced by the system itself. Clarifying the origin of our preferences is crucial, because it goes to the heart of how structures and agents affect one another. If agents bring clear, unalterable preferences to their encounters with media, they will bend media structures to their will. If, however, our preferences are shaped by our encounters with the media, we might bend in conformity to those structures. The problem, as Bowles pointed out, is that "we know surprisingly little about how we come to have the preferences we do."[33]

Exogenous Preferences

Anthony Giddens noted that social scientists often treat individuals "as the prime focus of social analysis. That is to say, the main concern of the social sciences is held to be the purposeful, reasoning actor."[34] The primacy of purposeful, reasoning actors is apparent in the many disciplines that offer explanations of media use. Each, as we've seen, has its own perspective on the subject.

Economists assume that utility-maximizing individuals have clear-cut preferences that determine their choices.[35] Sociologists argue that a person's place in society cultivates specific tastes that shape their cultural consumption, especially their appetite for different genres.[36] In communications, researchers have been enamored with a uses and gratifications model. It sees media use as a way to gratify needs that have "social and psychological origins."[37] Psychologists have placed an emphasis on individual attitudes, often explaining media use in terms of selective exposure to materials that minimize "cognitive dissonance."[38] More recently, social scientists have suggested that people bring different moods and hedonic impulses to their encounters with media, which explain their choices.[39]

Despite their varied origins, all these models of media choice focus on the psychological predispositions of agents to explain their actions. Sometimes preferences are tied to social structures, such as taste cultures or social networks.[40] Sometimes they're just there, such as program type preferences or mood states. In either event, predispositions show themselves as well-formed preferences that exist *prior to* a person's encounters with media. Those preferences might affect the operation of a media system, but they are unaffected by the system itself. In essence, these models assume that preferences cause exposure, as depicted in figure 6.2.[41]

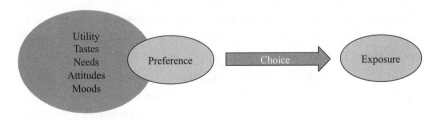

Figure 6.2
Traditional Models of Exposure

In this model, individuals bring their preferences to the media, which in turn determine their choices. The media are passive—like fruit waiting to be picked from the tree. By this reckoning, a person's diet of media is, for better or worse, of their own doing. This mind-set runs deep in the social sciences. More than one hundred years ago, the great philosopher and psychologist William James wrote, "*My experience is what I agree to attend to. Only those items which I notice shape my mind*—without selective interest, my experience is an utter chaos."[42] But putting all our faith in selective agents is an incomplete and misleading way to explain our encounters with media.

We know, for example, that people struggle with bounded rationality, especially in an abundant media environment. We know the tools they use to cope with abundance (e.g., repertoires, heuristics, recommender systems, etc.) can be biased and often produce suboptimal results. We also know from our own experiences that our interests and media preferences change. We become fans of a new band and lose interest in another. We encounter a new TV show and return for more. Or we become interested in someone or something just reported in the news. Surely some of these freshly minted preferences begin with an unintended encounter. A more realistic and ultimately useful model of exposure would account for all the factors that shape our exposure to media and would allow room for the possibility that people's preferences might be endogenous. That is, what we like and do is affected by the media systems within which we operate.

Endogenous Preferences

To explore that possibility, let's take stock of what we know about exposure to media. Traditional models, which suggest people's interests and desires motivate their choices, are in keeping with the "pull" model of audience building described in chapter 3. Although that undoubtedly happens some of the time, as we've seen, the media are hardly like fruit trees waiting to be picked. They actively try to manage our attention and cultivate our preferences. There are many ways in which media push content in our direction.

The most aggressive is advertising. Messages are directed to specific segments of the audience or, in some cases, specific individuals. Digital media are capable of targeting in ways that were unimaginable in broadcasting.[43] Although people have some power to avoid advertising, if a marketer applies enough resources it's difficult for media users to escape the advertiser's message completely. As Malcolm McCullough at the University of Michigan pointed out, "advertising stops at nothing. As a cultural force, it has few equals. And as environmental experience, it often leaves you little choice but to tune out the world."[44]

But advertising isn't the only way media are pushed in our direction. Linear systems introduce people to new and sometimes unexpected content. Audiences flow from one program to the next. Within programs, they flow from one story to the next. Editors and search engines place items at the top of the page, increasing their salience, and, at least tacitly, recommend them to our attention. Services such as Pandora now play the role of programmers. News aggregators such as Google News play the role of editors. They tailor a menu of what's to be consumed. Other recommender systems filter out all but the most "relevant" options.[45]

And in a somewhat less calculated and manageable way, certain things cascade through the culture, enforcing exposure almost as effectively as a well-financed ad campaign. For example, in their description of the massive attention that Susan Boyle's performance of "I Dreamed a Dream" received, Henry Jenkins and colleagues noted, "Some may have heard conversations about it and searched on YouTube; for many more, the message came in the midst of other social exchanges, much as an advertisement comes as part of the commercial television flow."[46] Many things spread like a contagion through social networks and reverberate across traditional media platforms. Who knows what will have erupted by the time you read this, but you'd have to be living in a cave for them to elude your notice.[47]

People aren't powerless in the face of this onslaught. In the digital environment, they can easily choose to direct their attention elsewhere. As a rule, media providers don't try to force users to consume a diet for which they have no appetite. That tactic would be doomed to failure. Rather, they try to anticipate what people might like. They assess user preferences and predispositions. They coax people, encourage their loyalties, and monitor the results with a variety of media measures. Strategies that work recur. Those that fail disappear. But quite often, the process begins with an encounter that wasn't of the user's choosing. This dynamic relationship between preference and exposure is depicted in figure 6.3.

The unanswered question embedded in this model is whether media that are pushed at people can actually alter preferences. If not, then traditional models based on exogenous preferences emerge relatively unscathed.

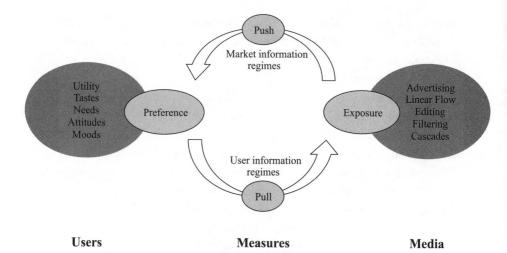

Users   **Measures**   **Media**

Figure 6.3
A Dynamic Model of Exposure.

Although it may be that not all exposures are chosen, our "selective interests" might still deflect what's unwelcome and accept only what comports with preexisting preferences. In that case, preferences still determine exposure and the media systems, which desperately seek public attention, will eventually come to heel.

If, however, exposure can affect preference formation, then media have the potential to move cultural consumption in different directions, perhaps changing what people like and attend to on a wide range of issues. In this model, preferences evolve through interactions with the media environment. So, what evidence supports the case for endogenous preferences?

There are several strains of research that shed light on how exposure affects preference. One of the oldest is in advertising. In chapter 1, I noted that we often assume advertising works by moving people through a "hierarchy of effects." That is, ads must produce an emotional response, such as liking or desire, before consumers make a purchase. In this "learning hierarchy," preference still precedes choice. By the 1970s, however, advertising researchers began to question the universality of this hierarchy and proposed two alternatives.[48]

The first was a "dissonance-attribution" model, which reversed the stages in the hierarchy entirely. That is, sometimes consumers choose among closely matched alternatives, and only afterward do they form a preference to "bolster their choice."[49] Psychologists have also noted "choice-induced preference change" in which people alter future preferences to match past behaviors.[50] Behavioral economists, who are dubious about rational choice, have documented similar "preference reversals."[51] As Ariely and Norton explained, "people observe their past behavior, infer some amount of utility and act in accordance with that inference of utility, despite the fact that this behavior can be based not on an initial choice driven by hedonic utility but on any host of trivial situational factors that impacted that first decision."[52] So it might be that a person intent on watching television finds herself choosing among new and barely distinguishable programs only to develop a preference afterward.

The second, rather common model is the "low-involvement" hierarchy. Here, consumers are repeatedly exposed to an ad and act on the basis of that awareness alone. This model benefits from an "availability" or recognition heuristic.[53] We pick what is familiar and only afterward develop a preference for it. As the name suggests, this model typically applies when people are making casual, uninvolved choices, which is true of many products, media selections, and even some voting behaviors.[54] Here again, psychologists have reported a similar phenomenon referred to as "mere exposure."[55] In all of these instances, exposure leads to preference formation.

Relatedly, there's a good deal of evidence in political science and communication that exposure can also promote any number of "effects."[56] For example, Prior noted that the low-choice environment of broadcast-only television gently enforced exposure to news.[57] That exposure led to incidental learning, which encouraged voting and benefited democracy. More broadly, George Gerbner and his colleagues have long argued that repeated exposure to the inescapable themes and stories of media culture have the ability to cultivate beliefs and distorted perceptions of reality.[58] It seems likely that they might cultivate preferences as well.

The relationship between exposure and preference, then, is not a one-way street but one of reciprocal influence. There are times when well-formed preferences drive the process, as traditional models suppose. But many encounters don't flow directly from our predispositions. We all see media that don't comport with our interests. They introduce us to new things and, in at least some instances, cultivate preferences and understandings that wouldn't otherwise exist. So agents, just like structures, are malleable. Our encounters with media can structure our preferences. But what preferences are susceptible to change, how do media act on them, and how long does that process take?

Structuring Preferences

Preferences can change quickly or not at all. Some materialize overnight. We can develop a fondness for a new television program or a catchy song on the basis of one chance encounter. Other preferences are less susceptible to change. One of the foundational works in communication noted long ago that media have the power to "canalize" behaviors.[59] That is, they can be quite effective at moving us along a path that we're already inclined to travel. So if you like one metal band, it's not surprising that you develop a taste for another. But media have a much harder time promoting fundamental changes in deeply held beliefs. Those enduring preferences are often tied to social structures, which can be nearly impervious to change.

Nor are the media themselves inclined to promote radical change. Commercial media have long been accused of impeding change by reinforcing the status quo.[60] Because their success depends on attracting an audience, they are unlikely to produce things for which there is no demonstrated market or to promote ideas deeply offensive to social norms. We saw in chapter 3 how creative industries are motivated to offer audiences something familiar. Users certainly can't develop a taste for cultural products or ideas they never encounter. Although new media make a far wider range of offerings available, it seems likely that incremental change will be the norm.

But even small, incremental changes in what we do and do not like can accumulate over time.[61] Those changes gradually reshape our encounters with media. It's here that the dimensions of structure are likely to encourage or squelch certain outcomes. If those structures are relatively open, they will be less likely to steer people in one direction or another. If they are relatively closed, they may be able to nudge people along a particular path. To explore these possibilities more thoroughly, let's consider how media and social structures might encourage preference formation.

The media systems with the greatest potential for cultivating preferences are those with closed, unobtrusive structures. They are the most active at filtering and targeting content to specific groups of users. At the risk of oversimplifying things, these systems do one of three things; they give us what *we want*, they give us what *they want*, or they give us what *they think we want*.

The first is more a goal than a reality. Often, people don't know exactly what they want. Users sometimes make whimsical, seemingly irrational choices based on their moods and the circumstances they confront at the time. If true all-knowing filters existed, they would leave enough room for serendipitous encounters. Some designers think that can happen, but we're not there yet and there's reason to doubt we ever will be.[62]

The second mode of filtering—giving us what they want—is the most worrisome. This is the stuff of surveillance, targeting, and deliberate attempts at manipulation. It's been an ongoing concern of academics and policy makers around the world,[63] and it isn't going away any time soon. Perhaps savvy users will be able to detect and resist overt attempts to target and manipulate them. Perhaps governments will intervene to protect people from exploitation. But these are open questions.

The third kind of filter gives us what they think we want. These include most of the competitors in what Eli Pariser called the "race for relevance."[64] Many of the best-known names in the business, such as Google and Facebook, fall into this category. Although they're not completely selfless, they cultivate an air of trustworthiness. Google, for instance, is well known for its motto "Don't be evil," although not everyone is convinced.[65]

For the sake of this argument, however, let's assume away all of the evil intentions that are ascribed to the second and third kinds of filters. Instead, let's pretend that we live in a world of well-intentioned filtering systems that only want to cater to our needs and desires. That hardly seems cause for alarm. Indeed, given the "user's dilemma," most people would welcome those filters with open arms. But should we? The answer, in my view, depends on the filter's ability to cultivate, rather than simply cater to, our preferences.

Even the most sophisticated algorithms and mining the biggest of big data have a way of reducing multidimensional people into simplified models of themselves. As Reed Hastings, CEO of Netflix admitted, "Human beings are very quirky and individualistic, and wonderfully idiosyncratic, … it makes it hard to figure out what they like."[66] Filters inevitably create caricatures of real people by inferring the existence of cleaner, more coherent dimensions of preference than actually exist. They then cater to those caricatures. We've all had these encounters. You get recommendations from Amazon that are rooted in some activity on your account, but suggest a cartoonish notion of who you are. Or, as some have reported, you begin to suspect that TiVo has made erroneous assumptions about your politics or sexual orientation.[67] Although recommender systems will undoubtedly improve their ability to figure out what we want, they'll never get it completely right.

What they will do is impose a comfortable discipline on our choices, making our encounters with media a bit more orderly and rational. Our benevolent filters will happily lead us down paths we're inclined to travel. No more silly detours and dead ends. But if this comfortable discipline also cultivates more orderly likes and dislikes, it's possible that these systems could turn us into the caricatures they imagine us to be.

That's the kind of mechanism that Pariser fears: "personalization algorithms can cause identity loops, in which what the code knows about you constructs your media environment, and your media environment helps shape your future preferences."[68] Right now, we know too little about the origins of our preferences to understand this mechanism completely. But in a closed system it's certainly possible that filters will cultivate preferences that are more stable, well defined, and, ultimately, manageable. Encouraging and then satisfying those appetites could make people less inclined to venture out into the larger marketplace. And the unobtrusive nature of these structures means we probably won't notice that it's happening.

Social structures also have the potential to cultivate preferences. Social structures are typically exogenous factors that influence our encounters with media "from the outside." For example, our socioeconomic status or social networks might encourage exposure to different genres.[69] But sometimes, social structures become so deeply embedded in the media that they are effectively endogenous influences—and they tend to create another type of closed system.

One of the more interesting examples is language. Although it isn't usually thought of as a filtering mechanism, language circumscribes populations of media users like nothing else. English speakers attend to English media, Mandarin speakers attend to Chinese media, and so it goes. With the exception of those who are actively multilingual, most people probably don't think about the many worlds of media that exist outside their own language. We're like fish who don't know our world is wet. But as the public sphere becomes more global[70] and individual nations, such as those in Western Europe and North America, become more multilingual the operation language-bound media environments is likely to grow in importance. The Internet and broadband television systems make it easier than ever for any diaspora to stay in touch with media from home.

Of course it's possible that although users are segregated by language, the media they encounter offer essentially the same constellation of ideas and concepts as all the others. There's certainly evidence that popular films, programming formulas, and at least some news travel across borders. But we're a far cry from the "global consensus hypothesis" that stipulates each language offers its users access to essentially the same set of concepts. Analyses of *Wikipedia* entries across languages, for example, demonstrate that there is surprisingly little overlap in the concepts they cover. And that the concepts described across multiple languages are often framed in very different ways.[71] Languages seem to create media environments different from the "massively overlapping cultures" typical of linguistically uniform societies.

Within a language, different frames and points of emphasis might be expected among the users of specialized media. But under those circumstances "outsiders" who speak the language can at least encounter and, potentially, confront the differences. Unfortunately, speaking different languages is more likely to blind people to the fact that others may see the world in very different ways and dampen deliberation.[72] If language creates a closed system, effectively eliminating crosscutting encounters, it could structure preferences and encourage global polarization. And once again, we might not notice that it's happening.

It's the structures we can't see that seem to have the greatest potential to cultivate preferences. Users are often willing "co-conspirators" in reproducing these structures. People welcome filtering technologies into their lives and use them with scarcely a thought. People gravitate to more culturally proximate materials. If these offerings are sufficiently enticing, users have little reason to look elsewhere, further closing the media environment. From an individual's perspective, these actions are perfectly sensible, but they can create durable, pervasive structures that could shape preferences, with potentially undesirable consequences. Even purposeful, reasoning agents can be the authors of unintentional outcomes.

The Swing Vote

The marketplace of attention is constructed through the interactions of users and the media resources that surround them. Although digital technologies seem to empower people to do what they want, the media play an important role in shaping those encounters. The structures that characterize the user's world aren't passive. They can promote certain outcomes and discourage others. But they rarely work in concert to achieve a single purpose. In fact, they often operate at cross purposes, pulling users in different directions. Some structures promote an open media environment, and others support the creation of enclaves. Under these circumstances, users exercise a kind of "swing vote" that can tilt the media environment in one direction or another.

Just how they'll decide to cast those votes isn't entirely clear. Some will undoubtedly stick with old allegiances. Others will develop new interests and appetites that they'll bring to their media choices. But it seems likely that many of the things that media push our way will cultivate preferences that wouldn't otherwise exist. If the latter became prevalent, the media could "rig the vote," and reshape popular culture. But as long as people don't become unwitting prisoners of closed systems that concern seems overstated. I see ample evidence of a massively overlapping culture and the openness that implies. For now, people seem to be voting for a variety of reasons, which produces a somewhat unpredictable quirkiness in cultural consumption.

Throughout this book I've noted the wildly different expectations that writers have about how digital media will affect society. Optimists see a rebirth of participatory culture. Pessimists see society being polarized into enclaves or silos. So what should we expect? The answer depends largely on how people use these new resources and the patterns of public attention that result.

We've learned a good deal about audience behavior: how users and structures interact to produce different audience formations. I hope that provides useful insights into how media systems operate, but the purpose of this last chapter is to address the larger question of what impact digital media will have on society. To do that, we'll consider the role of public attention in "the marketplace of ideas."

The marketplace of ideas is well-worn metaphor that offers a prescription for how media ought to function in a democracy. In the pages that follow, I'll note the philosophical underpinnings of the marketplace and how, ideally, we'd like audiences to behave. We'll review the arguments that lead some writers to believe that digital media will enliven the marketplace and others to believe they will eviscerate it. Finally, I'll apply our knowledge of audiences—theoretical and empirical—to suggest what might actually happen.

The Marketplace of Ideas

The "marketplace of ideas" is a phrase used by journalists, academics, and lawyers to describe how we hope citizens will encounter and weigh ideas. The underlying concept is often attributed to the seventeenth-century philosopher John Milton, who viewed open debate as a way to discover truth. As he put it, "Let [Truth] and Falsehood grapple; who ever knew Truth put to the worse in a free and open encounter."[1] That argument suggests media should support a free and open marketplace, and in the United States it provides a theoretical justification for guaranteeing freedom of speech and freedom of the press.

The marketplace metaphor expresses a particular philosophy, or "normative theory," about how the media should function. It was refined in the work of libertarian thinkers, such as John Locke and John Stuart Mill, who were suspicious of governments picking winners and losers in the marketplace of ideas. Although it's been a guiding principle in much policy making, it's certainly not the only model for how media might serve the public. As societies industrialized and media consolidated into large business enterprises, another normative theory called "social responsibility" began to moderate this purely libertarian approach.[2] That is, governments in most Western democracies began to view the media as public trustees who had an affirmative obligation to provide their audiences with an appropriate array of news and cultural offerings. This philosophical shift has opened the door for publicly funded media and some forms of regulation.[3]

Still, the notion of a marketplace of ideas remains a foundational concept for many academics and policy makers. Over the years, it's appeared in different guises. Most notably, the German philosopher Jürgen Habermas popularized the idea of a "public sphere."[4] Although each term has its own lineage, here I use them interchangeably. They both imagine a space where citizens freely assemble to present and weigh diverse ideas, perhaps finding common ground or some semblance of the truth. And they both recognize that in the modern world, the presentation and critique of ideas is often enacted in a media environment.[5]

In the United States, the Federal Communication Commission (FCC) has been charged by Congress with making sure that electronic media operate in the "public interest." To that end, a long-standing goal has been maintaining the marketplace of ideas by making sure that audiences have access to diverse viewpoints on issues of public importance. Historically, the commission has promoted diversity with policies that encouraged diverse sources (e.g., ownership or workforce diversity) and diverse content (e.g., program type or idea diversity).[6] As long as people had a limited number outlets from which to choose, making sure that those outlets offered some diversity seemed to be the best way to serve the marketplace of ideas.

But having a limited number of outlets is no longer an issue. Although mainstream media might privilege some stories or points of view, it's hard to argue that, taken together, digital media don't offer a wealth of information and forums where people can engage with diverse ideas. Further, much of the world has access to broadband television systems and the Internet, making it easy to hear and share those points of view. But does that mean that the marketplace of ideas will now function as theorists hope?

Not necessarily. What it does mean is that the operation of the marketplace is no longer dependent on what media provide, or what's been called "diversity as sent." Rather, the onus has now shifted to the audience and "diversity as received."[7] In other words, the media can provide all the diversity imaginable, but it's all for naught if people don't benefit from that diversity in their day-to-day encounters with media. In the end, each person's version of the marketplace of ideas will be circumscribed by what he or she attends to. We know how we'd like audiences to behave—but will they? It's on this question that the optimists and pessimists part ways.

There is a fairly broad consensus about what patterns of media use would best serve democracy. Cass Sunstein has argued that people should have serendipitous encounters where they happen on "views and topics they have not specifically selected." Additionally, citizens "should have a range of common experiences," traditionally provided by "general interest intermediaries" such as newspapers and broadcasters.[8] Similarly, Elihu Katz has noted that a well-designed democracy should have multiple spaces for deliberation including "generalized media dedicated to the polity as a whole, and specialized media dedicated to the citizens' need to know what like- or right-minded others are thinking."[9] Yochai Benkler envisions a world in which digital networks allow diverse communities of interest to weigh ideas and move the most meritorious along an "attention backbone" to broader audiences.[10] The ideal, then, sees people moving between outlets devoted to specialized topics and more popular forums where they assemble to hear from and engage with larger publics. But that's not what the pessimists fear will happen.

A particularly worrisome alternative is that people will use abundant choice to avoid arenas where "truth and falsehood grapple" and simply retreat into spaces offering one uncontested version of the truth. As Habermas himself warned, "the rise of millions of fragmented chat rooms across the world tend ... to lead to the fragmentation of large but politically focused mass audiences into a huge number of isolated issue publics."[11] Indeed, it's entirely possible that the emergence of enclaves could move their participants to ever-more extreme positions on whatever issue has brought them together.[12]

So the efficacy of the marketplace of ideas now depends on the behavior of audiences and that is very much in doubt. Diverse offerings have the potential to enrich the public sphere, if they are used in the right way. Even media outlets that encourage extremism have a role to play in democracies. As Sunstein himself noted, "The American Revolution, the civil rights movement, and the fall of both communism and apartheid"[13] all grew from groups tending toward extremes. But exposure to extreme viewpoints is best tempered by encounters with other perspectives and an appreciation of what people have in common. The goal, then, is to have media systems that encourage people and ideas to circulate.

Stories of Hope and Despair

The problem is, there has been very little consensus on what patterns of public attention are likely to emerge in this new, abundant digital marketplace. Some find reason for hope, others despair. One way to assess these divergent expectations about what audiences will do is to clarify how each line of argument sees the forces that shape the public attention—the users, the media, and the media measures they both depend on. In making that assessment, I'll gloss over many nuances in each writer's treatment, highlighting only what seem to be recurring themes. As you'll see, optimists focus on those features of the marketplace that support a more hopeful prognosis. Conversely, pessimists emphasize those that support a grimmer narrative. We'll begin by summarizing the arguments that suggest digital media will promote a healthy marketplace. We'll then assess how a different reading of those forces might weaken it.

The Case for a Healthy Marketplace

Optimistic treatments about the impact of digital media make fewer overt assumptions about the role of individual preferences in shaping media use. There is often a subtext that, although individuals might have an affinity for something, such as a particular cause or genre, they are for the most part omnivorous. However, much is made about people's penchant for making and sharing media as well as their skill at doing so. These relatively new practices enable users to play a much more active, participatory role in the media environment.[14]

As a result, the hero of many of these accounts is social media. These platforms offer people unprecedented opportunities to create and share ideas with the far larger networks now within their reach. As Williams and Delli Carpini note, "By allowing almost anyone to create his or her own media—through websites, blogs, Facebook pages, or YouTube videos—the new environment significantly blurs the line between producers and consumers of political information."[15] And even if people don't actually create things, social media allow them to freely share "compelling bits of news, information, and entertainment."[16] These features of digital media have led many, such as Yochai Benkler, to conclude that citizens "are no longer constrained to occupy the role of mere readers, viewers, and listeners. They begin to free the public agenda setting from dependence on the judgments of managers, whose job it is to assure that the maximum number of readers, viewers, and listeners are sold in the market for eyeballs."[17]

The optimistic accounts are more ambivalent about traditional mass media. Some see them as contributing to the empowerment of individual media users. For example, Rainie and Wellman note the growth in linear and nonlinear TV platforms and argue that "these changes allow for more flexible TV viewing tailored to personal interests, scheduling and time constraints. In contrast to the previous generation's 'must see' appointment TV, this has become an era of 'my playlist' TV."[18] In their celebration of spreadable media, Jenkins and colleagues acknowledged that "none of this supposes an end to the role of commercial mass media as perhaps the most powerful force in our collective cultural lives."[19] But others see mass media as a more problematic force that limits access to the public sphere, discourages diversity, and impoverishes the marketplace of ideas.[20]

In some of these accounts, media measures contribute to the health of marketplace. They are yet another tool that empowers ordinary users. Chris Anderson, for example, argued recommender systems are "the new tastemakers," that embody the "wisdom of the crowd," and are essential if people are to reap the benefits of the long tail. As he explained, "The new tastemakers are simply people whose opinions are respected. They influence the behavior of others, often encouraging them to try things they wouldn't otherwise pursue."[21] Similarly, the well-known legal scholar

Larry Lessig noted, "The *New York Times* used to have the power to say who was most significant. A much more democratic force does that now."[22]

In this vision of our future, people operate in a structurally open environment with a host of empowering tools. They don't use these resources to hide away in some enclave. For the most part, they wield their tools in a constructive way; creating media, expressing their opinions, and sharing what they find noteworthy within ever-expanding social networks. The "new tastemakers" encourage discovery and eventually bring worthwhile things to wider public notice. The net effect is a media system in which ideas circulate freely and public attention is concentrated on the most meritorious offerings, all of which produces a robust marketplace of ideas.

The Case for a Weakened Marketplace

In pessimistic accounts of digital media's impact, people's preferences are often a lynchpin of the argument. Users are seen as purposeful—even rational—consumers of media who have well-defined likes and dislikes that determine what they pay attention to. Those preferences trump all else. People use the abundance of the marketplace to seek out only what they're predisposed to like. If they encounter anything different, it's simply deflected or discredited.[23] Exposure to media actually reinforces attitudes and beliefs, perhaps making them more implacable and extreme over time.[24] As they become more pronounced, they will form the fault lines along which society fractures. There will be no serendipitous encounters, no shared experiences with people having a different point of view, only dissonance-free enclaves where people see what they want to see.

Our social networks will only exacerbate these tendencies. We've known for a long time that the groups we belong to are homophilous and likely to promote selective exposure. As digital media make those social networks exponentially larger, they include acquaintances and influentials whose recommendations are constantly before us. Scholars at the University of Pennsylvania have noted that "the popularity of social media platforms such as Facebook has created an ideal means by which people can exercise opinion leadership within social networks," but, unlike Anderson, they view this as a particularly "ominous" source of influence, because it's highly effective at reinforcing group predispositions.[25]

The media are generally happy to encourage whatever audience loyalties can be turned to their advantage. Linear media, such as television, do all they can to manage audience flow in their favor, usually by offering up one agreeable program after another. All but a handful of television networks offer specialized programming that caters to specific market segments or taste publics. Each user's repertoire of preferred "brands" will crowd out unwelcome encounters. These forces have the effect of creating the equivalent of "gated communities."[26] Nonlinear media, such as the web, provide even more specialized content and may direct users to like-minded sites or products through the use of hyperlinks.[27] Push media, such as ad networks, go one step further by targeting messages to certain types of people, further segregating them into "reputation silos."[28]

Media measures and the increasing use of big data contribute to these processes in two ways. First, market information helps media, both linear and nonlinear, accomplish the targeting of specific messages to specific kinds of users. In the process, they make the media more beholding to advertisers than the public interest.[29] Second, user information regimes are in a race to personalize their recommendations.[30] Google tailors its search results. Amazon and Netflix use collaborative filtering to encourage people to see or read things they're bound to like. These systems learn each user's preferences and filter out unwanted content. In fact, Cass Sunstein's grim assessment of digital media's impact on democracy noted "the unifying issue throughout will be the various problems, for a democratic society, that might be created by the power of complete filtering."[31]

All of these forces conspire to create closed structures that encourage people to consume a steady diet of what they are predisposed to like or agree with. Sometimes people will be willing participants in creating these comfortable enclaves. They will use only a handful of reliable outlets or apps to systematically avoid certain genres such as hard news.[32] Sometimes the filtering is done without their knowledge, but because these systems typically pander to their predispositions, they'll probably be welcomed and may well go unnoticed.[33] The net effect is a marketplace that loses a common, rough-and-tumble, public sphere and devolves into what Todd Gitlin called "sphericules."[34] In the process, the crosscutting encounters so essential to the marketplace of ideas largely disappear.

Questioning Our Assumptions

I noted in chapter 1 that new media often beget predictions that, with the wisdom of hindsight, seem overblown. In the present circumstance, we might temper our predictions by revisiting the major components of the marketplace and using that framework to question our assumptions about how we encounter ideas. But let's begin by considering where people can find political ideas.

Encountering Ideas

For decades, it's been widely assumed that political ideas circulated primarily in news and public affairs reporting. As a result, it was people's exposure to news and information that was most germane to understanding the marketplace of ideas. But that way of thinking seems bound to a particular moment in history, one that I believe defines the relevant public sphere too narrowly.

In the twentieth century, during the "age of broadcast news" when a few outlets dominated the audience, the news was what professional journalists determined it to be. It was they who differentiated facts from opinions and set the public agenda. Political ideas were reported in the news; everything else was just entertainment. That focus on the news persists. As well-known communication researchers argued, "unless Lisa Simpson becomes a mouthpiece for some clever political consultant, the larger utility of understanding communication effects through such entertainment programming seems greatly diminished."[35]

But other students of political communication have argued that sharp distinctions between news and entertainment characterized only one, rather fleeting "media regime."[36] A more useful way to think about the political consequences of media, then and certainly now, is that people encounter politically consequential ideas throughout the media environment.

Some years ago, the noted sociologist Herbert Gans described various taste publics, each with an appetite for its own menu of cultural offerings.[37] These included the usual high-brow and low-brow distinctions as well as various ethnic and youth cultures. Although the media these groups encountered didn't necessarily sort out along partisan dimensions, it often contained "political" ideas. As Gans explained,

One of the more important relationships between taste culture and the larger society is political. Although most taste cultures are not explicitly political, all cultural content expresses values that can become political or have political consequences. Even the simplest television family comedy, for example, says something about the relations between men and women and parents and children, and insofar as these relations involve values and questions of power they are political.[38]

Entertainment television, movies, and popular music all make ample use of socially controversial themes (e.g., sexuality, drug use, politics, etc.) and stories "ripped from the headlines." Talk shows, magazines, and other "softer" news formats highlight and frame a steady stream of issues. These inevitably affect what people think and talk about.[39] Affinity groups and user-generated content put even more ideas in circulation. All in all, we've entered "a new marketplace of ideas that makes no clear-cut distinction between fact and opinion or news and entertainment."[40]

Including entertainment among the places where people encounter political ideas is important for two reasons. First, for most people news is a small part of their diet. For some people, it's missing altogether.[41] Media users spend far more time with entertainment, and although that may not offer carefully researched facts, it is loaded with messages about social reality.[42] Second, the "politics" of entertainment are more difficult for casual users to detect. Entertainment doesn't seem to trigger people's skepticism the way that news or political advertising does. For that reason, it's been suggested that entertainment may be a more potent vehicle for affecting attitude change.[43] For instance, someone might watch a cop show or play a video game that was laden with implicit messages about gun violence. But they "willingly suspend disbelief" as the action unfolds. In this way, the pursuit of entertainment could slip through ideological filters. So when we consider how the marketplace of ideas is working, we should assume that all forms of media, not just news and information, are at work.

Media Users

Many of the more pessimistic expectations about the social impact of digital media rely heavily on psychological theories of how people make choices. Unfortunately, those theories don't do a particularly good job of explaining audience behaviors.[44] Many studies of the power of program preferences or selective exposure, or "uses and gratifications," particularly those conducted outside the lab, explain only modest amounts of variation in actual behaviors.

The assumption that stable, coherent individual preferences guide a person's choices is well entrenched. It's an article of faith for those who believe in "rational choice." And it has encouraged study after study to focus on some dimension of preference (attitudes, gratifications sought, etc.) in the belief that it offers a powerful way to explain exposure. The red media–blue media debate is illustrative. People are often conceived as falling along a continuum ranging from conservative to liberal, which determines their choice of news and information. If researchers find a statistically significant relationship between partisanship and news consumption, it supports a claim of selective exposure.

A problem with this approach is that most people don't have simple one-dimensional predispositions guiding their choices. On some matters they are conservative, on others a bit more liberal.[45] Sometimes they're interested in hearing the other side, sometimes they are indifferent. Sometimes their circumstances produce a kind of "de facto" selectivity that has very little to do with their attitudes.[46] And even if they do prefer one and only one way to frame events, their filtering mechanisms are often quite porous. Many studies find only modest evidence of politically motivated selective exposure.[47] So even if statistically significant differences are found, they aren't necessarily enough to compromise a robust public sphere.

In fact, the psychological factors that determine people's real world media choices are often in flux. Many people are "omnivores" who like variety in their media diets. With imperfect information, they navigate the media environment, "satisficing" as best they can. Occasionally they'll bump into something unexpected and perhaps develop a taste for it. None of these arguments suggests a slavish devotion to consuming only like-minded speech or any other single genre. It seems doubtful that people's preferences alone will eliminate varied or serendipitous encounters within the marketplace of ideas.

The Media

The ideas circulating in the digital media environment are less diverse than is widely assumed. Risky, high-cost productions encourage creators to use a limited pool of proven talent in formulaic ways.[48] Audiences often "punish" providers who stray too far from what's familiar.[49] Even inexpensive user-generated content often builds on what's already popular.[50] The producers of news and information aren't much different. Digital newsrooms constantly monitor and imitate their competitors, and virtually all news outlets and bloggers rely on a surprisingly small number of primary sources for their stories.[51] Although something truly new can occasionally be found, as a rule there is a follow-the-leader sameness in cultural production. This alone would tend to mitigate social polarization.

Pessimists, and even some optimists, doubt that commercial outlets, which are in the business of pursuing eyeballs, can make much of a contribution to the marketplace of ideas. Despite the media's propensity for encouraging audience loyalties that might balkanize the audience, they also have motives and strategies that lead to more widely shared experiences that might serve the marketplace.

First, push media can force people to confront things they're not inclined to seek out. The best example is political advertising. Who among us hasn't seen ads singing the praises of a candidate we dislike or attacking one we admire? Commercials make us aware of a great many things, whether we like it or not. Similarly, although their techniques are less heavy-handed than traditional advertising, most media outlets push things at us we haven't selected in advance: a news flash, a new pop star, or the latest thing to grab attention on YouTube. In doing so, they provide us with "reliable surprises"[52] that most of us appreciate.

Second, we shouldn't assume that best sellers are going away. Although Chris Anderson[53] derides the "hit-driven culture" of the past, the desire to create blockbusters or to "go viral" remains strong. In fact, Harvard's Anita Elberse claims "rather than a shift of demand to the long tail, we are witnessing an increased level of concentration in the marketplace for digital entertainment goods."[54] Although it may be difficult for the media to know in advance exactly how to make a winner, each year—without fail—winners there will be. These, by definition, concentrate widespread public

attention on a small number of movies, books, recording artists, news stories, and hit TV shows. Similarly, if Yochai Benkler is right, a relatively
small number of the most meritorious ideas will percolate their way up the
"attention backbone" of the web and achieve widespread notice.[55] Taken
together, these practices can create a common media culture that any user
would find hard to miss.

Media Measures

The ability of media measures to target messages and steer people in
specific directions has received most of the attention in critiques of the
marketplace. The "personalization bias," as I've called it, has some proponents and a good many critics. Less carefully considered is the "popularity
bias." Within any given category, recommendation systems generally point
people to the most popular offerings. Users find these popularity-driven
rankings helpful. If you believe they capture the "wisdom of crowds," they
provide at least some measure of quality. But even if popularity doesn't
always point you to the best of its kind, knowing that something is widely
used among a network of your friends or "people like you" suggests it
could be useful fodder for conversation. The popularity bias, then, tends to
counteract the personalization bias. Rather than herding people into small
homogeneous camps or niches, it concentrates public attention, increasing
the likelihood of more broadly shared cultural experiences.

The Shape of Things to Come

So, how will public attention take shape in the digital media environment
and how will that affect the operation of the public sphere? Before taking a stab at an answer, a bit of stocktaking is in order. Just as we've had
hopes and fears about each communication revolution, we've also never
been completely satisfied with whatever marketplace of ideas is operating
at the moment.

Be Careful What You Wish For

At its height, the age of broadcast news was regularly derided by academics
and media critics, if not the general public. With just three networks competing for the audience, their newscasts were faulted for being too uniform,
covering too few issues in too little depth, and being too unwilling to take

a stance. As Williams and Delli Caprini noted, "With few exceptions, the makeup of the audience for any program was quite similar to that for any other broadcast during the same time slot. In short, not only were audiences for any one broadcast likely to be large, but also audiences across these broadcasts were somewhat interchangeable, as was the content of what they were watching: the very definition of a mass audience."[56]

Although these programs operated with a sense of social responsibility and within the norms of professional journalism, at the time, many critics wanted something else. Mutz and Young put it this way: "Instead of an emphasis on facts and objectivity, the diversity they wanted was one of antagonistic vested interests, one in which reporters were advocates for their positions without any pretense of neutrality. This view of diversity is probably the closest to the one John Stuart Mill had in mind when advocating a marketplace of ideas."[57]

By the end of the twentieth century, the situation had changed dramatically. Most viewers in most Western nations had access to hundreds of channels. As economic theory—and common sense—would predict, these new outlets usually carved out a specialized niche. Among those outlets were networks that offered more ideologically extreme versions of news and information.[58] The web, of course, has only added to the many disparate voices now addressing the public. But rather than alleviating concerns about too much uniformity and blandness, it has created other causes for worry, many of which we've encountered.

So, as Mutz and Young advised their readers, you should "be careful what you wish for."[59] The larger lesson we can take from this turn of events is that although the marketplace of ideas might be a useful metaphor, it is an abstraction. It offers an ideal to be pursued but never fully realized. There will inevitably be too much of one thing and too little of another. The best we can hope for is to have a reasonable balance between the forces that unite us and the forces that pull us apart.

For many, that means a marketplace that offers specialized media and more broadly based general interest outlets. This idealized marketplace imagines citizens moving among those spaces, alternately learning from encounters with like-minded people and testing what they believe in a larger, more varied arena. We certainly have a growing wealth of specialized media but the fate of generalized media seems in doubt. If these spaces wither away, will that hobble the marketplace of ideas?

Out with the Old

In an article entitled "And Deliver Us from Segmentation," the noted scholar Elihu Katz explained his concern about the fate of a common public forum: "With the rapid multiplication of channels, television has all but ceased to function as a shared public space. Except for occasional media events, the nation no longer gathers together. Unlike the replacement of radio by television as radio underwent a similar process of segmentation, there is no new medium in the wings to replace television that is likely to promote national political integration."[60] In a similar vein, Williams and Delli Carpini noted that the old regime "developed a nightly ritual of citizenship—watching the evening news—which engaged most Americans and created a common political agenda, an achievement that seems increasingly remarkable in light of an increasingly fragmented media that seems to reinforce polarization and make civil engagement across political difference difficult."[61]

In retrospect, there's little doubt that major print and broadcast outlets served a unifying function. Although news and entertainment were fairly criticized for "excessive sameness," they provided a kind of cultural ballast that helped society stay on an even keel. We may mourn or celebrate their passing but, for all their faults, they drew people together in easily recognized public spaces. Clearly, digital media have forever changed the way public attention comes together, but it would be wrong to assume that what we are left with is a "massively parallel" culture that consists of a multitude of enclaves and tribal eddies.

In with the New

I think the cultural ballast provided by old media will remain with us. The forces that threaten to polarize society are, for the most part, overstated. The forces that will concentrate public attention are underappreciated. If I'm right, media will continue to provide a unifying function, although it will result less from the work of a few outlets and more from the ways in which people use the resources now at their disposal. The outcome will be a massively overlapping culture.

Although people's wants and interests will continue to shape their media use, those preferences are too varied and imperfectly enacted to support the creation of impermeable enclaves. Perhaps we should breathe a sigh of relief that people aren't completely "rational" in their choices and are therefore susceptible to surprises and serendipitous encounters. Although our social networks might incline us to see or read media that cater to our predispositions, those networks are often varied and multidimensional as well.

Although some people might religiously seek out or avoid certain kinds of media, most are more omnivorous. They indulge in their favorites, but still have variety in their diets. This is true even when it comes to ideologically charged content. Studies of online news use indicate people move across many sites. Those who visit the more extreme, sparsely attended sites routinely use mainstream outlets. As researchers at the University of Chicago concluded, people's "omnivorousness outweighs their ideological extremity, preventing their overall news diet from becoming too skewed."[62] Similarly, a wide-ranging report on the future of journalism by Columbia University argued that "choice in available media outlets will continue to expand, leading not so much to echo chambers as to a world of many overlapping publics of varying sizes."[63]

Although determined users have the tools to avoid these overlapping spaces, there's very little evidence that they do so. The niches that populate the long tail of media consumption are not sanctuaries that people never leave; they are way stations where most spend very little time. In fact, the existence of a "fat head" to that distribution virtually guarantees it. Popular media products will, by definition, get the attention of wide swaths of the public. As a rule, audiences flow easily between the popular and the obscure.[64] So although the structures that house the marketplace of ideas are changing, at present people seem to use them in a way that's generally consistent with the hopes of normative theory.

But that doesn't mean that we have no causes for concern. The most worrisome "preference-driven" loyalty we do see is the systematic avoidance of news. Many studies around the world have documented that large minorities of the adult population are uninterested in traditional news. This is discouraging for those of us who believe that the news, for all its faults, is a useful thing for citizens to encounter. Still, many bits of news have a way of resonating throughout popular culture and, if we believe the argument that all genres can carry politically consequential ideas, news avoiders may not be as tuned out as they appear. At least they're likely to hear of important developments and be able to seek further information as need be.[65]

A bigger threat to the happy untidiness of a massively overlapping culture is our unthinking reliance on structures we can't see. Writers such as Eli Pariser and Joe Turow are right to draw our attention to the invisible hand of recommender systems and targeted advertising. Unobtrusive structures, when skillfully executed, impose a kind of discipline on our encounters with media. Even if we aren't completely rational, they are. If our preferences can indeed be cultivated by a steady diet of the goodies they are likely to serve us, we may unwittingly become those caricatures that they imagine us to be, more easily sorted and managed.

Language and geographic proximity are the other unobtrusive structures that deserve our attention. Most of us live in media environments that are bounded by these factors, although we scarcely notice them. People in Chicago will encounter a different assortment of news and information than people in Houston and a vastly different menu than people in Amsterdam or Beijing. These differences create a geography of local knowledge. It's unclear whether Internet services that facilitate sharing will effectively span these geographies. Eric Schmidt and Jared Cohen think that "through the power of technology, age-old obstacles to human interaction, like geography, language and limited information, are falling and a new wave of creativity and potential is rising."[66] But in practice, border-spanning technologies haven't produced a bonanza of transnational encounters. As MIT's Ethan Zuckerman has pointed out, "Information may flow globally, but our attention tends to be highly local and highly tribal; we care more deeply about those with whom we share a group identity and much less about the distant 'other.'"[67]

Unobtrusive structures, then, have the greatest potential to segregate people into relatively isolated groups. The counterweight to these forces of polarization is, for the most part, the users themselves. Unobtrusive structures work most effectively when they operate as closed systems. It's only under those circumstances that a person's media diet can be purged of unplanned encounters and disciplined to maximum effect. But enclosing people within such structures is harder than it appears. We have varied needs and interests. We're using more media platforms than ever before. We rely on a host of mechanisms to choose among our options. We confront a variety of competitors using every trick in the book to grab our attention. And more than anything else, we participate in a culture that privileges popularity.

We've seen that many factors contribute to the persistence of popularity, which is an attribute that often gets a bad rap. Cultural critics, for instance, have long taken popularity as an indication of crass, "lowest common denominator" content. I dare say we can all think of disheartening examples of widespread public attention that seems misplaced. But popularity has its virtues. In the new media environment, it provides an important corrective to the forces of polarization. It concentrates public attention rather than dividing it. Popular outlets are necessarily in the repertoires of a great many people and so provide a kind of common ground. And there is no reason to believe long tails or power law distributions will change their basic shape anytime soon.

Popularity is valued by the media and users, who mutually create the cultural ballast that pulls society together. Most media providers seek public attention. Although some hope to achieve that goal by going to extremes, their offerings usually attract small, disloyal audiences.[68] The most popular outlets for news and entertainment remain mainstream media.[69] As a rule, the recipe for success discourages media from straying too far from what is familiar. To be popular, media must cater to widely held tastes and sensibilities.

And popularity appeals to users, too. Although it may not be a fail-safe indicator of quality or cultural relevance, oftentimes it is. Media makers will invest more in products that they believe will attract large audiences.[70] And those investments will buy higher production values. If the resulting offerings are anointed by the wisdom of crowds, which recommender systems make visible, ordinary users have good cause to choose what is popular.

So a broadly encompassing cultural forum will survive. It's just harder to locate within the confines of a few broadcast networks or newspapers. It exists across platforms providing widely shared encounters that focus public attention on the most salient news and entertainment. These will be the things that people talk about and share through social networks. The new public sphere will be constructed on the fly by the media and their audiences. It will never be exactly the same for any two users. But it will rarely be worlds apart. In this way, the marketplace of attention should promote a reasonable balance between the forces that unite and divide us.

NOTES

Preface

1. James G. Webster, Patricia F. Phalen, and Lawrence W. Lichty, *Ratings Analysis: Audience Measurement and Analytics*, 4th ed. (New York: Routledge, 2014).

2. James G. Webster, "User Information Regimes: How Social Media Shape Patterns of Consumption," *Northwestern University Law Review* 104, no. 2 (2010); Webster, "The Duality of Media: A Structurational Theory of Public Attention," *Communication Theory* 21, no. 1 (2011); James G. Webster and Thomas B. Ksiazek, "The Dynamics of Audience Fragmentation: Public Attention in an Age of Digital Media," *Journal of Communication* 62 (2012).

Chapter 1

1. Noteworthy examples include Chris Anderson, *The Long Tail: Why the Future of Business Is Selling Less of More*, 1st ed. (New York: Hyperion, 2006); Lee Rainie and Barry Wellman, *Networked: The New Social Operating System* (Cambridge, MA: MIT Press, 2012); Henry Jenkins, Sam Ford, and Joshua Green, *Spreadable Media: Creating Value and Meaning in a Networked Culture* (New York: New York University Press, 2013); Yochai Benkler, *The Wealth of Networks: How Social Production Transforms Markets and Freedom* (New Haven, CT: Yale University Press, 2006); J. Jarvis, *Public Parts: How Sharing in the Digital Age Improves the Way We Work and Live* (New York: Simon and Schuster, 2011); Clay Shirky, *Cognitive Surplus: Creativity and Generosity in a Connected Age* (New York: Penguin Press, 2010).

2. Markus Prior, *Post-broadcast Democracy: How Media Choice Increases Inequality in Political Involvement and Polarizes Elections* (Cambridge, UK: Cambridge University Press, 2007); Cass R. Sunstein, *Republic.com 2.0* (Princeton, NJ: Princeton University Press, 2007); N. J. Stroud, *Niche News: The Politics of News Choice* (New York: Oxford

University Press, 2011); Farhad Manjoo, *True Enough: Learning to Live in a Post-fact Society* (New York: Wiley, 2008).

3. E. Pariser, *The Filter Bubble: What the Internet is Hiding from You* (New York: Penguin Press, 2011); Joseph Turow, *The Daily You: How the New Advertising Industry Is Defining Your Identity and Your Worth* (New Haven, CT: Yale University Press, 2012); Andrew Keen, *Digital Vertigo: How Today's Online Social Revolution Is Dividing, Diminishing, and Disorienting Us* (New York: St. Martin's Press, 2012).

4. For an analysis of why utopian visions recur see Patrice Filchy, *The Internet Imaginaire* (Cambridge, MA: MIT Press, 2007).

5. Paul Starr, *The Creation of the Media: Political Origins of Modern Communications* (New York: Basic Books, 2004), 4.

6. Walter J. Ong, *Orality and Literacy: The Technologizing of the Word* (London: Routledge, 1982), 79.

7. For example, Walter Lippmann, *Public Opinion* (New York: Harcourt, Brace, 1927); John Dewey, *The Public and Its Problems* (New York: Henry Holt, 1927); Richard Butsch, *The Citizen Audience: Crowds, Publics, and Individuals* (New York: Routledge, 2008).

8. Sloan Commission on Cable Communications, *On the Cable: The Television of Abundance* (New York: McGraw-Hill, 1972); Thomas Streeter, "The Cable Fable Revisited: Discourse, Policy, and the Making of Cable Television," *Critical Studies in Mass Communication* 4, no. 2 (1987): 174–200; Anne W. Branscomb, "The Cable Fable: Will It Come True?" *Journal of Communication* 25, no. 1 (1975): 44–56.

9. Diana C. Mutz and Lori Young, "Communication and Public Opinion," *Public Opinion Quarterly* 75, no. 5 (2011): 1021.

10. Susanna Kim, "Twitter's IPO Filing Shows 215 Million Monthly Active Users," *ABC News* (October 3, 2013), http://abcnews.go.com/Business/twitter-ipo-filing-reveals-500-million-tweets-day/story?id=20460493.

11. YouTube, "Statistics." http://www.youtube.com/t/press_statistics.

12. For an admittedly "back-of-the-napkin" calculation see Clive Thompson, *Smarter Than You Think: How Technology Is Changing Our Minds for the Better* (New York: Penguin Press, 2013), 47.

13. John G. Palfrey and Urs Gasser, *Interop: The Promise and Perils of Highly Interconnected Systems* (New York: Basic Books, 2012).

14. Nielsen, "Television Audience: 2010–2011" (New York: Author, 2011b).

15. B. Garfield, *The Chaos Scenario* (Nashville: Stielstra Publishing, 2009).

16. Nielsen, "Anywhere Anytime Media Measurement" (New York: Author, 2006); James G. Webster, Patricia F. Phalen, and Lawrence W. Lichty, *Ratings Analysis: Audience Measurement and Analytics,* 4th ed. (New York: Routledge, 2014); Carol Edwards, *Arbitron's Single Source, Three-Screen Measurement Approach for CIMM* (New York: Arbitron, 2012).

17. Saul J. Berman, Bill Battino, and Karen Feldman, "Beyond Content: Capitalizing on the New Revenue Opportunities," in *Media and Entertainment* (Somers, NY: IBM Global Business Services, 2010); Philip M. Napoli, *Audience Evolution: New Technologies and the Transformation of Media Audiences* (New York: Columbia University Press, 2011).

18. C. W. Anderson, Emily Bell, and Clay Shirky, *Post-industrial Journalism: Adapting to the Present* (New York: Tow Center for Digital Journalism, Columbia University Journalism School, 2012), 16.

19. Roger E. Bohn and James E. Short, "How Much Information? 2009: Report on American Consumers" (San Diego: Global Information Industry Center, University of California, San Diego, 2009).

20. Nielsen, "A Look across Screens: The Cross-Platform Report," *Nielsen Newswire* (2013d).

21. Cotton Delo, "U.S. Adults Now Spending More Time on Digital Devices Than Watching TV," *Ad Age* (August 1, 2013), http://adage.com/article/digital/americans-spend-time-digital-devices-tv/243414/?utm_source=mediaworks&utm_medium=newsletter&utm_campaign=adage&ttl=1375984415.

22. Aaron Smith, "Smartphone Ownership—2013 Update," Pew Internet & American Life Project (June 5, 2013).

23. One recent report predicts that by 2015 Americans will spend more than fifteen hours a day with media, not counting media use at work. Although newer forms of media, such as gaming, are adding to the total, radio and television in its various guises will continue to account for the majority of time spent with media. See James E. Short, *How Much Media? 2013: Report on American Consumers* (Los Angeles: Institute for Communications Technology Management, University of California, 2013).

24. Council for Research Excellence, "Video Consumer Mapping Study," (New York: Author, 2009); Jumptap, "Screen Jumping: Understanding Today's Cross-Screen Consumer" (Jumptap and comScore, September 5, 2013).

25. Susan Whiting, "The Additive Effect of Tablet Reading," Economist Group (July 19, 2012).

26. M. Proulx and S. Shepatin, *Social TV: How Marketers Can Reach and Engage Audiences by Connecting Television to the Web, Social Media, and Mobile* (Hoboken, NJ: Wiley, 2012);

David Goetzl, "Media Industry Can Look to U.K. for New Terminology," in *TV Blog: Small Screen Big Picture* (MediaPost, 2013), http://www.mediapost.com/publications/article/205896/media-industry-can-look-to-uk-for-new-terminolog.html?edition=62934#axzz2akAw9ATq.

27. Nielsen, "The Full Twitter TV Picture Revealed," *Nielsen Newswire* (2013c). http://www.nielsen.com/us/en/newswire/2013/the-full-twitter-tv-picture-revealed.html.

28. Benkler, *The Wealth of Networks,* 240.

29. H. Simon, "Computers, Communications and the Public Interest," in *Computers, Communications, and the Public Interest,* ed. M. Greenberger (Baltimore: Johns Hopkins Press, 1971), 41.

30. Thomas H. Davenport and John C. Beck, *The Attention Economy: Understanding the New Currency of Business* (Boston: Harvard Business Press, 2001); J. Falkinger, "Attention Economies," *Journal of Economic Theory* 133, no. 1 (2007): 266–294; M. H. Goldhaber, "The Attention Economy and the Net," *First Monday* 2, no. 4–7 (1997); Tom Hayes, "Jump Point: How Network Culture Is Revolutionizing Business (New York: McGraw-Hill, 2008), 240; Richard Lanham, *The Economics of Attention: Style and Substance in the Age of Information* (Chicago: University of Chicago Press, 2006); Bernardo A. Huberman and Fang Wu, "The Economics of Attention: Maximizing User Value in Information-Rich Environments," in *Proceedings of the 1st International Workshop on Data Mining and Audience Intelligence for Advertising* (San Jose, CA: ACM, 2007); Eszter Hargittai, "Open Portals or Closed Gates? Channeling Content on the World Wide Web," *Poetics* 27, no. 4 (2000): 233–253.

31. Sunstein, *Republic.com 2.0,* 206–207.

32. Lanham, *The Economics of Attention,* 46.

33. For example, see Robert F. Potter and Paul Bolls, *Psychophysiological Measurement and Meaning: Cognitive and Emotional Processing of Media* (New York: Routledge, 2011); Malcolm McCullough, *Ambient Commons: Attention in the Age of Embodied Information* (Cambridge, MA: MIT Press, 2013).

34. A good practical example can be found in S. Weinschenk, *100 Things Every Designer Needs to Know about People* (Berkeley, CA: New Riders, 2011).

35. Noteworthy examples include Cathy N. Davidson, *Now You See It: How the Brain Science of Attention Will Transform the Way We Live, Work, and Learn* (New York: Viking Press, 2011); Rainie and Wellman, *Networked*; Nicholas Carr, *The Shallows: What the Internet Is Doing to Our Brains* (New York: W. W. Norton, 2011); Maggie Jackson, *Distracted: The Erosion of Attention and the Coming Dark Age* (Amherst, NY: Prometheus Books, 2009).

36. Albert-Laszlo Barabasi, "The Origin of Bursts and Heavy Tails in Human Dynamics," *Nature* 435, no. 7039 (2005): 207–211; D. J. Watts, *Everything Is Obvious: Once You Know the Answer; How Common Sense Fails* (New York: Penguin Press, 2011).

37. Sonia M. Livingstone, *Audiences and Publics: When Cultural Engagement Matters for the Public Sphere* (London: Intellect Books, 2005).

38. For example, M. L. Ray, "Marketing Communication and the Hierarchy of Effects," in *New Models of Communication Research,* vol. 2, ed. P. Clarke (Beverly Hills: Sage, 1973), 47–176; Anthony G. Greenwald and Clark Leavitt, "Audience Involvement in Advertising: Four Levels," *Journal of Consumer Research* 11, no. 1 (1984): 581–592.

39. WPP, "GroupM Forecasts 2012 Global Ad Spending to Increase 6.4% U.S.," press release, London, http://www.wpp.com/wpp/press/press/default.htm?guid ={23ebd8df-51a5-4a1d-b139-576d711e77ac.

40. Benkler, *The Wealth of Networks,* 254.

41. Davenport and Beck, *The Attention Economy,* 9.

42. J. Carey, *Culture as Communication: Essays on Media and Society* (New York: Routledge, 1989), 43.

43. Daniel Dayan and Elihu Katz, *Media Events: The Live Broadcasting of History* (Cambridge, MA: Harvard University Press, 1992), 14.

44. Harold D. Lasswell, "The Structure and Function of Communication in Society," in *The Communication of Ideas,* ed. Lyman Bryson (New York: Coopers Square Publishers, 1948), 37.

45. Bruce A. Williams and Michael X. Delli Carpini, *After Broadcast News: Media Regimes, Democracy, and the New Information Environment* (Cambridge, UK: Cambridge University Press, 2011), 44.

46. Anderson, Bell, and Shirky, *Post-industrial Journalism,* 38.

47. James G. Webster, "The Role of Structure in Media Choice," in *Media Choice: A Theoretical and Empirical Overview,* ed. T. Hartmann (New York: Routledge, 2009), 221–233; Anke Wonneberger, Klaus Schoenbach, and Lex van Meurs, "Dynamics of Individual Television Viewing Behavior: Models, Empirical Evidence, and a Research Program," *Communication Studies* 60, no. 3 (2009): 235–252; Roger Cooper and Tang Tang, "Predicting Audience Exposure to Television in Today's Media Environment: An Empirical Integration of Active-Audience and Structural Theories," *Journal of Broadcasting & Electronic Media* 53, no. 3 (2009): 400–418.

48. Anthony Giddens, *The Constitution of Society: Outline of the Theory of Structuration* (Berkeley: University of California Press, 1984).

49. James G. Webster, "The Duality of Media: A Structurational Theory of Public Attention," *Communication Theory* 21, no. 1 (2011): 43–66.

50. R. Williams, *Culture and Society, 1780–1950* (New York: Columbia University Press, 1958), 300.

51. James S. Ettema and D. Charles Whitney, "The Money Arrow: An Introduction to Audiencemaking," in *Audiencemaking: How the Media Create the Audience*, ed. J. S. Ettema and D. C. Whitney (Thousand Oaks, CA: Sage, 1994), 5.

52. Ethan Zuckerman, *Rewire: Digital Cosmopolitans in the Age of Connection* (New York: Norton, 2013), 93.

53. Watts, *Everything Is Obvious*, 79.

54. Zach Gottlieb, "In Online Media, Consumer is King," *Wired* (June 29, 2010), http://www.wired.com/2010/06/in-online-media-consumer-is-king/; Steven H. Chaffee and Miriam J. Metzger, "The End of Mass Communication?" *Mass Communication and Society* 4, no. 4 (2001): 365–379; P. Markillie, "Crowned at Last," *The Economist* 2 (2005), http://www.economist.com/node/3785166.

55. For example, B. M. Owen and S. S. Wildman, *Video Economics* (Cambridge, MA: Harvard University Press, 1992); Roland T. Rust, Wagner A. Kamakura, and Mark I. Alpert, "Viewer Preference Segmentation and Viewing Choice Models for Network Television," *Journal of Advertising* 21, no. 1 (1992): 1–18; Markus Prior, "News vs. Entertainment: How Increasing Media Choice Widens Gaps in Political Knowledge and Turnout," *American Journal of Political Science* 49, no. 3 (2005): 577–592.

56. For example, Stroud, *Niche News*; J. L. Cotton, "Cognitive Dissonance in Selective Exposure," in *Selective Exposure to Communication*, ed. D. Zillmann and J. Bryant (Hillsdale, NJ: Erlbaum, 1985), 11–33.

57. For example, Peter Vorderer, Christoph Klimmt, and Ute Ritterfeld, "Enjoyment: At the Heart of Media Entertainment," *Communication Theory* 14, no. 4 (2004): 388–408; D. Zillmann, "Mood Management in the Context of Selective Exposure Theory," in *Communication Yearbook*, ed. M. E. Roloff (Thousand Oaks, CA: Sage, 2000), 103–124.

58. For example, A. M. Rubin, "The Uses-and-Gratifications Perspective of Media Effects," in *Media Effects: Advances in Theory and Research*, 2nd ed., ed. J. Bryant and D. Zillmann (Mahwah, NJ: Lawrence Erlbaum, 2002), 525–548; T. E. Ruggiero, "Uses and Gratifications Theory in the 21st Century," *Mass Communication and Society* 3, no. 1 (2000): 3–37.

59. For example, Richard A. Peterson, "Problems in Comparative Research: The Example of Omnivorousness," *Poetics* 33, no. 5–6 (2005): 257–282; P. Bourdieu, *Distinction: A Social Critique of the Judgment of Taste,* trans. Richard Nice (Cambridge, MA: Harvard University Press, 1984).

60. Elihu Katz and Paul F. Lazarsfeld, *Personal Influence: The Part Played by People in the Flow of Mass Communications* (Glencoe, IL: Free Press, 1955).

61. James G. Webster, "User Information Regimes: How Social Media Shape Patterns of Consumption," *Northwestern University Law Review* 104, no. 2 (2010): 593–612; Mutz and Young, "Communication and Public Opinion."

62. Robert LaRose, "The Problem of Media Habits," *Communication Theory* 20, no. 2 (2010): 194–222; A. W. Rosenstein and A. E. Grant, "Reconceptualizing the Role of Habit: A New Model of Television Audience Activity," *Journal of Broadcasting & Electronic Media* 41, no. 3 (1997): 324–344; Alan M. Rubin, "Ritualized and Instrumental Television Viewing," *Journal of Communication* 34, no. 3 (1984): 67–77.

63. Harsh Taneja, James G. Webster, Edward C. Malthouse, and Thomas B. Ksiazek, "Media Consumption across Platforms: Identifying User-Defined Repertoires," *New Media & Society* (2012): 951–968.

64. H. A. Simon, *Administrative Behavior,* 4th ed. (New York: The Free Press, 1997).

65. Richard E. Caves, *Creative Industries: Contracts between Art and Commerce* (Cambridge, MA: Harvard University Press, 2000); James Hamilton, *All the News That's Fit to Sell: How the Market Transforms Information into News* (Princeton, NJ: Princeton University Press, 2004).

66. For example, Uwe Hasebrink and Jutta Popp, "Media Repertoires as a Result of Selective Media Use: A Conceptual Approach to the Analysis of Patterns of Exposure," *Communications: The European Journal of Communication Research* 31, no. 3 (2006): 369–387; Kimberly A. Neuendorf, David J. Atkin, and Leo W. Jeffres, "Reconceptualizing Channel Repertoire in the Urban Cable Environment," *Journal of Broadcasting & Electronic Media* 45, no. 3 (2001): 464–482; Kees van Rees and Koen van Eijck, "Media Repertoires of Selective Audiences: The Impact of Status, Gender, and Age on Media Use," *Poetics* 31, no. 5–6 (2003): 465–490; Elaine J. Yuan and James G. Webster, "Channel Repertoires: Using PeopleMeter Data in Beijing," *Journal of Broadcasting & Electronic Media* 50, no. 3 (2006): 524–536.

67. For example, Amos Tversky and Daniel Kahneman, "Judgment under Uncertainty: Heuristics and Biases," *Science* 185, no. 4157 (1974): 1124–1131; J. N. Marewski, M. Galesic, and G. Gigerenzer, "Fast and Frugal Media Choices," in *Media*

Choice: A Theoretical and Empirical Overview, ed. T. Hartmann (New York: Routledge, 2009), 107–128.

68. Claire Cain Miller, "As Web Search Goes Mobile, Competitors Chip at Google's Lead," *New York Times* (April 3, 2013).

69. A. Lenhart, "Adults and Social Network Websites," Pew Internet and American Life Project (January 14, 2009).

70. Benkler, *The Wealth of Networks*, 43.

71. Alice E. Marwick and danah boyd, "I Tweet Honestly, I Tweet Passionately: Twitter Users, Context Collapse, and the Imagined Audience," *New Media & Society* 13, no. 1 (2011): 114–133.

72. See William Goldman, *Adventures in the Screen Trade: A Personal View of Hollywood and Screenwriting*, vol. 92 (New York: Warner Books, 1983); Caves, *Creative Industries*.

73. Owen and Wildman, *Video Economics*.

74. N. Anand and A. Richard Peterson, "When Market Information Constitutes Fields: Sensemaking of Markets in the Commercial Music Industry," *Organization Science* 11, no. 3 (2000): 272.

75. Miller, "As Web Search Goes Mobile, Competitors Chip at Google's Lead."

76. By this I mean data drawn from meters or servers rather than self-reports. Although there's some debate about the accuracy of these approaches (see Markus Prior, "The Challenge of Measuring Media Exposure: Reply to Dilliplane, Goldman, and Mutz," *Political Communication* 30, no. 4 [2013a]: 620–634; Seth K. Goldman, Diana C. Mutz, and Susanna Dilliplane, "All Virtue Is Relative: A Response to Prior," *Political Communication* 30, no. 4 [2013]: 635–653), the latter are better at tracking what people actually do.

77. M. Hindman, *The Myth of Digital Democracy* (Princeton, NJ: Princeton University Press, 2009); Jungsu Yim, "Audience Concentration in the Media: Cross-Media Comparisons and the Introduction of the Uncertainty Measure," *Communication Monographs* 70, no. 2 (2003): 114–128.

78. Anderson, *The Long Tail*.

79. Ibid.; Todd Gitlin, "Public Sphere or Public Sphericules?" in *Media, Ritual, Identity*, ed. T. Liebes and James Curran (London: Routledge, 1998), 168–175; Pariser, *The Filter Bubble*; Stroud, *Niche News*; J. Turow, *Breaking Up America: Advertisers and the New Media World* (Chicago: University of Chicago Press, 1997); M. Van Alstyne and E. Brynjolfsson, "Global Village or Cyber-Balkans? Modeling and Measuring the

Integration of Electronic Communities," *Management Science* 51 (6) (2005): 851–868; Kathleen H. Jamieson and Joseph N. Cappella, *Echo Chamber: Rush Limbaugh and the Conservative Media Establishment* (New York: Oxford University Press, 2009); Turow, *The Daily You*.

80. James G. Webster and Thomas B. Ksiazek, "The Dynamics of Audience Fragmentation: Public Attention in an Age of Digital Media," *Journal of Communication* 62 (2012): 39–56; Matthew Gentzkow and Jesse M. Shapiro, "Ideological Segregation Online and Offline," *The Quarterly Journal of Economics* 126, no. 4 (2011): 1799–1839; Michael J. LaCour, "A Balanced News Diet, Not Selective Exposure: Evidence from a Real World Measure of Media Exposure," Presented at the Annual Midwest Political Science Association, Chicago, April 2012.

81. Philip M. Napoli, *Foundations of Communications Policy: Principles and Process in the Regulation of Electronic Media* (Cresskill, NJ: Hampton Press, 2001).

Chapter 2

1. José Van Dijck, "Users Like You? Theorizing Agency in User-Generated Content," *Media, Culture, and Society* 31, no. 1 (2009): 41.

2. P. Markillie, "Crowned at Last," *The Economist* 2 (2005), http://www.economist.com/node/3785166; Zach Gottlieb, "In Online Media, Consumer Is King," *Wired* (June 29, 2010), http://www.wired.com/2010/06/in-online-media-consumer-is-king/.

3. Jay Rosen, "The People Formerly Known as the Audience," *Huffington Post* (June 30, 2006), http://www.huffingtonpost.com/jay-rosen/the-people-formerly-known_1_b_24113.html; Dan Gillmor, *We the Media: Grassroots Journalism by the People, for the People* (Sebastopol, CA: O'Reilly Media, 2006).

4. Henry Jenkins, *Convergence Culture: Where Old and New Media Collide* (New York: New York University Press, 2006), 24.

5. Elihu Katz, "And Deliver Us from Segmentation," *Annals of the American Academy of Political and Social Science* 546 (1996): 29.

6. Neil Vidmar and Milton Rokeach, "Archie Bunker's Bigotry: A Study in Selective Perception and Exposure," *Journal of Communication* 24, no. 1 (1974): 36–47; Joseph T. Klapper, *The Effects of Mass Communication: Foundations of Communications Research* (Glencoe, IL: Free Press, 1960); Eunice Cooper and Marie Jahoda, "The Evasion of Propaganda: How Prejudiced People Respond to Anti-prejudice Propaganda," *Journal of Psychology* 23, no. 1 (1947): 15–25.

7. Kathleen H. Jamieson and Joseph N. Cappella, *Echo Chamber: Rush Limbaugh and the Conservative Media Establishment* (New York: Oxford University Press, 2009).

8. Stuart Hall, "Encoding/Decoding," in *Culture, Media, Language*, ed. Stuart Hall, Dorothy Hobson, Andrew Lowe, and Paul Willis (London: Unwin Hyman, 1980), 107–116; David Morley, *The Nationwide Audience: Structure and Decoding*, vol. 11 (London: British Film Institute, 1980).

9. Lee Rainie and Barry Wellman, *Networked: The New Social Operating System* (Cambridge, MA: MIT Press, 2012), 157.

10. Herbert A. Simon, "Rationality in Psychology and Economics," in *Rational Choice: The Contrast between Economics and Psychology*, ed. Robin M. Hograth and Melvin W. Reder (Chicago: University of Chicago Press, 1986), 25.

11. John G. Palfrey and Urs Gasser, *Interop: The Promise and Perils of Highly Interconnected Systems* (New York: Basic Books, 2012), 70.

12. John Jannarone and Rebecca Smith, "Super Bowl Audience Totaled 108.4 Million," *Wall Street Journal* (February 4, 2013).

13. R. Williams, *Culture and Society, 1780–1950* (New York: Columbia University Press, 1958); Richard Butsch, *The Citizen Audience: Crowds, Publics, and Individuals* (New York: Routledge, 2008); Steven H. Chaffee and Miriam J. Metzger, "The End of Mass Communication?" *Mass Communication and Society* 4, no. 4 (2001): 365–379.

14. Herbert Blumer, "The Field of Collective Behavior," in *New Outline of the Principles of Sociology*, ed. A. M. Lee (New York: Barnes & Noble, 1946); James G. Webster and Patricia F. Phalen, *The Mass Audience: Rediscovering the Dominant Model* (Mahwah, NJ: Erlbaum, 1997).

15. David Easley and Jon Kleinberg, *Networks, Crowds, and Markets: Reasoning about a Highly Connected World* (Cambridge, UK: Cambridge University Press, 2010); Philip Ball, *Critical Mass: How One Thing Leads to Another* (New York: Farrar, Straus & Giroux, 2004).

16. Alice E. Marwick and danah boyd, "I Tweet Honestly, I Tweet Passionately: Twitter Users, Context Collapse, and the Imagined Audience," *New Media & Society* 13, no. 1 (2011): 114–133.

17. Yochai Benkler, *The Wealth of Networks: How Social Production Transforms Markets and Freedom* (New Haven, CT: Yale University Press, 2006); Clay Shirky, *Here Comes Everybody: The Power of Organizing without Organizations* (New York: Penguin Books, 2008); W. Lance Bennett and Alexandra Segerberg, "The Logic of Connective Action," *Information, Communication & Society* 15, no. 5 (2012): 739–768.

18. Van Dijck, "Users Like You?" 49.

19. Dan Ariely and Michael I. Norton, "How Actions Create—Not Just Reveal—Preferences," *Trends in Cognitive Sciences* 12, no. 1 (2008): 13–16.

20. Dan Ariely, *Predictably Irrational: The Hidden Forces That Shape Our Decisions*, rev. and expanded ed. (New York: Harper, 2008), xx.

21. Bruce M. Owen and Steven S. Wildman, *Video Economics* (Cambridge, MA: Harvard University Press, 1992).

22. See Mark S. Fowler and Daniel L. Brenner, "Marketplace Approach to Broadcast Regulation," *Texas Law Review* 60 (1982): 207–257; Bruce Owen, *Economics and Freedom of Expression* (Cambridge, MA: Ballinger, 1975).

23. For example, Tilo Hartmann, "Action Theory, Theory of Planned Behavior and Media Choice," in *Media Choice: A Theoretical and Empirical Overview*, ed. T. Hartmann (New York: Routledge, 2009a); Robert LaRose, "Social Cognitive Theories of Media Selection," in *Media Choice: A Theoretical and Empirical Overview*, ed. T. Hartmann (New York: Routledge, 2009), 10–31.

24. For example, John W. Payne, James R. Bettman, and David A. Schkade, "Measuring Constructed Preferences: Towards a Building Code," *Journal of Risk and Uncertainty* 19, no. 1 (1999): 243–270; Paul Slovic, "The Construction of Preference," *American Psychologist* 50, no. 5 (1995): 364–371; Ariely and Norton, "How Actions Create—Not Just Reveal—Preferences."

25. G. Hsu, M. T. Hannan, and Ö. Koçak, "Multiple Category Memberships in Markets: An Integrative Theory and Two Empirical Tests," *American Sociological Review* 74, no. 1 (2009): 150–169.

26. Some of the more noteworthy studies include Andrew S. C. Ehrenberg, "The Factor Analytic Search for Program Types," *Journal of Advertising Research* 8, no. 1 (1968): 55–63; A. D. Kirsch and S. Banks, "Program Types Defined by Factor Analysis," *Journal of Advertising Research* 2, no. 3 (1962): 29–31; Roland T. Rust, Wagner A. Kamakura, and Mark I. Alpert, "Viewer Preference Segmentation and Viewing Choice Models for Network Television," *Journal of Advertising* 21, no. 1 (1992): 1–18; Ronald E. Frank, James C. Becknell, and James D. Clokey, "Television Program Types," *Journal of Marketing Research* 8, no. 2 (1971): 204–211; Dennis H. Gensch and B. Ranganathan, "Evaluation of Television Program Content for the Purpose of Promotional Segmentation," *Journal of Marketing Research* 11, no. 4 (1974): 390–398; V. J. Jones and F. H. Siller, "Factor Analysis of Media Exposure Data Using Prior Knowledge of the Medium," *Journal of Marketing Research* 15, no. 1 (1978): 137–144; Manouche Tavakoli and Martin Cave, "Modelling Television Viewing Patterns," *Journal of Advertising* 25, no. 4 (1996): 71–86; Byron Sharp, Virginia Beal, and Martin Collins, "Television: Back to the Future," *Journal of Advertising Research* 49, no. 2

(2009): 211–219; Gary W. Bowman and John U. Farley, "TV Viewing: Application of Formal Choice Model," *Applied Economics* 4, no. 4 (1972): 245–259.

27. G. J. Goodhardt, A. S. C. Ehrenberg, and M. A. Collins, *The Television Audience: Patterns of Viewing; An Update* (Aldershot, Hampshire, UK: Gower Publishing, 1987), 45.

28. Thomas B. Ksiazek, Edward C. Malthouse, and James G. Webster, "News-Seekers and Avoiders: Exploring Patterns of Total News Consumption across Media and the Relationship to Civic Participation," *Journal of Broadcasting & Electronic Media* 54, no. 4 (2010): 551–568; Anke Wonneberger, Klaus Schoenbach, and Lex Van Meurs, "Tuning Out? TV News Audiences in the Netherlands 1990–2010," presented at the 61st Annual Meeting of the International Communication Association, Boston, May 2011; Jung Su Kim, Young Min Baek, Sung Dong Cho, and Namjun Kang, "News Audience Polarization across TV and the Internet in South Korea," Paper presented at the annual meeting of the International Communication Association, Phoenix, AZ, May 2012; T. Aalberg, A. Blekesaune, and E. Elvestad, "Media Choice and Informed Democracy: An Empirical Study of Increasing Information Gaps in Europe," paper presented at the APSA annual meeting, New Orleans, LA, September 2012; Markus Prior, *Post-broadcast Democracy: How Media Choice Increases Inequality in Political Involvement and Polarizes Elections* (Cambridge, UK: Cambridge University Press, 2007); Kevin Arceneaux and Martin Johnson, *Changing Minds or Changing Channels? Partisan News in an Age of Choice* (Chicago: University of Chicago Press, 2013).

29. Byrony Jardine, "Retaining the Primetime TV Audience: Examining Adjacent Program Audience Duplication across Markets," master's thesis, University of South Australia, 2012; James G. Webster, "Audience Flow Past and Present: Television Inheritance Effects Reconsidered," *Journal of Broadcasting & Electronic Media* 50, no. 2 (2006): 323–337.

30. Eszter Hargittai and Eden Litt, "The Tweet Smell of Celebrity Success: Explaining Variation in Twitter Adoption among a Diverse Group of Young Adults," *New Media & Society* 13, no. 5 (2011): 824–842.

31. James G. Webster and Jacob J. Wakshlag, "A Theory of Television Program Choice," *Communication Research* 10, no. 4 (1983): 430–446.

32. T. Patrick Barwise and Andrew S. C. Ehrenberg, "The Liking and Viewing of Regular TV Series," *Journal of Consumer Research* 14, no. 1 (1987): 68.

33. Goodhardt, Ehrenberg, and Collins, *The Television Audience*; Rust, Kamakura, and Alpert, "Viewer Preference Segmentation and Viewing Choice Models for Network Television."

34. Andreas Fahr and Eabea Bocking, "Media Choice and Avoidance Behavior: Avoidance Motivations During Television Use," in *Media Choice: A Theoretical and Empirical Overview*, ed. T. Hartmann (New York: Routledge, 2009), 185–202.

35. P. Bourdieu, *Distinction: A Social Critique of the Judgment of Taste*, trans. Richard Nice (Cambridge, MA: Harvard University Press, 1984).

36. Herbert J. Gans, *Popular Culture and High Culture: An Analysis and Evaluation of Taste*, rev. and updated ed. (New York: Basic Books, 1999).

37. Richard A. Peterson, "Understanding Audience Segmentation: From Elite and Mass to Omnivore and Univore," *Poetics* 21, no. 4 (1992): 243–258.

38 Richard A. Peterson, "Problems in Comparative Research: The Example of Omnivorousness," *Poetics* 33, no. 5–6 (2005): 257–282; David Wright, "Making Tastes for Everything: Omnivorousness and Cultural Abundance," *Journal for Cultural Research* 15, no. 4 (2011): 355–371; A. Goldberg, "Mapping Shared Understandings Using Relational Class Analysis: The Case of the Cultural Omnivore Reexamined," *American Journal of Sociology* 116, no. 5 (2011): 1397–1436.

39. Bethany Bryson, " 'Anything But Heavy Metal': Symbolic Exclusion and Musical Dislikes," *American Sociological Review* 61, no. 5 (1996): 884–899.

40. Mike Savage, "The Musical Field," *Cultural Trends* 15, no. 2/3 (2006): 167.

41. Alan M. Rubin, "The Uses-and-Gratifications Perspective on Media Effects," in *Media Effects: Advances in Theory and Research*, 2nd ed., ed. Jennings Bryant and Mary B. Oliver (New York: Routledge, 2009), 525–548; Marina Krcmar and Yuliya Strizhakova, "Uses and Gratification as Media Choice," in *Media Choice: A Theoretical and Empirical Overview*, ed. T. Hartmann (New York: Routledge, 2009), 53–69.

42. Elihu Katz, Jay G. Blumler, and Michael Gurevitch, "Utilization of Mass Communication by the Individual," in *The Uses of Mass Communications: Current Perspectives on Gratifications Research*, ed. Jay G. Blumler and Elihu Katz (Beverly Hills: Sage, 1974), 20.

43. Alan M. Rubin, "Television Uses and Gratifications: The Interactions of Viewing Patterns and Motivations," *Journal of Broadcasting & Electronic Media* 27, no. 1 (1983): 37–51.

44. Alan M. Rubin, "Ritualized and Instrumental Television Viewing," *Journal of Communication* 34, no. 3 (1984): 67–77.

45. For example, see Angela M. Lee, "News Audiences Revisited: Theorizing the Link between Audience Motivations and News Consumption," *Journal of Broadcasting & Electronic Media* 57, no. 3 (2013): 300–317; Beverly A. Bondad-Brown, Ronald E. Rice, and Katy E. Pearce, "Influences on TV Viewing and Online User-Shared

Video Use: Demographics, Generations, Contextual Age, Media Use, Motivations, and Audience Activity," *Journal of Broadcasting & Electronic Media* 56, no. 4 (2012): 471–493; T. Charney and B. S. Greenberg, "Uses and Gratifications of the Internet," in *Communication Technology and Society: Audience Adoption and Uses*, ed. Carolyn Lin and David Adkin (Cresskill, NJ: Hampton Press, 2002), 379–407.

46. Robin L. Nabi, Carmen R. Stitt, Jeff Halford, and Keli L. Finnerty, "Emotional and Cognitive Predictors of the Enjoyment of Reality-Based and Fictional Television Programming: An Elaboration of the Uses and Gratifications Perspective," *Media Psychology* 8, no. 4 (2006): 444.

47. Leon Festinger, *A Theory of Cognitive Dissonance* (Stanford, CA: Stanford University Press, 1957); Wolfgang Donsbach, "Cognitive Dissonance Theory: A Roller Coaster Career," in *Media Choice: A Theoretical and Empirical Overview*, ed. T. Hartmann (New York: Routledge, 2009), 128–148.

48. David O. Sears and Jonathan L. Freedman, "Selective Exposure to Information: A Critical Review," *Public Opinion Quarterly* 31, no. 2 (1967): 194.

49. Natalie J. Stroud, *Niche News: The Politics of News Choice* (Oxford: Oxford University Press, 2011).

50. Dolf Zillmann and Jennings Bryant, eds., *Selective Exposure to Communication* (Hillsdale, NJ: Erlbaum, 1985).

51. Jamieson and Cappella, *Echo Chamber*, 75.

52. Stroud, *Niche News*; Shanto Iyengar and Kyusup Hahn, "Red Media, Blue Media: Evidence of Ideological Selectivity in Media Use," *Journal of Communication* 59, no. 1 (2009): 19–39.

53. J. L. Cotton, "Cognitive Dissonance in Selective Exposure," in *Selective Exposure to Communication*, ed. D. Zillmann and J. Bryant (Hillsdale, NJ: Erlbaum, 1985), 11–33; R. Kelly Garrett, "Politically Motivated Reinforcement Seeking: Reframing the Selective Exposure Debate," *Journal of Communication* 59, no. 4 (2009): 676–699.

54. Russ Clay, Jessica M. Barber, and Natalie J. Shook, "Techniques for Measuring Selective Exposure: A Critical Review," *Communication Methods and Measures* 7, no. 3 (2013): 221–245; Lauren Feldman, Natalie Jomini Stroud, Bruce Bimber, and Magdalena Wojcieszak, "Assessing Selective Exposure in Experiments: The Implications of Different Methodological Choices," *Communication Methods and Measures* 7, no. 3 (2013): 198–220; Shanto Iyengar, "Laboratory Experiments in Political Science," in *Handbook of Experimental Political Science*, ed. James N. Druckman, Donald P. Green, James H. Kuklinski, and Arthur Lupia (New York: Cambridge University Press, 2011), 73–88.

55. Markus Prior, "The Immensely Inflated News Audience: Assessing Bias in Self-Reported News Exposure," *Public Opinion Quarterly* 73, no. 1 (2009): 130–143; Michael J. LaCour, "A Balanced News Diet, Not Selective Exposure: Evidence from a Real World Measure of Media Exposure," presented at the Annual Midwest Political Science Association, Chicago, April 2012; Anke Wonneberger, Klaus Schoenbach, and Lex Van Meurs, "Dimensionality of TV-News Exposure: Mapping News Viewing Behavior with People-Meter Data," *International Journal of Public Opinion Research* 21 (1) (2012): 87–107; Markus Prior, "Media and Political Polarization," *Annual Review of Political Science* 16, no. 1 (2013b): 101–127.

56. LaCour, "A Balanced News Diet, Not Selective Exposure"; Matthew Gentzkow and Jesse M. Shapiro, "Ideological Segregation Online and Offline," *The Quarterly Journal of Economics* 126, no. 4 (2011): 1799–1839.

57. A sampler of the many works that wrestle with this topic include W. Lance Bennett and Shanto Iyengar, "A New Era of Minimal Effects? The Changing Foundations of Political Communication," *Journal of Communication* 58, no. 4 (2008): 707–731; R. L. Holbert, R. K. Garrett, and L. S. Gleason, "A New Era of Minimal Effects? A Response to Bennett and Iyengar," *Journal of Communication* 60, no. 1 (2010) : 15–34; W. Lance Bennett and Shanto Iyengar, "The Shifting Foundations of Political Communication: Responding to a Defense of the Media Effects Paradigm," *Journal of Communication* 60, no. 1 (2010): 35–39; Jamieson and Cappella, *Echo Chamber*; Stroud, *Niche News*; Diana C. Mutz and Lori Young, "Communication and Public Opinion," *Public Opinion Quarterly* 75, no. 5 (2011): 1018–1044; Prior, "Media and Political Polarization"; Matthew Levendusky, *How Partisan Media Polarize America* (Chicago: University of Chicago Press, 2013); Arceneaux and Johnson, *Changing Minds or Changing Channels?*

58. Sears and Freedman, "Selective Exposure to Information"; Silvia Knobloch-Westerwick and Steven B. Kleinman, "Preelection Selective Exposure: Confirmation Bias versus Informational Utility," *Communication Research* 39, no. 2 (2012): 170–193; Nicholas A. Valentino, Antoine J. Banks, Vincent L. Hutchings, and Anne K. Davis, "Selective Exposure in the Internet Age: The Interaction between Anxiety and Information Utility," *Political Psychology* 30, no. 4 (2009) : 591–613; William Hart, Dolores Albarracín, Alice H. Eagly, Inge Brechan, Matthew J. Lindberg, and Lisa Merrill, "Feeling Validated versus Being Correct: A Meta-Analysis of Selective Exposure to Information," *Psychological Bulletin* 135, no. 4 (2009): 555–588.

59. Peter Vorderer, Christoph Klimmt, and Ute Ritterfeld, "Enjoyment: At the Heart of Media Entertainment," *Communication Theory* 14, no. 4 (2004): 388–408; Mary B. Oliver, "Affect as a Predictor of Entertainment Choice: The Utility of Looking beyond Pleasure," in *Media Choice: A Theoretical and Empirical Overview*, ed. T. Hartmann (New York: Routledge, 2009), 167–184.

60. D. Zillmann, "Mood Management in the Context of Selective Exposure Theory," in *Communication Yearbook*, ed. M. E. Roloff (Thousand Oaks, CA: Sage, 2000), 103–124; Silvia Knobloch-Westerwick, "Mood Management: Theory, Evidence, and Advancements," in *Psychology of Entertainment*, ed. Jennings Bryant and Peter Vorderer (Mahwah, NJ: Erlbaum, 2006), 239–254.

61. One measurement company called TouchPoints has a panel of people with smartphones use an app to report their emotions at intervals throughout the day. Other researchers are divining emotions by looking at the language used in "tweets." See Scott A. Golder and Michael W. Macy, "Diurnal and Seasonal Mood Vary with Work, Sleep, and Daylength Across Diverse Cultures," *Science* 333, no. 6051 (2011): 1878–1881.

62. Oliver, "Affect as a Predictor of Entertainment Choice," 172.

63. Garrett, "Politically Motivated Reinforcement Seeking"; R. Kelly Garrett, Dustin Carnahan, and Emily Lynch, "A Turn toward Avoidance? Selective Exposure to Online Political Information, 2004–2008," *Political Behavior* 35 (1) (2013): 113–134.

64. Although they make a strong case for the existence of echo chambers, Jamieson and Cappella acknowledge that conservatives don't "barricade" themselves in conservative media. See Jamieson and Cappella, *Echo Chamber*, 240.

65. Herbert A. Simon, *Administrative Behavior*, 4th ed. (New York: The Free Press, 1997); Herbert A. Simon, "Rational Choice and the Structure of the Environment," *Psychological Review* 63, no. 2 (1956): 129–138.

66. Richard E. Caves, *Creative Industries: Contracts between Art and Commerce* (Cambridge, MA: Harvard University Press, 2000); James Hamilton, *All the News That's Fit to Sell: How the Market Transforms Information into News* (Princeton, NJ: Princeton University Press, 2004).

67. Simon, *Administrative Behavior*, 118.

68. Carrie Heeter, "Program Selection with Abundance of Choice—a Process Model," *Human Communication Research* 12, no. 1 (1985): 126–152; Douglas A. Ferguson and Elizabeth M. Perse, "Media and Audience Influences on Channel Repertoire," *Journal of Broadcasting & Electronic Media* 37, no. 1 (1993): 31–47; Kimberly A. Neuendorf, David J. Atkin, and Leo W. Jeffres, "Reconceptualizing Channel Repertoire in the Urban Cable Environment," *Journal of Broadcasting & Electronic Media* 45, no. 3 (2001): 464–482; Uwe Hasebrink and Hanna Domeyer, "Media Repertoires as Patterns of Behaviour and as Meaningful Practices: A Multimethod Approach to Media Use in Converging Media Environments," *Participations: Journal of Audience & Reception Studies* 9, no. 2 (2012): 757–779.

69. Nielsen, "Television Audience Report 2008" (New York: Author, 2009).

70. Elaine J. Yuan and James G. Webster, "Channel Repertoires: Using PeopleMeter Data in Beijing," *Journal of Broadcasting & Electronic Media* 50, no. 3 (2006): 524–536.

71. K. Van Eijck and K. Van Rees, "The Internet and Dutch Media Repertoires," *It&Society* 1, no. 2 (2002): 86–99; Harsh Taneja, James G. Webster, Edward C. Malthouse, and Thomas B. Ksiazek, "Media Consumption across Platforms: Identifying User-Defined Repertoires," *New Media & Society* (2012): 951–968; Hasebrink and Domeyer, "Media Repertoires as Patterns of Behaviour and as Meaningful Practices."

72. M. J. Metzger, A. J. Flanagin, and R. B. Medders, "Social and Heuristic Approaches to Credibility Evaluation Online," *Journal of Communication* 60, no. 3 (2010): 413–439.

73. Ibid.

74. Stroud, *Niche News*; R. P. Vallone, L. Ross, and M. R. Lepper, "The Hostile Media Phenomenon: Biased Perception and Perceptions of Media Bias in Coverage of the Beirut Massacre," *Journal of Personality and Social Psychology* 49, no. 3 (1985): 577–585.

75. Hsu, Hannan, and Koçak, "Multiple Category Memberships in Markets."

76. J. N. Marewski, M. Galesic, and G. Gigerenzer, "Fast and Frugal Media Choices," in *Media Choice: A Theoretical and Empirical Overview*, ed. T. Hartmann (New York: Routledge, 2009), 107–128.

77. Metzger, Flanagin, and Medders, "Social and Heuristic Approaches to Credibility Evaluation Online."

78. Ibid.

79. Marewski, Galesic, and Gigerenzer, "Fast and Frugal Media Choices," 120.

80. Amos Tversky and Daniel Kahneman, "Judgment under Uncertainty: Heuristics and Biases," *Science* 185, no. 4157 (1974): 1124–1131.

81. James Lull, "The Social Uses of Television," *Human Communication Research* 6, no. 3 (1980): 197–209.

82. Nathanael J. Fast, Chip Heath, and George Wu, "Common Ground and Cultural Prominence," *Psychological Science* 20, no. 7 (2009): 904–911.

83. Bourdieu, *Distinction*; N. B. Ellison, C. Steinfield, and C. Lampe, "Connection Strategies: Social Capital Implications of Facebook-Enabled Communication Practices," *New Media & Society* 13, no. 6 (2011): 873–892; K. N. Hampton, L. S. Goulet, C. Marlow, and L. Rainie, "Why Most Facebook Users Get More Than They Give," *Pew Internet Report* (February 3, 2012); Kevin Lewis, Marco Gonzalez, and Jason Kaufman, "Social Selection and Peer Influence in an Online Social Network," *Proceedings of the National Academy of Sciences* 109, no. 1 (2012): 68–72; Marwick and boyd, "I Tweet Honestly, I Tweet Passionately."

84. Paul DiMaggio and Hugh Louch, "Socially Embedded Consumer Transactions: For What Kinds of Purchases Do People Most Often Use Networks?" *American Sociological Review* 63, no. 5 (1998): 619–637; Elihu Katz and Paul F. Lazarsfeld, *Personal Influence: The Part Played by People in the Flow of Mass Communications* (Glencoe, IL: The Free Press, 1955).

85. Steven J. Tepper and Eszter Hargittai, "Pathways to Music Exploration in a Digital Age," *Poetics* 37, no. 3 (2009): 227–249.

86. Rainie and Wellman, *Networked*, 37.

87. M. McPherson, L. Smith-Lovin, and J. M. Cook, "Birds of a Feather: Homophily in Social Networks," *Annual Review of Sociology* 27 (2001): 415–444; Noah Mark, "Birds of a Feather Sing Together," *Social Forces* 77, no. 2 (1998): 453–485.

88. Katz and Lazarsfeld, *Personal Influence.*

89. S. Wu, J. M. Hofman, W. A. Mason, and D. J. Watts, "Who Says What to Whom on Twitter," paper presented at the International World Wide Web Conference, Hyderabad, India, March 28–April 1, 2011; Nicholas Harrigan, Palakorn Achananuparp, and Ee-Peng Lim, "Influentials, Novelty, and Social Contagion: The Viral Power of Average Friends, Close Communities, and Old News," *Social Networks* 34, no. 4 (2012): 470–480; Meeyoung Cha, Hamed Haddadi, Fabricio Benevenuto, and Krishna P. Gummadi, "Measuring User Influence in Twitter: The Million Follower Fallacy," paper presented at the 4th International AAAI Conference on Weblogs and Social Media (ICWSM), Washington, DC, May 2010.

90. Mark S. Granovetter, "The Strength of Weak Ties," *American Journal of Sociology* 78, no. 6 (1973): 1360–1380.

91. Ibid.; Duncan J. Watts and Steven H. Strogatz, "Collective Dynamics of 'Small-World' Networks," *Nature* 393, no. 6684 (1998): 440–442.

92. D. Centola and Michael Macy, "Complex Contagions and the Weakness of Long Ties," *American Journal of Sociology* 113, no. 3 (2007): 702–734.

93. Harrigan, Achananuparp, and Lim, "Influentials, Novelty, and Social Contagion," 472.

94. Centola and Macy, "Complex Contagions and the Weakness of Long Ties"; Robert M. Bond, Christopher J. Fariss, Jason J. Jones, Adam D. I. Kramer, Cameron Marlow, Jaime E. Settle, and James H. Fowler., "A 61-Million-Person Experiment in Social Influence and Political Mobilization," *Nature* 489, no. 7415 (2012): 295–298; Sinan Aral, "Social Science: Poked to Vote," *Nature* 489, no. 7415 (2012): 212–214.

95. Nielsen, "The State of Media: The Social Media Report Q3 2011" (New York: Author, 2011a).

96. Aaron Smith, "Why Americans Use Social Media," Pew Internet & American Life Project (November 2011).

97. Cha et al., "Measuring User Influence in Twitter"; Wu et al., "Who Says What to Whom on Twitter."

98. Wu et al., "Who Says What to Whom on Twitter."

99. Nielsen, "The State of Media."

100. Sonini Sengupta, "For Search, Facebook Had to Go Beyond 'Robospeak,'" *New York Times* (January 28, 2013), http://www.nytimes.com/2013/01/29/business/how-facebook-taught-its-search-tool-to-understand-people.html?ref=technology&amp%3B_r=&nl=technology&emc=edit_tu_20130129&_r=0.

101. V. Waller, "Not Just Information: Who Searches for What on the Search Engine Google?" *Journal of the American Society for Information Science and Technology* 62, no. 4 (2011): 761–775.

102. M. Proulx and S. Shepatin, *Social TV: How Marketers Can Reach and Engage Audiences by Connecting Television to the Web, Social Media, and Mobile* (Hoboken, NJ: Wiley, 2012).

103. Mark J. Salganik, P. S. Dodds, and D. J. Watts, "Experimental Study of Inequality and Unpredictability in an Artificial Cultural Market," *Science* 311, no. 5762 (2006): 854.

104. For example see Centola and Macy, "Complex Contagions and the Weakness of Long Ties"; Easley and Kleinberg, *Networks, Crowds, and Markets*; Jure Leskovec, Lada A. Adamic, and Bernardo A. Huberman, "The Dynamics of Viral Marketing," *ACM Trans. Web* 1, no. 1 (2007): 5; Harrigan, Achananuparp, and Lim, "Influentials, Novelty, and Social Contagion"; Albert-László Barabási, "The Origin of Bursts and Heavy Tails in Human Dynamics," *Nature* 435, no. 7039 (2005): 207–211; Jonah Berger and Katherine L. Milkman, "What Makes Online Content Viral?" *Journal of Marketing Research* 49, no. 2 (2012): 192–205. Despite its widespread use, some object to the term *viral* because it suggests that "human agency" is not involved in the circulation of media texts. See Henry Jenkins, Sam Ford, and Joshua Green, *Spreadable Media: Creating Value and Meaning in a Networked Culture* (New York: New York University Press, 2013), 22.

105. Hampton et al., "Why Most Facebook Users Get More Than They Give."

106. Duncan J. Watts and Peter Sheridan Dodds, "Influentials, Networks, and Public Opinion Formation," *Journal of Consumer Research* 34, no. 4 (2007): 441–458; Clive Thompson, "Is the Tipping Point Toast?" *Fast Company* 122 (November 21, 2008b); Harrigan, Achananuparp, and Lim, "Influentials, Novelty, and Social Contagion"; R. Bandari, S. Asur, and B. Huberman, "The Pulse of News in Social Media: Forecasting

Popularity," paper presented at the Association for the Advancement of Artificial Intelligence, Dublin (http://www.aaai.org), June 2012; Leskovec, Adamic, and Huberman, "The Dynamics of Viral Marketing"; Berger and Milkman, "What Makes Online Content Viral?"

107. Malcolm Gladwell, *The Tipping Point: How Little Things Can Make a Big Difference* (New York: Little, Brown, 2000).

108. Duncan J. Watts, *Everything Is Obvious: Once You Know the Answer; How Common Sense Fails* (New York: Penguin Press, 2011), 91.

109. D. Romero, W. Galuba, S. Asur, and B. Huberman, "Influence and Passivity in Social Media," *Machine Learning and Knowledge Discovery in Databases,* European Conference, ECML PKDD 2011, Athens, Greece, September 5–9, 2011 (New York: Springer), 18–33; Harrigan, Achananuparp, and Lim, "Influentials, Novelty, and Social Contagion."

110. Wu et al., "Who Says What to Whom on Twitter"; Watts and Dodds, "Influentials, Networks, and Public Opinion Formation."

111. Watts, *Everything Is Obvious,* 101.

112. Jenkins, Ford, and Green, *Spreadable Media,* 80.

113. Bandari, Asur, and Huberman, "The Pulse of News in Social Media."

114. Jenkins, Ford, and Green, *Spreadable Media*; Limor Shifman, "An Anatomy of a YouTube Meme," *New Media & Society* 14, no. 2 (2012): 187–203.

115. Fang Wu and Bernardo A. Huberman, "Novelty and Collective Attention," *Proceedings of the National Academy of Sciences* 104, no. 45 (2007): 17599–17601; Harrigan, Achananuparp, and Lim, "Influentials, Novelty, and Social Contagion."

116. Berger and Milkman, "What Makes Online Content Viral?"

117. David Tewksbury and Jason Rittenberg, *News on the Internet: Information and Citizenship in the 21st Century* (Oxford: Oxford University Press, 2012), 23.

118. Paul DiMaggio, Eszter Hargittai, W. Russell Neuman, and John P. Robinson, "Social Implications of the Internet," *Annual Review of Sociology* 27, (2001): 307–336; Eszter Hargittai and Yuli Patrick Hsieh, "Digital Inequality," in *Oxford Handbook of Internet Studies,* ed. William H. Dutton (Oxford: Oxford University Press, 2013), 129–150.

119. Chris Anderson, *Free: The Future of a Radical Price* (New York: Hyperion, 2009).

120. Anthony Giddens, *Social Theory and Modern Sociology* (Stanford, CA: Stanford University Press, 1987), 221; Robert LaRose, "The Problem of Media Habits," *Communication Theory* 20, no. 2 (2010): 194–222; A. W. Rosenstein and A. E. Grant,

"Reconceptualizing the Role of Habit: A New Model of Television Audience Activity," *Journal of Broadcasting & Electronic Media* 41, no. 3 (1997): 324–344.

121. Bruce M. Owen, Jack H. Beebe, and Willard G. Manning, *Television Economics* (Lexington, MA: Lexington Books, 1974); George Comstock, *Television in America* (Beverly Hills: Sage, 1980).

122. Harold L. Vogel, *Entertainment Industry Economics: A Guide for Financial Analysis,* 8th ed. (Cambridge, UK: Cambridge University Press, 2011).

123. Rainie and Wellman, *Networked.*

124. For example, Peter J. Danaher, Tracey S. Dagger, and Michael S. Smith, "Forecasting Television Ratings," *International Journal of Forecasting* 27, no. 4 (2011): 1215–1240.

125. Jumptap, "Screen Jumping: Understanding Today's Cross-Screen Consumer" (Jumptap and comScore, September 5, 2013).

126. Taneja et al., "Media Consumption across Platforms."

127. Jeremy Nye, "Tapping out an Age Old Rhythm," *Viewing 24/7* (August 22, 2012).

128. David Kirkpatrick, *The Facebook Effect: The Inside Story of the Company That Is Connecting the World* (New York: Simon and Schuster, 2011), 296.

129. W. R. Tobler, "A Computer Movie Simulating Urban Growth in the Detroit Region," *Economic Geography* 46 (1970): 234–240.

130. B. Hecht and E. Moxley, "Terabytes of Tobler: Evaluating the First Law in a Massive, Domain-Neutral Representation of World Knowledge," presented at the 9th International Conference on Spatial Information Theory, Aber Wrac'h, France, September 21–25, 2009, 88–105 (New York: Springer).

131. Thomas B. Ksiazek and Elaine Yuan, "A Comparative Networks Analysis of Audience Fragmentation in China and the U.S.," paper presented at the annual meeting of the International Communication Association, Phoenix, AZ, May 2012; Damian Trilling and Klaus Schoenbach, "Patterns of News Consumption in Austria: How Fragmented Are They?" *International Journal of Communication*, no. 7 (2013).

132. J. D. Straubhaar, "Beyond Media Imperialism: Asymmetrical Interdependence and Cultural Proximity," *Critical Studies in Media Communication* 8, no. 1 (1991): 39–59.

133. Sharp, Beal, and Collins, "Television."

134. Thomas B. Ksiazek and James G. Webster, "Cultural Proximity and Audience Behavior: The Role of Language in Patterns of Polarization and Multicultural Fluency," *Journal of Broadcasting & Electronic Media* 52, no. 3 (2008): 485–503.

135. Ibid.; B. Hecht and D. Gergle, "The Tower of Babel Meets Web 2.0: User-Generated Content and Its Applications in a Multilingual Context," paper presented at the Conference on Human Factors in Computing Systems C&T, Atlanta, GA, April 2010; Ethan Zuckerman, "Serendipity, Echo Chambers, and the Front Page," *Nieman Reports* 62, No. 4 (2008): 16; Ethan Zuckerman, *Rewire: Digital Cosmopolitans in the Age of Connection* (New York: Norton, 2013).

Chapter 3

1. Thomas H. Davenport and John C. Beck, *The Attention Economy: Understanding the New Currency of Business* (Boston: Harvard Business Press, 2001); J. Falkinger, "Attention Economies," *Journal of Economic Theory* 133, no. 1 (2007): 266–294; M. H. Goldhaber, "The Attention Economy and the Net," *First Monday* 2, nos. 4–7 (1997); Tom Hayes, *Jump Point: How Network Culture Is Revolutionizing Business* (New York: McGraw-Hill, 2008); R. A. Lanham, *The Economics of Attention: Style and Substance in the Age of Information* (Chicago: University of Chicago Press, 2006); Bernardo A. Huberman and Fang Wu, "The Economics of Attention: Maximizing User Value in Information-Rich Environments," in *Proceedings of the 1st International Workshop on Data Mining and Audience Intelligence for Advertising* (San Jose, CA: ACM, 2007).

2. For example, L. Lessig, *Remix: Making Art and Commerce Thrive in the Hybrid Economy* (New York: Penguin Press, 2008).

3. Philip M. Napoli, *Audience Economics: Media Institutions and the Audience Marketplace* (New York: Columbia University Press, 2003).

4. Lisa Belkin, "Queen of the Mommy Bloggers," *New York Times* (February 23, 2011).

5. Harold Hotelling, "Stability in Competition," *The Economic Journal* 39, no. 153 (1929): 41–57; Andrea Mangani, "Profit and Audience Maximization in Broadcasting Markets," *Information Economics and Policy* 15, no. 3 (2003): 305–315.

6. Bruce M. Owen and Steven S. Wildman, *Video Economics* (Cambridge, MA: Harvard University Press, 1992), 65.

7. David Tewksbury and Jason Rittenberg, *News on the Internet: Information and Citizenship in the 21st Century* (Oxford: Oxford University Press, 2012), 36.

8. Home-Office, *Broadcasting in the '90s: Competition, Choice and Quality,* ed. Secretary of State for the Home Office (London: HMSO Books, 1988), 7.

9. N. Helberger, "Diversity by Design," *Journal of Information Policy* 1 (2011): 441–469; Ofcom, "Measuring Media Plurality: Ofcom's Advice to the Secretary of State for Culture, Media and Sport" (London2012), http://stakeholders.ofcom.org.uk/consultations/measuring-plurality/advice.

10. B. Gunter, *Media Research Methods: Measuring Audiences, Reactions and Impact* (London: Sage, 1999), 93.

11. R. E. Caves, *Creative Industries: Contracts between Art and Commerce* (Cambridge, MA: Harvard University Press, 2000).

12. Pablo J. Boczkowski and Eugenia Mitchelstein, *The News Gap: When the Information Preferences of the Media and the Public Diverge* (Cambridge, MA: MIT Press, 2013).

13. Ibid.; For example, Karl Polanyi, *The Great Transformation: Economic and Political Origins of Our Time* (New York: Rinehart, 1944); Yochai Benkler, *The Penguin and the Leviathan: How Cooperation Triumphs over Self-Interest* (New York: Crown Business, 2011); Russell Belk, "Sharing," *Journal of Consumer Research* 36, no. 5 (2010): 715–734.

14. For example, Lessig, *Remix*; Henry Jenkins, Sam Ford, and Joshua Green, *Spreadable Media: Creating Value and Meaning in a Networked Culture* (New York: New York University Press, 2013); Yochai Benkler, *The Wealth of Networks: How Social Production Transforms Markets and Freedom* (New Haven: Yale University Press, 2006).

15. J. Rosen, "The People Formerly Known as the Audience," *Huffington Post* (June 30, 2006), http://www.huffingtonpost.com/jay-rosen/the-people-formerly -known_1_b_24113.html.

16. Jenkins, Ford, and Green, *Spreadable Media,* 305.

17. Belk, "Sharing."

18. For example, Benkler, *The Wealth of Networks*; Lessig, *Remix*.

19. Benkler, *The Wealth of Networks*; Jenkins, Ford, and Green, *Spreadable Media*; D. Yvette Wohn and Eun-Kyung Na, "Tweeting about TV: Sharing Television Viewing Experiences via Social Media Message Streams," *First Monday* 16, no. 3 (2011): 1–29; Clay Shirky, *Here Comes Everybody: The Power of Organizing without Organizations* (New York: Penguin Books, 2008); W. Lance Bennett and Alexandra Segerberg, "The Logic of Connective Action," *Information, Communication & Society* 15, no. 5 (2012): 739–768.

20. N. B. Ellison, C. Steinfield, and C. Lampe, "Connection Strategies: Social Capital Implications of Facebook-Enabled Communication Practices," *New Media & Society* 13, no. 6 (2011): 873–892; Jenkins, Ford, and Green, *Spreadable Media*; Nicholas Harrigan, Palakorn Achananuparp, and Ee-Peng Lim, "Influentials, Novelty, and Social Contagion: The Viral Power of Average Friends, Close Communities, and Old News," *Social Networks* 34, no. 4 (2012): 470–480; Fang Wu, D. M. Wilkinson, and B. A. Huberman, "Feedback Loops of Attention in Peer Production," International Conference on Computational Science and Engineering, CSE '09 August 29–31, 2009.

21. Benkler, *The Wealth of Networks,* 43.

22. Chris Anderson, *Free: The Future of a Radical Price* (New York: Hyperion, 2009), 159.

23. Alice E. Marwick and danah boyd, "I Tweet Honestly, I Tweet Passionately: Twitter Users, Context Collapse, and the Imagined Audience," *New Media & Society* 13, no. 1 (2011): 122.

24. A. Lenhart, "Adults and Social Network Websites," Pew Internet and American Life Project (January 14, 2009).

25. Jenkins, Ford, and Green, *Spreadable Media,* 59. Unfortunately, the metrics amateurs use to gauge their audience are very accurate, so people who use social media typically underestimate the size of their audience. See Michael S. Bernstein, Eytan Bakshy, Moira Burke, and Brian Karrer, "Quantifying the Invisible Audience in Social Networks," paper presented at the Proceedings of the SIGCHI Conference on Human Factors in Computing Systems, Paris, April 27–May 2, 2013.

26. Steven S. Wildman and Stephen E. Siwek, *International Trade in Films and Television Programs* (Cambridge, MA: Ballinger, 1988); David Waterman, *Hollywood's Road to Riches* (Cambridge, MA: Harvard University Press, 2005); Steven S. Wildman, "One-Way Flows and the Economics of Audiencemaking," in *Audiencemaking: How the Media Create the Audience,* ed. James S. Ettema and D. C. Whitney (Thousand Oaks, CA: Sage, 1994), 115–141.

27. Andrew Wallerstein, "Netflix Series Spending Revealed," *Variety* (March 8, 2013); Tom Vanderbilt and Willa Paskin, "The Platinum Age of TV," *Wired* (April 2013).

28. Waterman, *Hollywood's Road to Riches.*

29. Caves, *Creative Industries.*

30. Steven Levy, "Power Hours: Deep inside a Google Data Center," *Wired* (November 2012): 174–181.

31. Benkler, *The Wealth of Networks.*

32. Nielsen, "Buzz in the Blogosphere: Millions More Bloggers and Blog Readers," *Nielsen Newswire* (March 8, 2012), http://www.nielsen.com/us/en/newswire/2012/buzz-in-the-blogosphere-millions-more-bloggers-and-blog-readers.html.

33. Caves, *Creative Industries.*

34. Ibid.; William Goldman, *Adventures in the Screen Trade: A Personal View of Hollywood and Screenwriting,* vol. 92 (New York: Warner Books, 1983), 39.

35. Harold L. Vogel, *Entertainment Industry Economics: A Guide for Financial Analysis,* 8th ed. (Cambridge, UK: Cambridge University Press, 2011).

36. William T. Bielby and Denise D. Bielby, "'All Hits Are Flukes': Institutionalized Decision Making and the Rhetoric of Network Prime-Time Program Development," *American Journal of Sociology* 99 (5) (1994): 1287–1313.

37. John Lawless, "The Interview: Nigel Newton; Is There Life after Harry Potter," *Independent (London)* (July 3, 2005).

38. Joseph Lampel, Theresa Lant, and Jamal Shamsie, "Balancing Act: Learning from Organizing Practices in Cultural Industries," *Organization Science* 11, no. 3 (2000): 263–269.

39. Ibid., 266.

40. Klaus Schoenbach, "'The Own in the Foreign': Reliable Surprise—an Important Function of the Media?" *Media, Culture & Society* 29, no. 2 (2007): 344–353.

41. Bielby and Bielby, "All Hits Are Flukes."

42. Caves, *Creative Industries*; Gabriel Rossman, Nicole Esparza, and Phillip Bonacich, "I'd Like to Thank the Academy, Team Spillovers, and Network Centrality," *American Sociological Review* 75, no. 1 (2010): 31–51.

43. Anita Elberse, *Blockbusters: Hit-making, Risk-taking, and the Big Business of Entertainment* (New York: Holt, 2013), 7–8.

44. Jean K. Chalaby, "At the Origin of a Global Industry: The TV Format Trade as an Anglo-American Invention," *Media, Culture & Society* 34, no. 1 (2012): 36–52.

45. Keach Hagey, "Creator of 'The Voice' Gets a Second Act: The Netherlands' John de Mol Was a Pioneer of Reality Television," *Wall Street Journal* (June 9, 2013).

46. Jean K. Chalaby, "The Making of an Entertainment Revolution: How the TV Format Trade Became a Global Industry," *European Journal of Communication* 26, no. 4 (2011): 306.

47. Ibid.; Silvio Waisbord, "McTV Understanding the Global Popularity of Television Formats," *Television & New Media* 5, no. 4 (2004): 359–383.

48. Greta Hsu, Giacomo Negro, and Fabrizio Perretti, "Hybrids in Hollywood: A Study of the Production and Performance of Genre-Spanning Films," *Industrial and Corporate Change* 21, no. 6 (2012): 1431.

49. Vanderbilt and Paskin, "The Platinum Age of TV," 102.

50. Hsu, Negro, and Perretti, "Hybrids in Hollywood"; G. Hsu, M. T. Hannan, and Ö. Koçak, "Multiple Category Memberships in Markets: An Integrative Theory and Two Empirical Tests," *American Sociological Review* 74, No. 1 (2009): 150–169.

51. Roger Ebert, "*Cowboys & Aliens*," *Chicago Sun Times* (July 27, 2011), http://rogerebert.suntimes.com/apps/pbcs.dll/article?AID=/20110727/REVIEWS/110729987.

52. James Hamilton, *All the News That's Fit to Sell: How the Market Transforms Information into News* (Princeton, NJ: Princeton University Press, 2004), 9–10.

53. Project for Excellence in Journalism, "State of the News Media 2006: An Annual Report on American Journalism" (New York: Pew Research Center, 2006).

54. Peter L. M. Vasterman, "Media-Hype Self-Reinforcing News Waves, Journalistic Standards and the Construction of Social Problems," *European Journal of Communication* 20, no. 4 (2005): 514.

55. Pablo J. Boczkowski, *News at Work: Imitation in an Age of Information Abundance* (Chicago: University of Chicago Press, 2010), 6.

56. Lampel, Lant, and Shamsie, "Balancing Act," 266.

57. N. Anand and R. A. Peterson, "When Market Information Constitutes Fields: Sensemaking of Markets in the Commercial Music Industry," *Organization Science* 11 (3) (2000): 270–284.

58. James G. Webster, Patricia F. Phalen, and Lawrence W. Lichty, *Ratings Analysis: Audience Measurement and Analytics,* 4th ed. (New York: Routledge, 2014); M. Balnaves, T. O'Regan, and B. Goldsmith, *Rating the Audience: The Business of Media* (London: Bloomsbury, 2011).

59. Robert Perkurny, "Coping with Television Production," in *Individuals in Mass Media Organizations,* ed. James S. Ettema and D.C. Whitney (Beverly Hills, CA: Sage, 1982), 131–144; Ingunn Hagen, "Slaves of the Ratings Tyranny? Media Images of the Audience," in *Rethinking the Media Audience,* ed. Pertti Alasuutari (London: Sage, 1999), 130–150; Dwight Dewerth-Pallmeyer, *The Audience in the News* (Mahwah, NJ: Erlbaum, 1997).

60. Brooke Barnes, "Solving Equation of a Hit Film Script, with Data," *New York Times* (May 5, 2013).

61. For example, Kate Kaye, "Welcome to the Era of the Data-Driven Programmer: Yet Algorithms Won't Replace Humans Any Time Soon," *Advertising Age* (April 8, 2013): 8.

62. Joseph Turow, *The Daily You: How the New Advertising Industry Is Defining Your Identity and Your Worth* (New Haven, CT: Yale University Press, 2012).

63. C. W. Anderson, "Between Creative and Quantified Audiences: Web Metrics and Changing Patterns of Newswork in Local US Newsrooms," *Journalism* 12, no. 5 (2011): 561.

64. Ibid., 563.

65. Herbert J. Gans, *Deciding What's News* (Evanston, IL: Northwestern University Press, 2004); Paul Espinosa, "The Audience in the Text: Ethnographic Observations

of a Hollywood Story Conference," *Media, Culture & Society* 4, no. 1 (1982): 77–86; Jarl A. Ahlkvist, "Programming Philosophies and the Rationalization of Music Radio," *Media, Culture & Society* 23, no. 3 (2001): 339–358.

66. Anderson, "Between Creative and Quantified Audiences," 564, emphasis in original.

67. Vanderbilt and Paskin, "The Platinum Age of TV," 101.

68. Ibid., 96.

69. Barnes, "Solving Equation of a Hit Film Script, with Data."

70. Ibid.

71. Paul M. Hirsch and Daniel M. Gruber, "Digitizing Fads and Fashions: How Technology Has 'Glocalized' the Market for Creative Products," in *Handbook on Creative Industries*, ed. Candace Jones and Mark Lorenzen (Oxford: Oxford University Press, 2014); Aymar Jean Christian, "Valuing Post-Network Television," in *Flow* (May 6, 2013).

72. Dan Gillmor, *We the Media: Grassroots Journalism by the People, for the People* (Sebastopol, CA: O'Reilly Media, 2006), xiv.

73. Eric Schmidt and Jared Cohen, *The New Digital Age: Reshaping the Future of People, Nations and Business* (New York: Knopf, 2013), 47–48.

74. Bennett and Segerberg, "The Logic of Connective Action"; Shirky, *Here Comes Everybody*.

75. Project for Excellence in Journalism, "How News Happens: A Study of the News Ecosystem of One American City" (New York: Pew Research Center, 2010), 3.

76. Simon Dumenco, "The Truth about Reddit: The Benefits of Neglectful Ownership, Where Gawker and BuzzFeed Get Their 'Inspiration,' and More," *Advertising Age* (May 6, 2013): 6.

77. Lessig, *Remix*; Limor Shifman, "An Anatomy of a Youtube Meme," *New Media & Society* 14, no. 2 (2012): 187–203.

78. Jenkins, Ford, and Green, *Spreadable Media*, 83.

79. Meeyoung Cha, J. Pérez, and Hamed Haddadi, "Flash Floods and Ripples: The Spread of Media Content through the Blogosphere," paper presented at the AAAI Conference on Weblogs and Social Media (ICWSM) Data Challenge Workshop, San Jose, May 2009.

80. Ben Zimmer, "Who First Put 'Lipstick on a Pig'?" *Slate* (September 10, 2008).

81. Jure Leskovec, Lars Backstrom, and Jon Kleinberg, "Meme-Tracking and the Dynamics of the News Cycle," in *Proceedings of the 15th ACM SIGKDD International Conference on Knowledge Discovery and Data Mining* (Paris: ACM, 2009), 505.

82. Jaewon Yang and Jure Leskovec, "Patterns of Temporal Variation in Online Media," in *Proceedings of the Fourth ACM International Conference on Web Search and Data Mining* (Hong Kong: ACM, 2011), 177–186.

83. Wildman, "One-Way Flows and the Economics of Audiencemaking"; Waterman, *Hollywood's Road to Riches*.

84. Waterman, *Hollywood's Road to Riches*; Owen and Wildman, *Video Economics*.

85. Mark R. Levy, ed. *The VCR Age: Home Video and Mass Communication* (Newbury Park, CA: Sage, 1989).

86. Jack Hitt, "Multiscreen Mad Men," *New York Times* (November 21, 2008).

87. Department for Culture, Media and Sport and Department for Business, Innovation and Skills. "Digital Britain: Final Report" (2009): 135–136, http://www.official-documents.gov.uk/document/cm76/7650/7650.pdf.

88. Nielsen, "The Cross-Platform Report: How Viewers Watch Time-Shifted Programming," *Nielsen Newswire* (2013a), http://www.nielsen.com/us/en/newswire/2013/the-cross-platform-report-how-viewers-watch-time-shifted-programming.html.

89. Byron Sharp, Virginia Beal, and Martin Collins, "Television: Back to the Future," *Journal of Advertising Research* 49, no. 2 (2009): 211–219; Patrick Barwise, "Waiting for ''Vodot':' Why "Video on 'Demand' Won't Happen," *Market Leader* (2011): 30–33; Stylianos Papathanassopoulos, Sharon Coen, James Curran, Toril Aalberg, David Rowe, Paul Jones, Hernando Rojas, and Rod Tiffen, "Online Threat, but Television Is Still Dominant," *Journalism Practice* 7 (6) (2013): 1–15.

90. Vanderbilt and Paskin, "The Platinum Age of TV," 94.

91. Kara Swisher, "Social Media + Pop Culture = ?" *Wall Street Journal* (June 3, 2013). Also see Helen A. S. Popkin, "Game of Spoilers: Social Media Is Killing DVR Culture," *NBC News*.

92. Marc Graser, "10 Insights from Studies of Binge Watchers," *Variety* (March 7, 2013).

93. WayneFriedman,"TimeWarnerFavorsTradTVoverStreaming,"*MediaPost*(March 4, 2013), http://www.mediapost.com/publications/article/194887/time-warner-favors-trad-tv-over-streaming.html#axzz2OBm8ElCj.

94. Brian Steinberg, "To Goose TV Audience, Scripps Uses the Web," *Advertising Age* (March 5, 2013).

95. Horace M. Newcomb and Paul M. Hirsch, "Television as a Cultural Forum: Implications for Research," *Quarterly Review of Film & Video* 8, no. 3 (1983): 45–55; Raymond Williams, *Television: Technology and Cultural Form* (New York: Schocken Books, 1974).

96. Jenkins, Ford, and Green, *Spreadable Media,* 44–45.

97. Ibid., 6.

98. Webster, Phalen, and Lichty, *Ratings Analysis.*

99. T. W. Farnam, "Obama Campaign Took Unorthodox Approach to Ad Buying," *Washington Post* (November 14, 2012).

100. Susan Tyler Eastman and Douglas A. Ferguson, *Media Programming: Strategies and Practices* (Belmont, CA: Wadsworth, 2012).

101. Hitt, "Multiscreen Mad Men."

102. Byrony Jardine, "Retaining the Primetime TV Audience: Examining Adjacent Program Audience Duplication across Markets," master's thesis, University of South Australia, 2012; James G. Webster, "Audience Flow Past and Present: Television Inheritance Effects Reconsidered," *Journal of Broadcasting & Electronic Media* 50, no. 2 (2006): 323–337.

103. Klaus Schoenbach, "Trap Effect," in *The International Encyclopedia of Communication,* ed. Wolfgang Donsbach (Malden, MA: Blackwell, 2008), 5176–5178.

104. Anke Wonneberger, Klaus Schoenbach, and Lex van Meurs, "Staying Tuned: TV News Audiences in the Netherlands 1988–2010," *Journal of Broadcasting & Electronic Media* 56, no. 1: 55–74.

105. For an extended discussion of how entertainment industries manage the hit making process see Elberse, *Blockbusters.*

106. Peter J. Danaher, Tracey S. Dagger, and Michael S. Smith, "Forecasting Television Ratings," *International Journal of Forecasting* 27, no. 4 (2011): 1215–1240.

107. Natasha Singer, "Your Online Attention, Bought in an Instant," *New York Times* (November 17, 2012): 1.

108. Turow, *The Daily You,* 118.

109. Viktor Mayer-Schonberger and Kenneth Cukier, *Big Data: A Revolution That Will Transform How We Live, Work and Think* (Boston: Houghton Mifflin Harcourt, 2013), 12.

110. J. Cho and S. Roy, "Impact of Search Engines on Page Popularity," paper presented at the Proceedings of the 13th International Conference on World Wide Web, New York, May 2004.

111. Alexander Halavais, *Search Engine Society* (Cambridge, UK: Polity Press, 2009), 71.

112. Michael D. Conover, Jacob Ratkiewicz, Matthew Francisco, Bruno Gonçalves, Alessandro Flammini, and Filippo Menczer, "Political Polarization on Twitter," paper presented at the AAAI 5th International Conference on Weblogs and Social Media Barcelona, July 2011.

113. Nielsen, "Television Audience Report 2008" (New York: Author, 2009); Elaine J. Yuan and James G. Webster, "Channel Repertoires: Using PeopleMeter Data in Beijing," *Journal of Broadcasting & Electronic Media* 50, no. 3 (2006): 524–536; Jakob Bjur, "Transforming Audiences: Patterns of Individualization in Television Viewing" (Gothenburg, Germany: University of Gothenburg, 2009).

114. Eli Pariser, *The Filter Bubble: What the Internet Is Hiding from You* (New York: Penguin Press, 2011), 67.

115. Elberse, *Blockbusters*, 4.

Chapter 4

1. Jon Gertner, "Our Ratings, Ourselves," *New York Times Magazine* (April 10, 2005): 35.

2. Hugh M. Beville, *Audience Ratings: Radio, Television, Cable* (Hillsdale, NJ: Erlbaum, 1988); B. Gunter, *Media Research Methods: Measuring Audiences, Reactions and Impact* (London: Sage, 1999); M. Balnaves, T. O'Regan, and B. Goldsmith, *Rating the Audience: The Business of Media* (London: Bloomsbury, 2011); James G. Webster, Patricia F. Phalen, and Lawrence W. Lichty, *Ratings Analysis: Audience Measurement and Analytics*, 4th ed. (New York: Routledge, 2014).

3. N. Anand and A. Richard Peterson, "When Market Information Constitutes Fields: Sensemaking of Markets in the Commercial Music Industry," *Organization Science* 11, no. 3 (2000): 271.

4. Ibid.

5. Kurt Andrews and Philip M. Napoli, "Changing Market Information Regimes: A Case Study of the Transition to the BookScan Audience Measurement System in the U.S. Book Publishing Industry," *Journal of Media Economics* 19, no. 1 (2006): 33–54; Beth Barnes and L. Thomson, "Power to the People (Meter): Audience Measurement Technology and Media Specialization," in *Audiencemaking: How the Media Create the Audience*, ed. J. S. Ettema and D. C. Whitney (Thousand Oaks, CA: Sage, 1994), 75–94.

6. Philip M. Napoli, *Audience Evolution: New Technologies and the Transformation of Media Audiences* (New York: Columbia University Press, 2011); Webster, Phalen, and Lichty, *Ratings Analysis.*

7. Harsh Taneja and Utsav Mamoria, "Measuring Media Use across Platforms: Evolving Audience Information Systems," *International Journal on Media Management* 14, no. 2 (2012): 121–140; Webster, Phalen, and Lichty, *Ratings Analysis.*

8. WPP, "GroupM Forecasts 2012 Global Ad Spending to Increase 6.4% U.S.," http://www.wpp.com/wpp/press/press/default.htm?guid={23ebd8df-51a5-4a1d-b1 39-576d711e77ac.

9. For example, Eszter Hargittai, "Digital Na(t)ives? Variation in Internet Skills and Uses among Members of the 'Net Generation,'" *Sociological Inquiry* 80, no. 1 (2010): 92–113; S. S. Sundar and C. Nass, "Conceptualizing Sources in Online News," *Journal of Communication* 51, no. 1 (2001): 52–72.

10. E. Pariser, *The Filter Bubble: What the Internet Is Hiding from You* (New York: Penguin Press, 2011), 40.

11. For a thoughtful collection of essays on the fallacy of "raw data," see Lisa Gitelman, ed. *"Raw Data" Is an Oxymoron* (Cambridge, MA: MIT Press, 2013).

12. WFA/EACA, *Guide to Organizing Audience Research* (Brussels: World Federation of Advertisers and European Association of Communications Agencies, 2008).

13. Karen Buzzard, *Tracking the Audience: The Ratings Industry from Analog to Digital* (New York: Routledge, 2012); Webster, Phalen, and Lichty, *Ratings Analysis.*

14. Philip M. Napoli, "Audience Measurement and Media Policy: Audience Economics, the Diversity Principle, and the Local People Meter," *Communication Law and Policy* 10, no. 4 (2005): 349–382.

15. R. Hernandez and S. Elliot, "Advertising: The Odd Couple vs. Nielsen," *New York Times* (June 14, 2004).

16. Tim O'Reilly, "What Is Web 2.0: Design Patterns and Business Models for the Next Generation of Software," *Communications & Strategies* 65, no. 1 (2007): 27.

17. Tim O'Reilly and John Battelle, "Web Squared: Web 2.0 Five Years On," Web 2.0 Summit, San Francisco, October 20–22, 2009.

18. Ibid., 3.

19. Claire Cain Miller, "Google Changes Search Algorithm, Trying to Make Results More Timely," *Bits* (November 3, 2011), http://bits.blogs.nytimes.com/2011/11/03/google-changes-search-algorithm.

20. David Segal, "The Dirty Little Secrets of Search," *New York Times* (February 12, 2011).

21. Eric Schmidt and Jared Cohen, *The New Digital Age: Reshaping the Future of People, Nations and Business* (New York: Knopf, 2013), 57.

22. Steve Stecklow and Julia Angwin, "House Releases "Do Not Track" Bill," *Wall Street Journal* (May 7, 2011), http://online.wsj.com/article/SB1000142405274870399 2704576307261709717734.html.

23. Jay Rosen, "The Right to Be Forgotten," *Stanford Law Review Online* 64 (2012): 88; Natasha Singer, "Data Protection Laws, an Ocean Apart," *New York Times* (February 2, 2013).

24. Napoli, *Audience Evolution*; Webster, Phalen, and Lichty, *Ratings Analysis*.

25. Pariser, *The Filter Bubble*, 7.

26. Webster, Phalen, and Lichty, *Ratings Analysis*.

27. Joseph Turow, *The Daily You: How the New Advertising Industry Is Defining Your Identity and Your Worth* (New Haven, CT: Yale University Press, 2012).

28. Webster, Phalen, and Lichty, *Ratings Analysis*.

29. For example, Andrew S. C. Ehrenberg, *Data Reduction: Analyzing and Interpreting Statistical Data* (London: Wiley, 1975).

30. Webster, Phalen, and Lichty, *Ratings Analysis*.

31. M. Proulx and S. Shepatin, *Social TV: How Marketers Can Reach and Engage Audiences by Connecting Television to the Web, Social Media, and Mobile* (Hoboken, NJ: Wiley, 2012); Webster, Phalen, and Lichty, *Ratings Analysis*; Napoli, *Audience Evolution*.

32. O'Reilly and Battelle, "Web Squared," 9.

33. E. Thorson, "Changing Patterns of News Consumption and Participation," *Information, Communication & Society* 11, no. 4 (2008): 473–489; S. Knobloch-Westerwick, N. Sharma, D. L. Hansen, and S. Alter, "Impact of Popularity Indications on Readers' Selective Exposure to Online News," *Journal of Broadcasting & Electronic Media* 49, no. 3 (2005): 296–313; James G. Webster, "User Information Regimes: How Social Media Shape Patterns of Consumption," *Northwestern University Law Review* 104, no. 2 (2010): 593–612; Carl Bialik, "Look at This Article: It's One of Our Most Popular," *Wall Street Journal* (May 20, 2009), http://online.wsj.com/article/SB12427781601703727 5.html?KEYWORDS=carl+bialik.

34. T. Gillespie, "Can an Algorithm Be Wrong? Twitter Trends, the Specter of Censorship, and Our Faith in the Algorithms around Us." *Culture Digitally* (October 19, 2011), http://culturedigitally.org/2011/10/can-an-algorithm-be-wrong.

35. Fang Wu, D. M. Wilkinson, and B. A. Huberman, "Feedback Loops of Attention in Peer Production," paper presented at the International Conference on Computational Science and Engineering, CSE '09, August 29–31, 2009.

36. K. N. Hampton, L. S. Goulet, C. Marlow, and L. Rainie, "Why Most Facebook Users Get More Than They Give," *Pew Internet Report* (February 3, 2012).

37. Christopher Steiner, *Automate This: How Algorithms Came to Rule Our World* (New York: Portfolio/Penguin Press, 2012).

38. Steven Levy, "Inside the Box," *Wired* (March 2010): 96–116; Miller, "Google Changes Search Algorithm, Trying to Make Results More Timely."

39. John Battelle, *The Search: How Google and Its Rivals Rewrote the Rules of Business and Transformed Our Culture* (New York: Portfolio Trade, 2006); Massimo Franceschet, "PageRank: Standing on the Shoulders of Giants," *Communications of the ACM* 54, no. 6 (2011): 92–101.

40. Steven Levy, "Power Hours: Deep inside a Google Data Center," *Wired* (November 2012): 174–181.

41. For example, Lada A. Adamic, "The Social Hyperlink," in *The Hyperlinked Society: Questioning Connections in the Digital Age,* ed. Joseph Turow and L. Tsui (Ann Arbor: University of Michigan Press, 2008), 227–249; Seth Finkelstein, "Google, Links, and Popularity versus Authority," in *The Hyperlinked Society: Questioning Connections in the Digital Age,* ed. Joseph Turow and L. Tsui (Ann Arbor: University of Michigan Press, 2008), 104–120.

42. Larry Page, S. Brin, R. Motwani, and T. Winograd, "The PageRank Citation Ranking: Bringing Order to the Web," Stanford Info Lab (1999).

43. Franceschet, "PageRank," 94.

44. Miller, "Google Changes Search Algorithm, Trying to Make Results More Timely"; J. Cho and S. Roy, "Impact of Search Engines on Page Popularity," paper presented at the Proceedings of the 13th International Conference on World Wide Web, May 2004.

45. O'Reilly and Battelle, "Web Squared," 2.

46. Pariser, *The Filter Bubble*.

47. Clara Shih, "What's a 'Like' Worth? Ask Facebook's Graph Search: Facebook Search Graph Optimization Becomes as Important as Google SEO," *Advertising Age* (February 14, 2013).

48. G. Adomavicius and A. Tuzhilin, "Toward the Next Generation of Recommender Systems: A Survey of the State-of-the-Art and Possible Extensions," *IEEE Transactions on Knowledge and Data Engineering* 17, no. 6 (2005): 734–749.

49. G. Adomavicius and A. Tuzhilin, "Context-Aware Recommender Systems," in *Recommender Systems Handbook*, ed. F. Ricci, L. Rokach, and B. Shapira (New York: Springer, 2011), 217–253; O'Reilly and Battelle, "Web Squared"; Claire Cain Miller, "Apps That Know What You Want, Before You Do," *New York Times* (July 29, 2013).

50. For example, Turow, *The Daily You.*

51. Balnaves, O'Regan, and Goldsmith, *Rating the Audience,* 22.

52. Webster, Phalen, and Lichty, *Ratings Analysis.*

53. P. A. Samuelson, "A Note on the Pure Theory of Consumer's Behaviour," *Economica* 5, no. 17 (1938): 61–71; Hal R. Varian, "Revealed Preference," in *Samuelsonian Economics and the Twenty-First Century*, ed. Michael Szenberg, Lall Ramrattan, and Aron A. Gottesman (Oxford: Oxford University Press, 2006); Frederic Vermeulen, "Foundations of Revealed Preference: Introduction," *The Economic Journal* 122, no. 560 (2012): 287–294.

54. Pariser, *The Filter Bubble,* 9.

55. Dan Ariely and Michael I. Norton, "How Actions Create—Not Just Reveal—Preferences," *Trends in Cognitive Sciences* 12, no. 1 (2008): 13–16; John W. Payne, James R. Bettman, and David A. Schkade, "Measuring Constructed Preferences: Towards a Building Code," *Journal of Risk and Uncertainty* 19, no. 1 (1999): 243–270; Paul Slovic, "The Construction of Preference," *American Psychologist* 50, no. 5 (1995): 364–371.

56. Pariser, *The Filter Bubble,* 24.

57. Google, "Personalized Search for Everyone," Google Blog (December 4, 2009), http://googleblog.blogspot.com/2009/12/personalized-search-for-everyone.html.

58. Sonini Sengupta, "For Search, Facebook Had to Go beyond 'Robospeak,'" *New York Times* (January 28, 2013), http://www.nytimes.com/2013/01/29/business/how-facebook-taught-its-search-tool-to-understand-people.html?ref=technology&amp%3B_r=&nl=technology&emc=edit_tu_20130129&_r=0.

59. Miller McPherson, Lynn Smith-Lovin, and James M. Cook, "Birds of a Feather: Homophily in Social Networks," *Annual Review of Sociology* 27 (2001): 415–444.

60. Jeff Wildman, "EdgeRank: A Guide to Facebook's Newsfeed Algorithm" (2013), http://edgerank.net; Taina Bucher, "Want to Be on the Top? Algorithmic Power and the Threat of Invisibility on Facebook," *New Media & Society* 14, no. 7 (2012): 1164–1180.

61. For example, Cass R. Sunstein, *Republic.com 2.0* (Princeton, NJ: Princeton University Press, 2007); Turow, *The Daily You.*

62. Pariser, *The Filter Bubble.*

63. Sinan Aral, Lev Muchnik, and Arun Sundararajan, "Distinguishing Influence-Based Contagion from Homophily-Driven Diffusion in Dynamic Networks," *Proceedings of the National Academy of Sciences* 106, no. 51 (2009): 21544–21549; Kevin Lewis, Marco Gonzalez, and Jason Kaufman, "Social Selection and Peer Influence in an Online Social Network," *Proceedings of the National Academy of Sciences* 109, no. 1 (2012): 68–72.

64. Sinan Aral, "Social Science: Poked to Vote," *Nature* 489, no. 7415 (2012): 212–214; Robert M. Bond, Christopher J. Fariss, Jason J. Jones, Adam D. I. Kramer, Cameron Marlow, Jaime E. Settle, and James H. Fowler, "A 61-Million-Person Experiment in Social Influence and Political Mobilization," *Nature* 489, no. 7415 (2012): 295–298.

65. Solomon Messing and Sean J. Westwood, "Selective Exposure in the Age of Social Media: Endorsements Trump Partisan Source Affiliation When Selecting News Online," *Communication Research* (2012).

66. Diana C. Mutz and Lori Young, "Communication and Public Opinion," *Public Opinion Quarterly* 75, no. 5 (2011): 1018–1044.

67. Bialik, "Look at This Article."

68. James Surowiecki, *The Wisdom of Crowds: Why the Many Are Smarter Than the Few and How Collective Wisdom Shapes Business, Economies, Societies and Nations* (New York: Doubleday, 2004).

69. R. I. M. Dunbar, "Neocortex Size as a Constraint on Group Size in Primates," *Journal of Human Evolution* 22, no. 6 (1992): 469–493; R. I. M. Dunbar, "The Social Brain: Mind, Language, and Society in Evolutionary Perspective," *Annual Review of Anthropology* 32 (2003): 163–181.

70. Bruno Gonçalves, Nicola Perra, and Alessandro Vespignani, "Modeling Users' Activity on Twitter Networks: Validation of Dunbar's Number," *PLoS ONE* 6, no. 8 (2011): e22656.

71. Barry Wellman, "Is Dunbar's Number Up?" *British Journal of Psychology* 103, no. 2 (2012): 174–176; Lee Rainie and B. Wellman, *Networked: The New Social Operating System* (Cambridge, MA: MIT Press, 2012).

72. Adomavicius and Tuzhilin, "Toward the Next Generation of Recommender Systems."

73. Ramsey M. Raafat, Nick Chater, and Chris Frith, "Herding in Humans," *Trends in Cognitive Sciences* 13, no. 10 (2009): 420–428; Lev Muchnik, Sinan Aral, and Sean J. Taylor, "Social Influence Bias: A Randomized Experiment," *Science* 341, no. 6146 (2013): 647–651.

74. Mark J. Salganik, P. S. Dodds, and D. J. Watts, "Experimental Study of Inequality and Unpredictability in an Artificial Cultural Market," *Science* 311, no. 5762 (2006): 854.

75. Nate Silver, *The Signal and the Noise: Why So Many Predictions Fail—but Some Don't* (New York: Penguin Press, 2012), 358.

76. Levy, "Power Hours."

77. Donna Tam, "Facebook Processes More Than 500 TB of Data Daily," CNET, http://news.cnet.com/8301-1023_3-57498531-93/facebook-processes-more-than -500-tb-of-data-daily/.

78. Manyika, James, Michael Chui, Brad Brown, Jacques Bughin, Richard Dobbs, Charles Roxburgh, and Angela Hung Byers. "Big Data: The Next Frontier for Innovation, Competition, and Productivity," McKinsey Global Institute (May 2011), http://www.mckinsey.com/insights/business_technology/ big_data_the_next_frontier_for_innovation.

79. For example, Chris Anderson, "The End of Theory: The Data Deluge Makes the Scientific Method Obsolete," *Wired* (June 23, 2008); D. Bollier, *The Promise and Peril of Big Data* (Washington, DC: Aspen Institute, Communications and Society Program, 2010); James Manyika, Michael Chui, Brad Brown, Jacques Bughin, Richard Dobbs, Charles Roxburgh, and Angela Hung Byers, "Big Data"; David Rogers and Don Sexton, "Marketing ROI in the Era of Big Data," in *BRITE-NYAMA Marketing in Transition* (New York: Columbia University Business School, 2012); Steve Lohr, "The Age of Big Data," *New York Times* (February 11, 2012); J. Anderson and L. Rainie, "The Impact of the Internet on Institutions in the Future," in *Pew Research Center's Internet and American Life Project and Elon University's Imagining the Internet Center* (Washington, DC: Pew Research Center's Internet and American Life Project, 2010); Viktor Mayer-Schonberger and Kenneth Cukier, *Big Data: A Revolution That Will Transform How We Live, Work and Think* (Boston: Houghton Mifflin Harcourt, 2013).

80. Anderson, "The End of Theory."

81. danah boyd and Kate Crawford, "Critical Questions for Big Data," *Information, Communication & Society* 15, no. 5 (2012): 668.

82. Steiner, *Automate This*, 61.

83. Michael Learmonth, "Digitas Unveils Tool to Find YouTube Stars before They're Stars: A Long Tail of YouTube Stars Is out There, but How to Find Them?" *Advertising Age* (May 2, 2013): 2.

84. Robert K. Merton, "The Self-Fulfilling Prophecy," *The Antioch Review* 8, no. 2 (1948): 195.

85. Peter J. Danaher, Tracey S. Dagger, and Michael S. Smith, "Forecasting Television Ratings," *International Journal of Forecasting* 27, no. 4 (2011): 1215–1240; Brian Christian, "The A/B Test: Inside the Technology That's Changing the Rules of Business," *Wired* (May 2012): 176–200.

86. Wendy N. Espeland and M. Sauder, "Rankings and Reactivity: How Public Measures Recreate Social Worlds," *American Journal of Sociology* 113, no. 1 (2007): 1–40.

87. Pariser, *The Filter Bubble*, 125.

88. Mayer-Schonberger and Cukier, *Big Data*.

Chapter 5

1. See for example Markus Prior, "The Immensely Inflated News Audience: Assessing Bias in Self-Reported News Exposure," *Public Opinion Quarterly* 73, no. 1 (2009): 130–143; Michael J. LaCour, "A Balanced News Diet, Not Selective Exposure: Evidence from a Real World Measure of Media Exposure," Presented at the Annual Midwest Political Science Association, Chicago, April 2012; James G. Webster, Patricia F. Phalen, and Lawrence W. Lichty, *Ratings Analysis: Audience Measurement and Analytics,* 4th ed. (New York: Routledge, 2014); Russ Clay, Jessica M. Barber, and Natalie J. Shook, "Techniques for Measuring Selective Exposure: A Critical Review," *Communication Methods and Measures* 7, no. 3 (2013): 221–245. For an exchange about the virtues of meters versus self-reports see Markus Prior, "The Challenge of Measuring Media Exposure: Reply to Dilliplane, Goldman, and Mutz," *Political Communication* 30, no. 4 (2013a): 620–634; Seth K. Goldman, Diana C. Mutz, and Susanna Dilliplane, "All Virtue Is Relative: A Response to Prior," *Political Communication* 30, no. 4 (2013): 635–653.

2. C. Anderson, *The Long Tail: Why the Future of Business Is Selling Less of More,* 1st ed. (New York: Hyperion, 2006); Yochai Benkler, *The Wealth of Networks: How Social Production Transforms Markets and Freedom* (New Haven, CT: Yale University Press, 2006).

3. Todd Gitlin, "Public Sphere or Public Sphericules?" in *Media, Ritual, Identity,* ed. T. Liebes and James Curran (London: Routledge, 1998), 168–175; Elihu Katz, "And Deliver Us from Segmentation," *Annals of the American Academy of Political and Social Science* 546 (1996): 22–33; Cass R. Sunstein, *Republic.com 2.0* (Princeton, NJ: Princeton University Press, 2007).

4. James G. Webster and T. B. Ksiazek, "The Dynamics of Audience Fragmentation: Public Attention in an Age of Digital Media," *Journal of Communication* 62 (2012): 39–56; Avery Holton, "Negating Nodes and Liquid Fragmentation: Extending

Conversations of Diffusion, Social Networks, and Fragmentation," *Communication Theory* 22, no. 3 (2012): 279–298.

5. D. Tewksbury, "The Seeds of Audience Fragmentation: Specialization in the Use of Online News Sites," *Journal of Broadcasting & Electronic Media* 49, no. 3 (2005): 332–348; Anderson, *The Long Tail*.

6. James G. Webster, "Beneath the Veneer of Fragmentation: Television Audience Polarization in a Multichannel World," *Journal of Communication* 55, no. 2 (2005): 366–382.

7. Jakob Bjur, *Transforming Audiences: Patterns of Individualization in Television Viewing* (Gothenburg, Germany: University of Gothenburg, 2009); Anke Wonneberger, "Coping with Diversity: Exposure to Public-Affairs TV in a Changing Viewing Environment," PhD diss., University of Amsterdam (2011); Elaine J. Yuan, "The New Multi-Channel Media Environment in China: Diversity of Exposure in Television Viewing," PhD diss., Northwestern University (2007); Su Jung Kim, "Emerging Patterns of News Media Use across Multiple Platforms and Their Political Implications in South Korea," PhD diss., Northwestern University (2011).

8. Anderson, *The Long Tail*.

9. M. Hindman, *The Myth of Digital Democracy* (Princeton, NJ: Princeton University Press, 2009); Webster and Ksiazek, "The Dynamic of Audience Fragmenation"; Arthur De Vany, *Hollywood Economics: How Extreme Uncertainty Shapes the Film Industry* (Routledge, 2003); Robert H. Frank and P. J. Cook, *The Winner-Take-All Society: Why the Few at the Top Get So Much More Than the Rest of Us* (New York: Penguin Press, 1996); Mark J. Salganik, P. S. Dodds, and D. J. Watts, "Experimental Study of Inequality and Unpredictability in an Artificial Cultural Market," *Science* 311, no. 5762 (2006): 854; W. Russell Neuman, *The Future of the Mass Audience* (Cambridge, UK: Cambridge University Press, 1991).

10. Hindman, *The Myth of Digital Democracy*; Jungsu Yim, "Audience Concentration in the Media: Cross-Media Comparisons and the Introduction of the Uncertainty Measure," *Communication Monographs* 70, no. 2 (2003): 114–128.

11. Anderson, *The Long Tail*, 181.

12. For example, Anita Elberse, "Should You Invest in the Long Tail?" *Harvard Business Review* 86, no. 7/8 (2008): 88–96; Frank and Cook, *The Winner-Take-All Society*.

13. Bernardo A. Huberman, *The Laws of the Web: Patterns in the Ecology of Information* (Cambridge, MA: MIT Press, 2003); Albert-László Barabási and Réka Albert, "Emergence of Scaling in Random Networks," *Science* 286, no. 5439 (1999): 509–512.

14. Alexander Halavais, *Search Engine Society* (Cambridge, UK: Polity Press, 2009), 60.

15. Chris Anderson, *Free: The Future of a Radical Price* (New York: Hyperion, 2009).

16. Frank and Cook, *The Winner-Take-All Society*, 33.

17. Anderson, *The Long Tail*, 22.

18. Nathanael J. Fast, Chip Heath, and George Wu, "Common Ground and Cultural Prominence," *Psychological Science* 20, no. 7 (2009): 904–911.

19. M. Proulx and S. Shepatin, *Social TV: How Marketers Can Reach and Engage Audiences by Connecting Television to the Web, Social Media, and Mobile* (Hoboken, NJ: Wiley, 2012); S. Wu, J. M. Hofman, W. A. Mason, and D. J. Watts, "Who Says What to Whom on Twitter," paper presented at the International World Wide Web Conference, Hyderabad, India, March 28–April 1, 2011; Nielsen, "The Follow-Back: Understanding the Two-Way Causal Influence between Twitter Activity and TV Viewership," *Nielsen Newswire* (August 6, 2013b).

20. Salganik, Dodds, and Watts, "Experimental Study of Inequality and Unpredictability in an Artificial Cultural Market."

21. James Surowiecki, *The Wisdom of Crowds: Why the Many Are Smarter Than the Few and How Collective Wisdom Shapes Business, Economies, Societies and Nations* (New York: Doubleday, 2004).

22. For example, Hindman, *The Myth of Digital Democracy*; De Vany, *Hollywood Economics*; W. W. Fu and C. C. Sim, "Aggregate Bandwagon Effect on Online Videos' Viewership: Value Uncertainty, Popularity Cues, and Heuristics," *Journal of the American Society for Information Science and Technology* 62, no. 12 (2011): 2382–2395.

23. Elberse, "Should You Invest in the Long Tail?"

24. Webster, "Beneath the Veneer of Fragmentation."

25. For example, Andrew S. C. Ehrenberg, "The Factor Analytic Search for Program Types," *Journal of Advertising Research* 8, no. 1 (1968): 55–63; A. D. Kirsch and S. Banks, "Program Types Defined by Factor Analysis," *Journal of Advertising Research* 2, no. 3 (1962): 29–31; Dennis H. Gensch and B. Ranganathan, "Evaluation of Television Program Content for the Purpose of Promotional Segmentation," *Journal of Marketing Research* 11, no. 4 (1974): 390–398; Roland T. Rust, Wagner A. Kamakura, and Mark I. Alpert, "Viewer Preference Segmentation and Viewing Choice Models for Network Television," *Journal of Advertising* 21, no. 1 (1992): 1–18; Manouche Tavakoli and Martin Cave, "Modelling Television Viewing Patterns," *Journal of Advertising* 25, no. 4 (1996): 71–86.

26. Jon Marks and Michael Hess, "Redefining Program Types Using Viewing Analysis," PowerPoint presentation for Nielsen 360, Turner Research, Atlanta, GA, 2012.

27. Kate Kaye, "Welcome to the Era of the Data-Driven Programmer: Yet Algorithms Won't Replace Humans Any Time Soon," *Advertising Age* (April 8, 2013): 8.

28. Markus Prior, *Post-broadcast Democracy: How Media Choice Increases Inequality in Political Involvement and Polarizes Election* (Cambridge, UK: Cambridge University Press, 2007).

29. Thomas B. Ksiazek, Edward C. Malthouse, and James G. Webster, "News-Seekers and Avoiders: Exploring Patterns of Total News Consumption across Media and the Relationship to Civic Participation," *Journal of Broadcasting & Electronic Media* 54, no. 4 (2010): 551–568.

30. Su Jung Kim and James G. Webster, "The Impact of a Multichannel Environment on Television News Viewing: A Longitudinal Study of News Audience Polarization in South Korea," *International Journal of Communication* 6 (1) (2012): 838–856; Anke Wonneberger, Klaus Schoenbach, and Lex van Meurs, "Dimensionality of TV-News Exposure: Mapping News Viewing Behavior with People-Meter Data," *International Journal of Public Opinion Research* 21 (1) (2012): 87–107; Anke Wonneberger, Klaus Schoenbach, and Lex van Meurs, "Staying Tuned: TV News Audiences in the Netherlands 1988–2010," *Journal of Broadcasting & Electronic Media* 56, no. 1 (2012): 55–74; T. Aalberg, A. Blekesaune, and E. Elvestad, "Media Choice and Informed Democracy: An Empirical Study of Increasing Information Gaps in Europe," paper presented at the APSA 2012 Annual Meeting (2012).

31. For a sample of this work see Markus Prior, "Media and Political Polarization," *Annual Review of Political Science* 16, no. 1 (2013): 101–127; N. J. Stroud, *Niche News: The Politics of News Choice* (Oxford: Oxford University Press, 2011); Kathleen H. Jamieson and Joseph N. Cappella, *Echo Chamber: Rush Limbaugh and the Conservative Media Establishment* (New York: Oxford University Press, 2009); Shanto Iyengar and Kyusup Hahn, "Red Media, Blue Media: Evidence of Ideological Selectivity in Media Use," *Journal of Communication* 59, no. 1 (2009): 19–39; B. Hollander, "Tuning out or Tuning Elsewhere? Partisanship, Polarization, and Media Migration from 1998 to 2006," *Journalism and Mass Communication Quarterly* 85, no. 1 (2008): 23–40; Matthew Gentzkow and Jesse M. Shapiro, "Ideological Segregation Online and Offline," *The Quarterly Journal of Economics* 126, no. 4 (2011): 1799–1839; Kevin Arceneaux, Martin Johnson, and John Cryderman, "Communication, Persuasion, and the Conditioning Value of Selective Exposure: Like Minds May Unite and Divide but They Mostly Tune Out," *Political Communication* 30, no. 2 (2013): 213–231; W. L. Bennett and S. Iyengar, "A New Era of Minimal Effects? The Changing Foundations of Political Communication," *Journal of Communication* 58, no. 4 (2008): 707–731.

32. LaCour, "A Balanced News Diet."

33. Gentzkow and Shapiro, "Ideological Segregation."

34. Ibid., 1821.

35. Hindman, *The Myth of Digital Democracy*.

36. Gentzkow and Shapiro, "Ideological Segregation," 1802.

37. Ibid.

38. Michael D. Conover, Jacob Ratkiewicz, Matthew Francisco, Bruno Gonçalves, Alessandro Flammini, and Filippo Menczer, "Political Polarization on Twitter," paper presented at the Proceedings of the 5th International Conference on Weblogs and Social Media (2011): 7.

39. K. Nahon and J. Hemsley, "Democracy.com: A Tale of Political Blogs and Content," paper presented at the System Sciences (HICSS), 2011 44th Hawaii International Conference (January 4–7, 2011); E. Hargittai, J. Gallo, and M. Kane, "Cross-Ideological Discussions Among Conservative and Liberal Bloggers," *Public Choice* 134, no. 1–2 (2008): 67–86.

40. Aaron Shaw and Yochai Benkler, "A Tale of Two Blogospheres: Discursive Practices on the Left and Right," *American Behavioral Scientist* 56, no. 4 (2012): 482.

41. Sunstein, *Republic.com 2.0*; Stroud, *Niche News*; Iyengar and Hahn, "Red Media, Blue Media."

42. Jamieson and Cappella, *Echo Chamber*, 240.

43. R. Kelly Garrett, Benjamin K. Jonshon, Rachel Neo, and Aysemur Dal, "Implications of Pro- and Counter-Attitudinal Information Exposure for Affective Polarization," presented at the Annual Meeting of the International Communication Association, London, June 2013; Shanto Iyengar, Gaurav Sood, and Yphtach Lelkes, "Affect, Not Ideology: A Social Identity Perspective on Polarization," *Public Opinion Quarterly* 76, no. 3 (2012): 405–431.

44. For example, G. J. Goodhardt, "Constant in Duplicated Television Viewing," *Nature* 212 (1966): 1616; Ehrenberg, "The Factor Analytic Search for Program Types."

45. Audience duplication is a measure of the extent to which the audiences for any pair of media offerings (e.g., TV programs, websites, etc.) overlap. For example, how many people watch one TV show and then another or what percentage of the population has visited two different websites.

46. G. J. Goodhardt, A. S. C. Ehrenberg, and M. A. Collins, *The Television Audience: Patterns of Viewing; An Update* (Aldershot, Hampshire, UK: Gower Publishing, 1987), 45.

47. James G. Webster, "Audience Flow Past and Present: Television Inheritance Effects Reconsidered," *Journal of Broadcasting & Electronic Media* 50, no. 2 (2006): 323–337; Byrony Jardine, "Retaining the Primetime TV Audience: Examining Adjacent

Program Audience Duplication across Markets," PhD diss., University of South Australia (2012).

48. Byron Sharp, Virginia Beal, and Martin Collins, "Television: Back to the Future," *Journal of Advertising Research* 49, no. 2 (2009): 211–219.

49. PBS, "Audience Insight 2012," CPB Webinar, June 18, 2012.

50. Ibid.

51. Andrew S. C. Ehrenberg, Gerald J. Goodhardt, and T. Patrick Barwise, "Double Jeopardy Revisited," *The Journal of Marketing* 54, no. 3 (1990): 82–91; William N. McPhee, *Formal Theories of Mass Behavior* (Glencoe, IL: Free Press 1963); Elberse, "Should You Invest in the Long Tail?"

52. Webster, "Beneath the Veneer of Fragmentation."

53. For example, Harsh Taneja, James G. Webster, Edward C. Malthouse, and Thomas B. Ksiazek, "Media Consumption across Platforms: Identifying User-Defined Repertoires," *New Media & Society* 14, no. 6 (2012): 951–968; Webster, Phalen, and Lichty, *Ratings Analysis.*

54. Sharp, Beal, and Collins, "Television"; Patrick Barwise and Andrew Ehrenberg, *Television and Its Audience* (Thousand Oaks, CA: Sage, 1988); James G. Webster, "Audience Behavior in the New Media Environment," *Journal of Communication* 36, no. 3 (1986): 77–91.

55. PPMs are small pagerlike devices that detect an inaudible piece of code embedded in the audio portion of a broadcast. For more see Webster, Phalen, and Lichty, *Ratings Analysis.*

56. Thomas B. Ksiazek and James G. Webster, "Cultural Proximity and Audience Behavior: The Role of Language in Patterns of Polarization and Multicultural Fluency," *Journal of Broadcasting & Electronic Media* 52, no. 3 (2008): 485–503.

57. For example, ibid.; George A. Barnett and Eunjung Sung, "Culture and the Structure of the International Hyperlink Network," *Journal of Computer-Mediated Communication* 11, no. 1 (2006): 217–238; Hanwoo Park, George A. Barnett, and Chung Chung, Joo "Structural Changes in the 2003–2009 Global Hyperlink Network," *Global Networks* 11, no. 4 (2011): 522–542.

58. For example, J. D. Straubhaar, *World Television: From Global to Local* (Thousand Oaks, CA: Sage, 2007); J. D. Straubhaar, "Beyond Media Imperialism: Asymmetrical Interdependence and Cultural Proximity," *Critical Studies in Media Communication* 8, no. 1 (1991): 39–59; Jae Kook Lee, "The Effect of the Internet on Homogeneity of the Media Agenda: A Test of the Fragmentation Thesis," *Journalism & Mass Communication Quarterly* 84, no. 4 (2007): 745–760.

59. Daniel Ford and Josh Batson, "Languages of the World (Wide Web)," http://googleresearch.blogspot.com/2011/07/languages-of-world-wide-web.html.

60. There will always be some audience overlap between outlets, even if it's just one or two people. In this approach, to declare an audience-defined link, audience overlap has to exceed what would be expected if chance alone was at work. For more see Thomas B. Ksiazek, "A Network Analytic Approach to Understanding Cross-Platform Audience Behavior," *Journal of Media Economics* 24, no. 4 (2011): 237–251.

61. Harsh Taneja, "Mapping an Audience Centric World Wide Web: A Departure from Hyperlink Analysis," paper presented at Association for Education in Journalism and Mass Communication, Washington, DC, August 2013.

62. This phrase takes liberties with the well-known book by Clifford Geertz, *Local Knowledge: Further Essays in Interpretive Anthropology* (New York: Basic Books, 1983).

63. Matthew Hale, Erika Franklin Fowler, and Kenneth M. Goldstein, "Capturing Multiple Markets: A New Method of Capturing and Analyzing Local Television News," *Electronic News* 1, no. 4 (2007): 227–243.

64. Damian Trilling and Klaus Schoenbach, "Patterns of News Consumption in Austria: How Fragmented Are They?" *International Journal of Communication* 7 (2013); Yuan, "The New Multi-Channel Media Environment in China."

65. LaCour, "A Balanced News Diet."

66. Ksiazek, Malthouse, and Webster, "News-Seekers and Avoiders."

67. Mark Jurkowitz and Katerina Eva Masta, "Despite Some Warning Signs, Local TV Stations Are Hot Commodities," Pew Research Journalism Project (August 5, 2013).

68. Hale, Fowler, and Goldstein, "Capturing Multiple Markets."

69. Prior, *Post-broadcast Democracy*.

70. Ksiazek, Malthouse, and Webster, "News-Seekers and Avoiders."

71. Anderson, *The Long Tail*, 183.

72. Farhad Manjoo, *True Enough: Learning to Live in a Post-fact Society* (New York: Wiley, 2008), 25.

73. Ksiazek, "A Network Analytic Approach to Understanding Cross-Platform Audience Behavior"; Webster and Ksiazek, "The Dynamic of Audience Fragmentation."

74. Gentzkow and Shapiro, "Ideological Segregation," 1823.

75. Webster, Phalen, and Lichty, *Ratings Analysis*; Prior, "Media and Political Polarization."

76. Kevin Arceneaux and Martin Johnson, *Changing Minds or Changing Channels? Partisan News in an Age of Choice* (Chicago: University of Chicago Press, 2013).

77. Webster, "Beneath the Veneer of Fragmentation."

78. Bill Carter, "Republicans Like Golf, Democrats Prefer Cartoons, TV Research Suggests," *New York Times* (October 11, 2012); Bruce Goerlich, "Political Ratings—a Nation Divided?" in *Thought Lobs from Goerlich's Frontal Lobe* (October 26, 2012), http://brucegoerlich.com/2012/10/26/political-ratings-a-nation-divided; Travis N. Ridout, Michael Franz, Kenneth M. Goldstein, and William J. Feltus, "Separation by Television Program: Understanding the Targeting of Political Advertising in Presidential Elections," *Political Communication* 29, no. 1 (2012): 1–23; Experian Simmons, "Simmons Consumer Segmentations: PoliticalPersonas" (New York: Author, 2011).

79. Carter, "Republicans Like Golf, Democrats Prefer Cartoons, TV Research Suggests."

80. Goerlich, "Political Ratings."

81. Rankings are often based on the average audience for every minute of the program. To be consistent with table 5.1, these rankings are based on reach. There is virtually no difference in the results. Further, five of the top seven programs were variations on the Oscars (e.g., "red carpet" coverage before and after the event). I eliminated these secondary Oscar broadcasts and the Thursday broadcast of *American Idol* to avoid redundancies.

82. This correlation is based on the reach of each program, not its rank, across some twenty-two thousand programs in the analysis. The correlation between MSNBC and CNN viewers is 0.90. The correlation between Fox News and CNN viewers is 0.77.

Chapter 6

1. Anthony Giddens, *The Constitution of Society: Outline of the Theory of Structuration* (Berkeley: University of California Press, 1984), xvi.

2. For example, James G. Webster, "The Duality of Media: A Structurational Theory of Public Attention," *Communication Theory* 21, no. 1 (2011): 43–66; Sharon Hays, "Structure and Agency and the Sticky Problem of Culture," *Sociological Theory* 12 (1994): 57–72; William H. Sewell, "A Theory of Structure: Duality, Agency, and Transformation," *American Journal of Sociology* 98, no. 1 (1992): 1–29; Mustafa Emirbayer and Ann Mische, "What Is Agency?" *American Journal of Sociology* 103, no. 4

(1998): 962–1023; Rob Stones, *Structuration Theory* (Basingstoke Hampshire, UK: Palgrave Macmillan, 2005).

3. Sewell, "A Theory of Structure," 2.

4. Anthony Giddens, *Social Theory and Modern Sociology* (Stanford, CA: Stanford University Press, 1987), 221.

5. For example, William J. Adams, "Scheduling Practices Based on Audience Flow: What Are the Effects on New Program Success?" *Journalism & Mass Communication Quarterly* 74, no. 4 (1997): 839–858.

6. Joseph Turow, *The Daily You: How the New Advertising Industry Is Defining Your Identity and Your Worth* (New Haven, CT: Yale University Press, 2012), 117.

7. Tarleton Gillespie, "Designed to 'Effectively Frustrate': Copyright, Technology and the Agency of Users," *New Media & Society* 8, no. 4 (2006): 651–669; Henry Jenkins, Sam Ford, and Joshua Green, *Spreadable Media: Creating Value and Meaning in a Networked Culture* (New York: New York University Press, 2013); Lawrence Lessig, *Remix: Making Art and Commerce Thrive in the Hybrid Economy* (New York: Penguin Press, 2008); John G. Palfrey and Urs Gasser, *Interop: The Promise and Perils of Highly Interconnected Systems* (New York: Basic Books 2012).

8. Michael D. Slater, "Reinforcing Spirals: The Mutual Influence of Media Selectivity and Media Effects and Their Impact on Individual Behavior and Social Identity," *Communication Theory* 17, no. 3 (2007): 288.

9. K. H. Jamieson and J. N. Cappella, *Echo Chamber: Rush Limbaugh and the Conservative Media Establishment* (New York: Oxford University Press, 2009).

10. Cass R. Sunstein, *Republic.com 2.0* (Princeton, NJ: Princeton University Press, 2007); Cass R. Sunstein, *Going to Extremes: How Like Minds Unite and Divide* (New York: Oxford University Press, 2009).

11. Palfrey and Gasser, *Interop*, 11–12.

12. Sunstein, *Republic.com 2.0*.

13. J. Turow, *Breaking Up America: Advertisers and the New Media World* (Chicago: University of Chicago Press, 1997).

14. Todd Gitlin, "Public Sphere or Public Sphericules?" in *Media, Ritual, Identity*, ed. T. Liebes and James Curran (London: Routledge, 1998), 168–175.

15. M. Van Alstyne and E. Brynjolfsson, "Global Village or Cyber-Balkans? Modeling and Measuring the Integration of Electronic Communities," *Management Science* 51 (6) (2005): 851–868.

16. Eli Pariser, *The Filter Bubble: What the Internet Is Hiding from You* (New York: Penguin Press, 2011).

17. Chris Anderson, *The Long Tail: Why the Future of Business Is Selling Less of More*, 1st ed. (New York: Hyperion, 2006).

18. For example, Eszter Hargittai, "Digital Na(t)ives? Variation in Internet Skills and Uses among Members of the 'Net Generation,'" *Sociological Inquiry* 80, no. 1 (2010): 92–113; Eszter Hargittai, "Second-Level Digital Divide," *First Monday* 7, no. 4–1 (2002).

19. Eszter Hargittai, L. Fullerton, E. Menchen-Trevino, and K. Y. Thomas, "Trust Online: Young Adults' Evaluation of Web Content," *International Journal of Communication* 4, no. 1 (2010): 468–494.

20. Hays, "Structure and Agency and the Sticky Problem of Culture," 62.

21. Yochai Benkler, *The Wealth of Networks: How Social Production Transforms Markets and Freedom* (New Haven, CT: Yale University Press, 2006).

22. Henry Jenkins, *Convergence Culture: Where Old and New Media Collide* (New York: New York University Press, 2006).

23. Benkler, *The Wealth of Networks*, 9.

24. Markus Prior, *Post-broadcast Democracy: How Media Choice Increases Inequality in Political Involvement and Polarizes Elections* (Cambridge, UK: Cambridge University Press, 2007), 17–18.

25. Sunstein, *Republic.com 2.0*, 6.

26. Pariser, *The Filter Bubble*.

27. Turow, *The Daily You*.

28. Pariser, *The Filter Bubble*, 218.

29. Bruce A. Williams and Michael X. Delli Carpini, *After Broadcast News: Media Regimes, Democracy, and the New Information Environment* (Cambridge, UK: Cambridge University Press, 2011), 17.

30. Ibid., 85.

31. Ernst Fehr and Karla Hoff, "Introduction: Tastes, Castes and Culture: The Influence of Society on Preferences," *The Economic Journal* 121, no. 556 (2011): F396–F412.

32. Samuel Bowles, "Endogenous Preferences: The Cultural Consequences of Markets and Other Economic Institutions," *Journal of Economic Literature* 36, no. 1 (1998): 75.

33. Ibid., 80.

34. Giddens, *Social Theory and Modern Sociology*, 59.

35. B. M. Owen and S. S. Wildman, *Video Economics* (Cambridge, MA: Harvard University Press, 1992).

36. For example, Herbert J. Gans, *Popular Culture and High Culture: An Analysis and Evaluation of Taste*, rev. and updated ed. (New York: Basic Books, 1999); P. Bourdieu, *Distinction: A Social Critique of the Judgment of Taste*, trans. Richard Nice (Cambridge, MA: Harvard University Press, 1984); Noah Mark, "Birds of a Feather Sing Together," *Social Forces* 77, no. 2 (1998): 453–485; Kevin Lewis, Marco Gonzalez, and Jason Kaufman, "Social Selection and Peer Influence in an Online Social Network," *Proceedings of the National Academy of Sciences* 109, no. 1 (2012): 68–72.

37. Elihu Katz, Jay G. Blumler, and Michael Gurevitch, "Utilization of Mass Communication by the Individual," in *The Uses of Mass Communications: Current Perspectives on Gratifications Research*, ed. Jay G. Blumler and Elihu Katz (Beverly Hills: Sage, 1974), 20.

38. Leon Festinger, *A Theory of Cognitive Dissonance* (Stanford, CA: Stanford University Press, 1957); D. Zillmann and J. Bryant, eds., *Selective Exposure to Communication* (Hillsdale, NJ: Erlbaum, 1985).

39. D. Zillmann, "Mood Management in the Context of Selective Exposure Theory," in *Communication Yearbook*, ed. M. E. Roloff (Thousand Oaks, CA: Sage, 2000), 103–124; Peter Vorderer, Christoph Klimmt, and Ute Ritterfeld, "Enjoyment: At the Heart of Media Entertainment," *Communication Theory* 14, no. 4 (2004): 388–408; Jinhee Kim and Mary Beth Oliver, "How Do We Regulate Sadness through Entertainment Messages? Exploring Three Predictions," *Journal of Broadcasting & Electronic Media* 57, no. 3 (2013): 374–391.

40. Gary S. Becker, *Accounting for Tastes* (Cambridge, MA: Harvard University Press, 1996).

41. In some theories preference causes choice; in others it causes exposure. Conceptually, these are different. Choice implies a deliberate act on the part of the user; exposure does not. Often, these terms are used interchangeably. In fact, exposure is often measured by acts of choice, such as tuning to a channel or requesting a web page. See James G. Webster, Patricia F. Phalen, and Lawrence W. Lichty, *Ratings Analysis: Audience Measurement and Analytics*, 4th ed. (New York: Routledge, 2014).

42. William James, *Principles of Psychology*, vol. 1 (Cambridge, MA: Harvard University Press, 1890), 402. (emphasis in the original).

43. Turow, *The Daily You*.

44. Malcolm McCullough, *Ambient Commons: Attention in the Age of Embodied Information* (Cambridge, MA: MIT Press, 2013), 12.

45. Pariser, *The Filter Bubble*.

46. Jenkins, Ford, and Green, *Spreadable Media*, 13.

47. My mother-in-law is a lovely ninety-year-old woman living in rural Kentucky. Out of curiosity, I asked her if she had heard of "gangnam style." She said no, but when my wife produced the video of Psy on her smartphone she said, "Oh yes, I've seen that. I don't understand what all the fuss is about."

48. M. L. Ray, "Marketing Communication and the Hierarchy of Effects," in *New Models of Communication Research*, vol. 2, ed. P. Clarke (Beverly Hills, CA: Sage, 1973), 47–176.

49. Ibid., 152.

50. J. W. Brehm, "Postdecision Changes in the Desirability of Alternatives," *The Journal of Abnormal and Social Psychology* 52, no. 3 (1956): 384; Petter Johansson, Lars Hall, and Nick Chater, "Preference Change through Choice," in *Neuroscience of Preference and Choice*, ed. Raymond Dolan and Tali Sharot (London: Academic Press, 2012), 121–141; Venkat Lakshminarayanan and Laurie R. Santos, "The Evolution of Our Preferences: Insights from Non-human Primates," in *Neuroscience of Preference and Choice*, ed. Raymond Dolan and Tali Sharot (London: Academic Press, 2012), 75–91.

51. Paul Slovic, "The Construction of Preference," *American Psychologist* 50, no. 5 (1995): 364–371.

52. Dan Ariely and Michael I. Norton, "How Actions Create—Not Just Reveal—Preferences," *Trends in Cognitive Sciences* 12, no. 1 (2008): 14.

53. Amos Tversky and Daniel Kahneman, "Judgment under Uncertainty: Heuristics and Biases," *Science* 185, no. 4157 (1974): 1124–1131; J. N. Marewski, M. Galesic, and G. Gigerenzer, "Fast and Frugal Media Choices," in *Media Choice: A Theoretical and Empirical Overview*, ed. T. Hartmann (New York: Routledge, 2009), 107–128.

54. Ray, "Marketing Communication and the Hierarchy of Effects."

55. R. B. Zajonc, "Attitudinal Effects of Mere Exposure," *Journal of Personality and Social Psychology* 9, no. 2 (1968): 1; R. B. Zajonc, "Mere Exposure: A Gateway to the Subliminal," *Current Directions in Psychological Science* 10, no. 6 (2001): 224–228.

56. Jennings Bryant and Mary B. Oliver, *Media Effects: Advances in Theory and Research*, 3rd ed. (New York: Routledge, 2009).

57. Prior, *Post-broadcast Democracy*.

58. George Gerbner, Larry Gross, Michael Morgan, Nancy Signorielli, and James Shanahn, "Growing Up with Television: Cultivation Processes," in *Media Effects: Advances in Theory and Research*, 2nd ed., ed. Jennings Bryant and Dolf Zillmann (Mahwah, NJ: Erlbaum, 2002), 43–68.

59. Paul F. Lazarsfeld and Robert K. Merton, "Mass Communication, Popular Taste and Organized Social Action," in *The Communication of Ideas*, ed. Lyman Bryson (New York: Harper & Row, 1948), 95–118.

60. Joseph T. Klapper, *The Effects of Mass Communication: Foundations of Communications Research* (Glencoe, IL: Free Press, 1960).

61. Bart J. Bronnenberg, Jean-Pierre H. Dubé, and Matthew Gentzkow, "The Evolution of Brand Preferences: Evidence from Consumer Migration," *The American Economic Review* 102, no. 6 (2012): 2472–2508.

62. For a variety of perspectives on this topic see R. Kelly Garrett and Paul Resnick, "Resisting Political Fragmentation on the Internet," *Daedalus* 140, no. 4 (2011): 676–699; Paul Resnick et al., "Bursting Your (Filter) Bubble: Strategies for Promoting Diverse Exposure," in *Proceedings of the 2013 Conference on Computer Supported Cooperative Work Companion* (San Antonio, TX: ACM, 2013), 95–100; Natalie Helberger, "Diversity by Design," *Journal of Information Policy* 1 (2011): 441–469; Ethan Zuckerman, *Rewire: Digital Cosmopolitans in the Age of Connection* (New York: Norton, 2013); Andrew Keen, *Digital Vertigo: How Today's Online Social Revolution Is Dividing, Diminishing, and Disorienting Us* (New York: St. Martin's Press, 2012).

63. Turow, *The Daily You*; Joseph Turow, *Niche Envy: Marketing Discrimination in the Digital Age* (Cambridge, MA: MIT Press, 2006); J. Rosen, "The Right to Be Forgotten," *Stanford Law Review Online* 64 (2012): 88; Natasha Singer, "Data Protection Laws, an Ocean Apart," *New York Times* (February 2, 2013); Mark Andrejevic, *Infoglut: How Too Much Information Is Changing the Way We Think and Know* (New York: Routledge, 2013).

64. Pariser, *The Filter Bubble*.

65. Siva Vaidhyanathan, *The Googlization of Everything (and Why We Should Worry)* (Berkeley: University of California Press, 2012).

66. Clive Thompson, "If You Liked This, You're Sure to Love That," *New York Times Magazine* (November 21, 2008a), http://www.nytimes.com/2008/11/23/magazine/23Netflix-t.html?pagewanted=6.

67. Jeffrey Zaslow, "If TiVo Thinks You Are Gay, Here's How to Set It Straight," *Wall Street Journal* (November 26, 2002).

68. Pariser, *The Filter Bubble*, 233.

69. Mark, "Birds of a Feather Sing Together"; Lewis, Gonzalez, and Kaufman, "Social Selection and Peer Influence in an Online Social Network"; Eszter Hargittai and Eden Litt, "The Tweet Smell of Celebrity Success: Explaining Variation in Twitter Adoption among a Diverse Group of Young Adults," *New Media & Society* 13, no. 5 (2011): 824–842.

70. Manuel Castells, "The New Public Sphere: Global Civil Society, Communication Networks, and Global Governance," *The Annals of the American Academy of Political and Social Science* 616, no. 1 (2008): 78–93.

71. Brent Hecht and Darren Gergle, "The Tower of Babel Meets Web 2.0: User-Generated Content and Its Applications in a Multilingual Context," paper presented at CHI 2010, April 10–15, Atlanta,, GA, 2010.

72. For a more extended discussion of global information flows see Zuckerman, *Rewire*.

Chapter 7

1. John Milton, *The Works of John Milton in Verse and Prose,* vol. 4 (London: William Pickering, 1851), 443.

2. See Clifford G. Christians, T. L. Glasser, D. McQuail, K. Nordenstreng, and R. White, *Normative Theories of the Media: Journalism in Democratic Societies* (Urbana: University of Illinois Press, 2009).

3. Philip M. Napoli, *Foundations of Communications Policy: Principles and Process in the Regulation of Electronic Media* (Cresskill, NJ: Hampton Press, 2001).

4. Craig Calhoun, ed., *Habermas and the Public Sphere* (Cambridge, MA: MIT Press, 1992); Jürgen Habermas, *The Structural Transformation of the Public Sphere: An Inquire into a Category of Bourgeois Society* (Cambridge, MA: MIT Press, 1991); R. Benson, "Shaping the Public Sphere: Habermas and Beyond," *The American Sociologist* 40, no. 3 (2009): 175–197.

5. For example, Manuel Castells, "The New Public Sphere: Global Civil Society, Communication Networks, and Global Governance," *The Annals of the American Academy of Political and Social Science* 616, no. 1 (2008): 78–93; W. Russell Neuman, Bruce Bimber, and Matthew Hindman, "The Internet and Four Dimensions of Citizenship," in *The Oxford Handbook of American Public Opinion and the Media,* ed. Robert Y. Shapiro and Lawrence R. Jacobs (New York: Oxford University Press, 2011), 22–42; Jürgen Habermas, "Political Communication in Media Society: Does Democracy Still Enjoy an Epistemic Dimension? The Impact of Normative Theory on Empirical Research," *Communication Theory* 16, no. 4 (2006): 411–426; Napoli, *Foundations of Communications Policy;* Maxwell E. McCombs and Donald L. Shaw, "The Evolution of Agenda-Setting Research: Twenty-Five Years in the Marketplace of Ideas," *Journal of Communication* 43, no. 2 (1993): 58–67; C. Edwin Baker, *Media, Markets, and Democracy* (Cambridge, UK: Cambridge University Press, 2001).

6. Napoli, *Foundations of Communications Policy.*

7. N. Helberger, "Diversity by Design," *Journal of Information Policy* 1 (2011): 444.

8. Cass R. Sunstein, *Republic.com 2.0* (Princeton, NJ: Princeton University Press, 2007), 6–8.

9. Elihu Katz, "And Deliver Us from Segmentation," *Annals of the American Academy of Political and Social Science* 546 (1996): 23.

10. Yochai Benkler, *The Wealth of Networks: How Social Production Transforms Markets and Freedom* (New Haven, CT: Yale University Press, 2006), 258.

11. Habermas, "Political Communication in Media Society," 423.

12. Cass R. Sunstein, *Going to Extremes: How Like Minds Unite and Divide* (New York: Oxford University Press, 2009).

13. Ibid., 149.

14. For example, J. Jarvis, *Public Parts: How Sharing in the Digital Age Improves the Way We Work and Live* (New York: Simon and Schuster, 2011); Benkler, *The Wealth of Networks*; Henry Jenkins, Sam Ford, and Joshua Green, *Spreadable Media: Creating Value and Meaning in a Networked Culture* (New York: New York University Press, 2013); Lawrence Lessig, *Remix: Making Art and Commerce Thrive in the Hybrid Economy* (New York: Penguin Press, 2008); Eric Schmidt and Jared Cohen, *The New Digital Age: Reshaping the Future of People, Nations and Business* (New York: Knopf, 2013).

15. Bruce A. Williams and Michael X. Delli Carpini, *After Broadcast News: Media Regimes, Democracy, and the New Information Environment* (Cambridge, UK: Cambridge University Press, 2011), 288.

16. Jenkins, Ford, and Green, *Spreadable Media*, 13.

17. Benkler, *The Wealth of Networks*, 272.

18. Lee Rainie and Barry Wellman, *Networked: The New Social Operating System* (Cambridge, MA: MIT Press, 2012), 157.

19. Jenkins, Ford, and Green, *Spreadable Media*, 259.

20. For example, Benkler, *The Wealth of Networks*; J. Rosen, "The People Formerly Known as the Audience," *Huffington Post* (June 30, 2006), http://www.huffingtonpost.com/jay-rosen/the-people-formerly-known_1_b_24113.html; Dan Gillmor, *We the Media: Grassroots Journalism by the People, for the People* (Sebastopol, CA: O'Reilly Media, 2006); Jarvis, *Public Parts*; Baker, *Media, Markets, and Democracy*.

21. Chris Anderson, *The Long Tail: Why the Future of Business Is Selling Less of More*, 1st ed. (New York: Hyperion, 2006), 106, 107.

22. Lessig, *Remix*, 61.

23. Kathleen H. Jamieson and Joseph N. Cappella, *Echo Chamber: Rush Limbaugh and the Conservative Media Establishment* (New York: Oxford University Press, 2009).

24. Sunstein, *Republic.com 2.0*.

25. Diana C. Mutz and Lori Young, "Communication and Public Opinion," *Public Opinion Quarterly* 75, no. 5 (2011): 1038, 1040.

26. Joseph Turow, *Breaking Up America: Advertisers and the New Media World* (Chicago: University of Chicago Press, 1997).

27. Lada A. Adamic and N. Glance, "The Political Blogosphere and the 2004 U.S. Election: Divided They Blog," paper presented at the Proceedings of the 3rd International Workshop on Link Discovery, Chicago, August 2005; K. Barzilai-Nahon and J. Hemsley, "Democracy.com: A Tale of Political Blogs and Content," paper presented at the Proceedings of the Hawaii International Conference on System Sciences, Kauai, HI, January 2011.

28. Joseph Turow, *The Daily You: How the New Advertising Industry Is Defining Your Identity and Your Worth* (New Haven, CT: Yale University Press, 2012).

29. Ibid.; Robert W. McChesney, *Digital Disconnect: How Capitalism Is Turning the Internet against Democracy* (New York: New Press, 2013).

30. E. Pariser, *The Filter Bubble: What the Internet Is Hiding from You* (New York: Penguin Press, 2011); Sunstein, *Republic.Com 2.0*.

31. Sunstein, *Republic.com 2.0*, 11.

32. Markus Prior, *Post-broadcast Democracy: How Media Choice Increases Inequality in Political Involvement and Polarizes Elections* (Cambridge, UK: Cambridge University Press, 2007).

33. Pariser, *The Filter Bubble*.

34. Todd Gitlin, "Public Sphere or Public Sphericules?" in *Media, Ritual, Identity*, ed. T. Liebes and James Curran (London: Routledge, 1998), 168–175.

35. W. Lance Bennett and Shanto Iyengar, "The Shifting Foundations of Political Communication: Responding to a Defense of the Media Effects Paradigm," *Journal of Communication* 60, no. 1 (2010): 35–39. Also see Kevin Arceneaux and Martin Johnson, *Changing Minds or Changing Channels? Partisan News in an Age of Choice* (Chicago: University of Chicago Press, 2013).

36. Williams and Delli Carpini, *After Broadcast News*.

37. Herbert J. Gans, *Popular Culture and High Culture: An Analysis and Evaluation of Taste*, rev. and updated ed. (New York: Basic Books, 1999).

38. Ibid., 13.

39. Matthew A. Baum, "Sex, Lies, and War: How Soft News Brings Foreign Policy to the Inattentive Public," *American Political Science Review* 96, no. 1 (2002): 91–109; James Hamilton, *All the News That's Fit to Sell: How the Market Transforms Information into News* (Princeton, NJ: Princeton University Press, 2004); R. Lance Holbert, Owen Pillion, David A. Tschida, Greg G. Armfield, Kelly Kinder, Kristin L. Cherry, and Amy R. Daulton, "The West Wing as Endorsement of the U.S. Presidency: Expanding the Bounds of Priming in Political Communication," *Journal of Communication* 53, no. 3 (2003): 427–443; Williams and Delli Carpini, *After Broadcast News*; Anke Wonneberger, Klaus Schoenbach, and Lex Van Meurs, "How Keeping up Diversifies: Watching Public Affairs TV in the Netherlands 1988–2010," *European Journal of Communication* 28, no. 6 (2013): 646–662.

40. Williams and Delli Carpini, *After Broadcast News*, 84.

41. Prior, *Post-broadcast Democracy*; Thomas B. Ksiazek, Edward C. Malthouse, and James G. Webster, "News-Seekers and Avoiders: Exploring Patterns of Total News Consumption across Media and the Relationship to Civic Participation," *Journal of Broadcasting & Electronic Media* 54, no. 4 (2010): 551–568; T. Aalberg, A. Blekesaune, and E. Elvestad, "Media Choice and Informed Democracy: An Empirical Study of Increasing Information Gaps in Europe," paper presented at the APSA 2012 Annual Meeting, New Orleans, August 30–September 2 2012; Arceneaux and Johnson, *Changing Minds or Changing Channels?*

42. See, for example, George Gerbner, Larry Gross, Michael Morgan, Nancy Signorielli, and James Shanahn, "Growing Up with Television: Cultivation Processes," in *Media Effects: Advances in Theory and Research*, ed. Jennings Bryant and Dolf Zillmann (Mahwah, NJ: Erlbaum, 2002), 43–68.

43. For example, Jay G. Blumler, "The Role of Theory in Uses and Gratifications Studies," *Communication Research* 6, no. 1 (1979): 9–36; Klaus Schoenbach and Edmund Lauf, "Another Look at the 'Trap' Effect of Television—and Beyond," *International Journal of Public Opinion Research* 16, no. 2 (2004): 169–182.

44. Tilo Hartmann, ed. *Media Choice: A Theoretical and Empirical Overview* (New York: Routledge, 2009b); James G. Webster, "The Role of Structure in Media Choice," in *Media Choice: A Theoretical and Empirical Overview*, ed. T. Hartmann (New York: Routledge, 2009), 221–233.

45. Pew, "Beyond Red vs. Blue: Political Typology" (Washington, DC: Pew Center for the People & the Press, 2011).

46. Mutz and Young, "Communication and Public Opinion"; David O. Sears and Jonathan L. Freedman, "Selective Exposure to Information: A Critical Review," *Public Opinion Quarterly* 31, no. 2 (1967): 194–213.

47. Michael J. LaCour, "A Balanced News Diet, Not Selective Exposure: Evidence from a Real World Measure of Media Exposure," presented at the Annual Midwest Political Science Association, Chicago, April 2012; D. Trilling and K. Schoenbach, "Challenging Selective Exposure: Do People Expose Themselves Only to Online Content That Fits Their Interests and Preferences?," paper presented at the WAPOR 65th Annual Conference, Hong Kong, June 2012; Matthew Gentzkow and Jesse M. Shapiro, "Ideological Segregation Online and Offline," *The Quarterly Journal of Economics* 126, no. 4 (2011); R. Kelly Garrett, "Politically Motivated Reinforcement Seeking: Reframing the Selective Exposure Debate," *Journal of Communication* 59, no. 4 (2009): 676–699; Markus Prior, "Media and Political Polarization," *Annual Review of Political Science* 16, no. 1 (2013): 101–127.

48. Richard E. Caves, *Creative Industries: Contracts between Art and Commerce* (Cambridge, MA: Harvard University Press, 2000); William T. Bielby and D. Denise Bielby, "Hits Are Flukes": Institutionalized Decision Making and the Rhetoric of Network Prime-Time Program Development," *American Journal of Sociology* (1994): 1287–1313; Gabriel Rossman, Nicole Esparza, and Phillip Bonacich, "I'd Like to Thank the Academy, Team Spillovers, and Network Centrality," *American Sociological Review* 75, no. 1 (2010): 31–51.

49. Greta Hsu, Giacomo Negro, and Fabrizio Perretti, "Hybrids in Hollywood: A Study of the Production and Performance of Genre-Spanning Films," *Industrial and Corporate Change* 21, no. 6 (2012): 1427–1450; Joseph Lampel, Theresa Lant, and Jamal Shamsie, "Balancing Act: Learning from Organizing Practices in Cultural Industries," *Organization Science* 11, no. 3 (2000): 263–269.

50. Lessig, *Remix*; Jenkins, Ford, and Green, *Spreadable Media*; Limor Shifman, "An Anatomy of a Youtube Meme," *New Media & Society* 14, no. 2 (2012): 187–203.

51. Project for Excellence in Journalism, "How News Happens: A Study of the News Ecosystem in One American City" (New York: Pew Research Center, 2010); Jae Kook Lee, "The Effect of the Internet on Homogeneity of the Media Agenda: A Test of the Fragmentation Thesis," *Journalism & Mass Communication Quarterly* 84, no. 4 (2007): 745–760; Pablo J. Boczkowski, *News at Work: Imitation in an Age of Information Abundance* (Chicago: University of Chicago Press, 2010).

52. Klaus Schoenbach, "'The Own in the Foreign': Reliable Surprise—an Important Function of the Media?" *Media, Culture & Society* 29, no. 2 (2007): 344–353.

53. Anderson, *The Long Tail*.

54. Anita Elberse, *Blockbusters: Hit-making, Risk-taking, and the Big Business of Entertainment* (New York: Holt, 2013), 163.

55. Benkler, *The Wealth of Networks*, 258.

56. Williams and Delli Carpini, *After Broadcast News,* 78.

57. Mutz and Young, "Communication and Public Opinion," 1023.

58. Matthew Gentzkow and Jesse M. Shapiro, "Competition and Truth in the Market for News," *The Journal of Economic Perspectives* 22, no. 2 (2008): 133–154; Daniel F. Stone, "Ideological Media Bias," *Journal of Economic Behavior & Organization* 78, no. 3 (2011): 256–271; N. J. Stroud, *Niche News: The Politics of News Choice* (Oxford: Oxford University Press, 2011).

59. Mutz and Young, "Communication and Public Opinion," 1021.

60. Katz, "And Deliver Us from Segmentation," 22.

61. Williams and Delli Carpini, *After Broadcast News,* 285.

62. Gentzkow and Shapiro, "Ideological Segregation," 1832.

63. C. W. Anderson, Emily Bell, and Clay Shirky, *Post-industrial Journalism: Adapting to the Present* (New York: Tow Center for Digital Journalism, Columbia University Journalism School, 2012), 108.

64. Gentzkow and Shapiro, "Ideological Segregation"; Anita Elberse, "Should You Invest in the Long Tail?" *Harvard Business Review* 86, no. 7–8 (2008): 88–96; James G. Webster and T. B. Ksiazek, "The Dynamics of Audience Fragmentation: Public Attention in an Age of Digital Media," *Journal of Communication* 62 (2012): 39–56.

65. John Zaller, "A New Standard of News Quality: Burglar Alarms for the Monitorial Citizen," *Political Communication* 20, no. 2 (2003): 109–130.

66. Schmidt and Cohen, *The New Digital Age,* 4.

67. Ethan Zuckerman, *Rewire: Digital Cosmopolitans in the Age of Connection* (New York: Norton, 2013), 58.

68. Elberse, "Should You Invest in the Long Tail?"; Gentzkow and Shapiro, "Ideological Segregation."

69. M. Hindman, *The Myth of Digital Democracy* (Princeton, NJ: Princeton University Press, 2009); Webster and Ksiazek, "The Dynamic of Audience Fragmentation."

70. Elberse, *Blockbusters.*

BIBLIOGRAPHY

Aalberg, T., A. Blekesaune, and E. Elvestad. "Media Choice and Informed Democracy: An Empirical Study of Increasing Information Gaps in Europe." Paper presented at the APSA 2012 Annual Meeting, August 30–September 2, New Orleans, 2012.

Adamic, Lada A. The Social Hyperlink. In *The Hyperlinked Society: Questioning Connections in the Digital Age*, ed. Joseph Turow and L. Tsui, 227–249. Ann Arbor: University of Michigan Press, 2008.

Adamic, Lada A., and N. Glance. "The Political Blogosphere and the 2004 U.S. Election: Divided They Blog." Paper presented at the 3rd International Workshop on Link Discovery, Chicago, August 2005.

Adams, William J. "Scheduling Practices Based on Audience Flow: What Are the Effects on New Program Success?" *Journalism & Mass Communication Quarterly* 74 (4) (1997): 839–858.

Adomavicius, G., and A. Tuzhilin. "Toward the Next Generation of Recommender Systems: A Survey of the State-of-the-Art and Possible Extensions." *IEEE Transactions on Knowledge and Data Engineering* 17 (6) (2005): 734–749.

Adomavicius, G., and A. Tuzhilin. Context-Aware Recommender Systems. In *Recommender Systems Handbook*, ed. F. Ricci, L. Rokach, and B. Shapira, 217–253. New York: Springer, 2011.

Ahlkvist, Jarl A. "Programming Philosophies and the Rationalization of Music Radio." *Media Culture & Society* 23 (3) (2001): 339–358.

Anand, N., and A. Richard Peterson. "When Market Information Constitutes Fields: Sensemaking of Markets in the Commercial Music Industry." *Organization Science* 11 (3) (2000): 270–284.

Anderson, C. W. "Between Creative and Quantified Audiences: Web Metrics and Changing Patterns of Newswork in Local US Newsrooms." *Journalism* 12 (5) (2011): 550–566.

Anderson, C. W., Emily Bell, and Clay Shirky. *Post-industrial Journalism: Adapting to the Present.* New York: Tow Center for Digital Journalism, Columbia University Journalism School, 2012.

Anderson, Chris. *The Long Tail: Why the Future of Business Is Selling Less of More.* 1st ed. New York: Hyperion, 2006.

Anderson, Chris. "The End of Theory: The Data Deluge Makes the Scientific Method Obsolete." *Wired* (June 23, 2008).

Anderson, Chris. *Free: The Future of a Radical Price.* New York: Hyperion, 2009.

Anderson, J., and L. Rainie. The Impact of the Internet on Institutions in the Future. In *Pew Research Center's Internet and American Life Project and Elon University's Imagining the Internet Center.* Washington, DC: Pew Research Center's Internet and American Life Project, 2010.

Andrejevic, Mark. *Infoglut: How Too Much Information Is Changing the Way We Think and Know.* New York: Routledge, 2013.

Andrews, Kurt, and Philip M. Napoli. "Changing Market Information Regimes: A Case Study of the Transition to the BookScan Audience Measurement System in the U.S. Book Publishing Industry." *Journal of Media Economics* 19 (1) (2006): 33–54.

Aral, Sinan. "Social Science: Poked to Vote." *Nature* 489 (7415) (2012): 212–214.

Aral, Sinan, Lev Muchnik, and Arun Sundararajan. "Distinguishing Influence-Based Contagion from Homophily-Driven Diffusion in Dynamic Networks." *Proceedings of the National Academy of Sciences of the United States of America* 106 (51) (2009): 21544–21549.

Arceneaux, Kevin, and Martin Johnson. *Changing Minds or Changing Channels? Partisan News in an Age of Choice.* Chicago: University of Chicago Press, 2013.

Arceneaux, Kevin, Martin Johnson, and John Cryderman. "Communication, Persuasion, and the Conditioning Value of Selective Exposure: Like Minds May Unite and Divide but They Mostly Tune Out." *Political Communication* 30 (2) (2013): 213–231.

Ariely, Dan. *Predictably Irrational: The Hidden Forces That Shape Our Decisions.* rev. and expanded ed. New York: Harper, 2008.

Ariely, Dan, and Michael I. Norton. "How Actions Create—Not Just Reveal—Preferences." *Trends in Cognitive Sciences* 12 (1) (2008): 13–16.

Atkinson, Clair. "How Commercial Ratings Changed the $70b TV Market: Commercial Ratings White Paper." *Advertising Age* (2008).

Baker, C. Edwin. *Media, Markets, and Democracy.* Cambridge, UK: Cambridge University Press, 2001.

Ball, Philip. *Critical Mass: How One Thing Leads to Another.* New York: Farrar, Straus & Giroux, 2004.

Balnaves, M., T. O'Regan, and B. Goldsmith. *Rating the Audience: The Business of Media.* London: Bloomsbury, 2011.

Bandari, R., S. Asur, and B. Huberman. "The Pulse of News in Social Media: Forecasting Popularity." Paper presented at the Association for the Advancement of Artificial Intelligence, Dublin (http://www.aaai.org), June 2012.

Barabási, Albert-László. "The Origin of Bursts and Heavy Tails in Human Dynamics." *Nature* 435 (7039) (2005): 207–211.

Barabási, Albert-László, and Réka Albert. "Emergence of Scaling in Random Networks." *Science* 286 (5439) (1999): 509–512.

Barnes, Beth, and L. Thomson. Power to the People (Meter): Audience Measurement Technology and Media Specialization. In *Audiencemaking: How the Media Create the Audience,* ed. J. S. Ettema and D. C. Whitney, 75–94. Thousand Oaks, CA: Sage, 1994.

Barnes, Brooke. "Solving Equation of a Hit Film Script, with Data." *New York Times* (May 5, 2013).

Barnett, George A., and Eunjung Sung. "Culture and the Structure of the International Hyperlink Network." *Journal of Computer-Mediated Communication* 11 (1) (2006): 217–238.

Barwise, Patrick. "Waiting for 'Vodot': Why 'Video on Demand' Won't Happen." *Market Leader* 2 (2011): 30–33.

Barwise, T. Patrick, and Andrew S. C. Ehrenberg. "The Liking and Viewing of Regular TV Series." *Journal of Consumer Research* 14 (1) (1987): 63–70.

Barwise, Patrick, and Andrew Ehrenberg. *Television and Its Audience.* Thousand Oaks, CA: Sage, 1988.

Barzilai-Nahon, K., and J. Hemsley. "Democracy.com: A Tale of Political Blogs and Content." Paper presented at the 44th Hawaii International Conference on System Sciences, Manoa, 2011.

Battelle, John. *The Search: How Google and Its Rivals Rewrote the Rules of Business and Transformed Our Culture.* New York: Portfolio Trade, 2006.

Baum, Matthew A. "Sex, Lies, and War: How Soft News Brings Foreign Policy to the Inattentive Public." *American Political Science Review* 96 (1) (2002): 91–109.

Becker, Gary S. *Accounting for Tastes.* Cambridge, MA: Harvard University Press, 1996.

Belk, Russell. "Sharing." *Journal of Consumer Research* 36 (5) (2010): 715–734.

Belkin, Lisa. "Queen of the Mommy Bloggers." *New York Times* (February 23, 2011).

Benkler, Yochai. *The Wealth of Networks: How Social Production Transforms Markets and Freedom.* New Haven, CT: Yale University Press, 2006.

Benkler, Yochai. *The Penguin and the Leviathan: How Cooperation Triumphs over Self-Interest.* New York: Crown Business, 2011.

Bennett, W. Lance, and Shanto Iyengar. "A New Era of Minimal Effects? The Changing Foundations of Political Communication." *Journal of Communication* 58 (4) (2008): 707–731.

Bennett, W. Lance, and Shanto Iyengar. "The Shifting Foundations of Political Communication: Responding to a Defense of the Media Effects Paradigm." *Journal of Communication* 60 (1) (2010): 35–39.

Bennett, W. Lance, and Alexandra Segerberg. "The Logic of Connective Action." *Information Communication and Society* 15 (5) (2012): 739–768.

Benson, Rodney. "Shaping the Public Sphere: Habermas and Beyond." *American Sociologist* 40 (3) (2009): 175–197.

Berger, Jonah, and Katherine L. Milkman. "What Makes Online Content Viral?" *Journal of Marketing Research* 49 (2) (2012): 192–205.

Berman, S. J., B. Battino, and K. Feldman. "Beyond Content: Capitalizing on the New Revenue Opportunities." In *Media and Entertainment.* Somers, NY: IBM Global Business Services, 2010.

Bernstein, Michael S., Eytan Bakshy, Moira Burke, and Brian Karrer. "Quantifying the Invisible Audience in Social Networks." Paper presented at the SIGCHI Conference on Human Factors in Computing Systems, Paris, April 27–May 2, 2013.

Beville, Hugh M. *Audience Ratings: Radio, Television, Cable*. Hillsdale, NJ: Erlbaum, 1988.

Bialik, Carl. "Look at This Article: It's One of Our Most Popular." *Wall Street Journal* (May 20, 2009). http://online.wsj.com/article/SB124277816017037275.html?KEYWORDS =carl+bialik.

Bielby, William T., and D. Denise Bielby. "'All Hits Are Flukes': Institutionalized Decision Making and the Rhetoric of Network Prime-Time Program Development." *American Journal of Sociology* 99 (5) (1994): 1287–1313.

Bjur, Jakob. *Transforming Audiences: Patterns of Individualization in Television Viewing*. Gothenburg, Germany: University of Gothenburg, 2009.

Blumer, Herbert. The Field of Collective Behavior. In *New Outline of the Principles of Sociology*, ed. A. M. Lee. New York: Barnes & Noble, 1946.

Blumler, Jay G. "The Role of Theory in Uses and Gratifications Studies." *Communication Research* 6 (1) (1979): 9–36.

Boczkowski, Pablo J. *News at Work: Imitation in an Age of Information Abundance*. Chicago: University of Chicago Press, 2010.

Boczkowski, Pablo J., and Eugenia Mitchelstein. *The News Gap: When the Information Preferences of the Media and the Public Diverge*. Cambridge, MA: MIT Press, 2013.

Bohn, Roger E., and James E. Short. "How Much Information? 2009: Report on American Consumers." San Diego: Global Information Industry Center, University of California, San Diego, 2009.

Bollier, D. *The Promise and Peril of Big Data*. Washington, DC: Aspen Institute, Communications and Society Program, 2010.

Bond, Robert M., Christopher J. Fariss, Jason J. Jones, Adam D. I. Kramer, Cameron Marlow, Jaime E. Settle, and James H. Fowler. "A 61-Million-Person Experiment in Social Influence and Political Mobilization." *Nature* 489 (7415) (2012): 295–298.

Bondad-Brown, Beverly A., Ronald E. Rice, and Katy E. Pearce. "Influences on TV Viewing and Online User-Shared Video Use: Demographics, Generations, Contextual Age, Media Use, Motivations, and Audience Activity." *Journal of Broadcasting & Electronic Media* 56 (4) (2012): 471–493.

Bourdieu, P. *Distinction: A Social Critique of the Judgement of Taste*. trans. Richard Nice. Cambridge, MA: Harvard University Press, 1984.

Bowles, Samuel. "Endogenous Preferences: The Cultural Consequences of Markets and Other Economic Institutions." *Journal of Economic Literature* 36 (1) (1998): 75–111.

Bowman, Gary W., and John U. Farley. "TV Viewing: Application of Formal Choice Model." *Applied Economics* 4 (4) (1972): 245–259.

boyd, danah, and Kate Crawford. "Critical Questions for Big Data." *Information Communication and Society* 15 (5) (2012): 662–679.

Branscomb, Anne W. "The Cable Fable: Will It Come True?" *Journal of Communication* 25 (1) (1975): 44–56.

Brehm, J. W. "Postdecision Changes in the Desirability of Alternatives." *Journal of Abnormal and Social Psychology* 52 (3) (1956): 384.

Bronnenberg, Bart J., Jean-Pierre H. Dubé, and Matthew Gentzkow. "The Evolution of Brand Preferences: Evidence from Consumer Migration." *American Economic Review* 102 (6) (2012): 2472–2508.

Bryant, Jennings, and Mary B. Oliver. *Media Effects: Advances in Theory and Research.* 3rd ed. New York: Routledge, 2009.

Bryson, Bethany. "'Anything but Heavy Metal': Symbolic Exclusion and Musical Dislikes." *American Sociological Review* 61 (5) (1996): 884–899.

Bucher, Taina. "Want to Be on the Top? Algorithmic Power and the Threat of Invisibility on Facebook." *New Media & Society* 14 (7) (2012): 1164–1180.

Butsch, Richard. *The Citizen Audience: Crowds, Publics, and Individuals.* New York: Routledge, 2008.

Buzzard, Karen. *Tracking the Audience: The Ratings Industry from Analog to Digital.* New York: Routledge, 2012.

Calhoun, Craig, ed. *Habermas and the Public Sphere.* Cambridge, MA: MIT Press, 1992.

Carey, J. *Culture as Communication: Essays on Media and Society, Media and Popular Culture.* New York: Routledge, 1989.

Carr, Nicholas. *The Shallows: What the Internet Is Doing to Our Brains.* New York: W. W. Norton, 2011.

Carter, Bill. "Republicans Like Golf, Democrats Prefer Cartoons, TV Research Suggests." *New York Times* (October 11, 2012).

Castells, Manuel. "The New Public Sphere: Global Civil Society, Communication Networks, and Global Governance." *Annals of the American Academy of Political and Social Science* 616 (1) (2008): 78–93.

Caves, Richard E. *Creative Industries: Contracts between Art and Commerce.* Cambridge, MA: Harvard University Press, 2000.

Centola, Damon, and Michael Macy. "Complex Contagions and the Weakness of Long Ties." *American Journal of Sociology* 113 (3) (2007): 702–734.

Cha, Meeyoung, Hamed Haddadi, Fabricio Benevenuto, and Krishna P. Gummadi. "Measuring User Influence in Twitter: The Million Follower Fallacy." Paper presented at the 4th International AAAI Conference on Weblogs and Social Media (ICWSM), Washington, DC, May 2010.

Cha, Meeyoung, J. Pérez, and Hamed Haddadi. "Flash Floods and Ripples: The Spread of Media Content through the Blogosphere." Paper presented at the AAAI Conference on Weblogs and Social Media (ICWSM) Data Challenge Workshop, San Jose, May 2009.

Chaffee, Steven H., and Miriam J. Metzger. "The End of Mass Communication?" *Mass Communication & Society* 4 (4) (2001): 365–379.

Chalaby, Jean K. "The Making of an Entertainment Revolution: How the TV Format Trade Became a Global Industry." *European Journal of Communication* 26 (4) (2011): 293–309.

Chalaby, Jean K. "At the Origin of a Global Industry: The TV Format Trade as an Anglo-American Invention." *Media Culture & Society* 34 (1) (2012): 36–52.

Charney, T., and B. S. Greenberg. Uses and Gratifications of the Internet. In *Communication Technology and Society: Audience Adoption and Uses*, ed. Carolyn Lin and David Adkin, 379–407. Cresskill, NJ: Hampton Press, 2002.

Cho, J., and S. Roy. "Impact of Search Engines on Page Popularity." Paper presented at the 13th International Conference on World Wide Web, New York, May 2004.

Christian, Aymar Jean. "Valuing Post-Network Television." *Flow* (May 6, 2013).

Christian, Brian. "The A/B Test: Inside the Technology That's Changing the Rules of Business." *Wired* (May 2012).

Christians, Clifford G., T. L. Glasser, D. McQuail, K. Nordenstreng, and R. White. *Normative Theories of the Media: Journalism in Democratic Societies*. Urbana: University of Illinois Press, 2009.

Clay, Russ, Jessica M. Barber, and Natalie J. Shook. "Techniques for Measuring Selective Exposure: A Critical Review." *Communication Methods and Measures* 7 (3) (2013): 221–245.

Comstock, George. *Television in America*. Beverly Hills: Sage, 1980.

Conover, Michael D., Jacob Ratkiewicz, Matthew Francisco, Bruno Gonçalves, Alessandro Flammini, and Filippo Menczer. "Political Polarization on Twitter." Paper presented at the 5th International Conference on Weblogs and Social Media, Barcelona, July 2011.

Cooper, Eunice, and Marie Jahoda. "The Evasion of Propaganda: How Prejudiced People Respond to Anti-prejudice Propaganda." *Journal of Psychology* 23 (1) (1947): 15–25.

Cooper, Roger, and Tang Tang. "Predicting Audience Exposure to Television in Today's Media Environment: An Empirical Integration of Active-Audience and Structural Theories." *Journal of Broadcasting & Electronic Media* 53 (3) (2009): 400–418.

Cotton, J. L. "Cognitive Dissonance in Selective Exposure." In *Selective Exposure to Communication*, ed. D. Zillmann and J. Bryant, 11–33. Hillsdale, NJ: Erlbaum, 1985.

Council for Research Excellence. *Video Consumer Mapping Study*. Author, 2009.

Department for Culture, Media and Sport and Department for Business, Innovation and Skills. "Digital Britain: Final Report" (2009). http://www.official-documents.gov
.uk/document/cm76/7650/7650.pdf.

Danaher, Peter J., Tracey S. Dagger, and Michael S. Smith. "Forecasting Television Ratings." *International Journal of Forecasting* 27 (4) (2011): 1215–1240.

Davenport, Thomas H., and John C. Beck. *The Attention Economy: Understanding the New Currency of Business*. Boston: Harvard Business Press, 2001.

Davidson, Cathy N. *Now You See It: How the Brain Science of Attention Will Transform the Way We Live, Work, and Learn*. New York: Viking Press, 2011.

Dayan, Daniel, and Elihu Katz. *Media Events: The Live Broadcasting of History*. Cambridge, MA: Harvard University Press, 1992.

Delo, Cotton. "U.S. Adults Now Spending More Time on Digital Devices Than Watching TV." *AdAge* (August 1, 2013). http://adage.com/article/digital/americans-spend-time
-digital-devices-tv/243414/?utm_source=mediaworks&utm_medium=newsletter
&utm_campaign=adage&ttl=1375984415.

De Vany, Arthur. *Hollywood Economics: How Extreme Uncertainty Shapes the Film Industry*. New York: Routledge, 2003.

DeWerth-Pallmeyer, Dwight. *The Audience in the News*. Mahwah, NJ: Erlbaum, 1997.

Dewey, John. *The Public and Its Problems*. New York: Henry Holt, 1927.

DiMaggio, Paul, Eszter Hargittai, W. Russell Neuman, and John P. Robinson. "Social Implications of the Internet." *Annual Review of Sociology* 27 (2001): 307–336.

DiMaggio, Paul, and Hugh Louch. "Socially Embedded Consumer Transactions: For What Kinds of Purchases Do People Most Often Use Networks?" *American Sociological Review* 63 (5) (1998): 619–637.

Donsbach, Wolfgang. Cognitive Dissonance Theory: A Roller Coaster Career. In *Media Choice: A Theoretical and Empirical Overview*, ed. T. Hartmann, 128–148. New York: Routledge, 2009.

Dumenco, Simon. "The Truth about Reddit: The Benefits of Neglectful Ownership, Where Gawker and Buzzfeed Get Their 'Inspiration,' and More." *Advertising Age* (May 2013): 6.

Dunbar, R. I. M. "Neocortex Size as a Constraint on Group Size in Primates." *Journal of Human Evolution* 22 (6) (1992): 469–493.

Dunbar, R. I. M. "The Social Brain: Mind, Language, and Society in Evolutionary Perspective." *Annual Review of Anthropology* 32 (2003): 163–181.

Easley, David, and Jon Kleinberg. *Networks, Crowds, and Markets: Reasoning about a Highly Connected World*. Cambridge, UK: Cambridge University Press, 2010.

Eastman, Susan Tyler, and Douglas A. Ferguson. *Media Programming: Strategies and Practices*. Belmont, CA: Wadsworth, 2012.

Ebert, Roger. "*Cowboys & Aliens*." *Chicago Sun Times* (July 27, 2011). http://rogerebert.suntimes.com/apps/pbcs.dll/article?AID=/20110727/REVIEWS/110729987.

Edwards, Carol. *Arbitron's Single Source, Three-Screen Measurement Approach for CIMM*. New York: Arbitron, 2012.

Ehrenberg, Andrew S. C. "The Factor Analytic Search for Program Types." *Journal of Advertising Research* 8 (1) (1968): 55–63.

Ehrenberg, Andrew S. C. *Data Reduction: Analysing and Interpreting Statistical Data*. London: Wiley, 1975.

Ehrenberg, Andrew S. C., Gerald J. Goodhardt, and T. Patrick Barwise. "Double Jeopardy Revisited." *Journal of Marketing* 54 (3) (1990): 82–91.

Elberse, Anita. "Should You Invest in the Long Tail?" *Harvard Business Review* 86 (7–8) (2008): 88–96.

Elberse, Anita. *Blockbusters: Hit-making, Risk-taking, and the Big Business of Entertainment*. New York: Holt, 2013.

Ellison, N. B., C. Steinfield, and C. Lampe. "Connection Strategies: Social Capital Implications of Facebook-Enabled Communication Practices." *New Media & Society* 13 (6) (2011): 873–892.

Emirbayer, Mustafa, and Ann Mische. "What Is Agency?" *American Journal of Sociology* 103 (4) (1998): 962–1023.

Espeland, Wendy N., and M. Sauder. "Rankings and Reactivity: How Public Measures Recreate Social Worlds." *American Journal of Sociology* 113 (1) (2007): 1–40.

Espinosa, Paul. "The Audience in the Text: Ethnographic Observations of a Hollywood Story Conference." *Media Culture & Society* 4 (1) (1982): 77–86.

Ettema, James S., and D. Charles Whitney. The Money Arrow: An Introduction to Audiencemaking. In *Audiencemaking: How the Media Create the Audience*, ed. J. S. Ettema and D. C. Whitney, 1–18. Thousand Oaks, CA: Sage, 1994.

Experian Simmons. *Simmons Consumer Segmentations: PoliticalPersonas*. 2011. New York: Author.

Fahr, Andreas, and Eabea Bocking. Media Choice and Avoidance Behavior: Avoidance Motivations during Television Use. In *Media Choice: A Theoretical and Empirical Overview*, ed. T. Hartmann, 185–202. New York: Routledge, 2009.

Falkinger, J. "Attention Economies." *Journal of Economic Theory* 133 (1) (2007): 266–294.

Farnam, T. W. "Obama Campaign Took Unorthodox Approach to Ad Buying." *Washington Post* (November 14, 2012).

Fast, Nathanael J., Chip Heath, and George Wu. "Common Ground and Cultural Prominence." *Psychological Science* 20 (7) (2009): 904–911.

Fehr, Ernst, and Karla Hoff. "Introduction: Tastes, Castes and Culture: The Influence of Society on Preferences." *Economic Journal* 121 (556) (2011): F396–F412.

Feldman, Lauren, Natalie Jomini Stroud, Bruce Bimber, and Magdalena Wojcieszak. "Assessing Selective Exposure in Experiments: The Implications of Different Methodological Choices." *Communication Methods and Measures* 7 (3) (2013): 198–220.

Ferguson, Douglas A., and Elizabeth M. Perse. "Media and Audience Influences on Channel Repertoire." *Journal of Broadcasting & Electronic Media* 37 (1) (1993): 31–47.

Festinger, Leon. *A Theory of Cognitive Dissonance*. Stanford, CA: Stanford University Press, 1957.

Filchy, Patrice. *The Internet Imaginaire*. Cambridge, MA: MIT Press, 2007.

Finkelstein, Seth. Google, Links, and Popularity versus Authority. In *The Hyperlinked Society: Questioning Connections in the Digital Age*, ed. Joseph Turow and L. Tsui, 104–120. Ann Arbor: University of Michigan Press, 2008.

Ford, Daniel, and Josh Batson. "Languages of the World (Wide Web)" (2011). http://googleresearch.blogspot.com/2011/07/languages-of-world-wide-web.html.

Fowler, Mark S., and Daniel L. Brenner. "Marketplace Approach to Broadcast Regulation." *Texas Law Review* 60 (1982): 207–257.

Franceschet, Massimo. "PageRank: Standing on the Shoulders of Giants." *Communications of the ACM* 54 (6) (2011): 92–101.

Frank, Robert H., and P. J. Cook. *The Winner-Take-All Society: Why the Few at the Top Get So Much More Than the Rest of Us*. New York: Penguin Press, 1996.

Frank, Ronald E., James C. Becknell, and James D. Clokey. "Television Program Types." *Journal of Marketing Research* 8 (2) (1971): 204–211.

Friedman, Wayne. "Time Warner Favors Trad TV over Streaming." *Media Post* (March 4, 2013). http://www.mediapost.com/publications/article/194887/time-warner-favors-trad-tv-over-streaming.html#axzz2OBm8ElCj.

Fu, Wayne W., and C. C. Sim. "Aggregate Bandwagon Effect on Online Videos' Viewership: Value Uncertainty, Popularity Cues, and Heuristics." *Journal of the American Society for Information Science and Technology* 62 (12) (2011): 2382–2395.

Gans, Herbert J. *Popular Culture and High Culture: An Analysis and Evaluation of Taste*. rev. and updated ed. New York: Basic Books, 1999.

Gans, Herbert J. *Deciding What's News*. Evanston, IL: Northwestern University Press, 2004.

Garfield, Bob. *The Chaos Scenario*. Nashville: Stielstra Publishing, 2009.

Garrett, R. Kelly. "Politically Motivated Reinforcement Seeking: Reframing the Selective Exposure Debate." *Journal of Communication* 59 (4) (2009): 676–699.

Garrett, R. Kelly, Dustin Carnahan, and Emily Lynch. "A Turn toward Avoidance? Selective Exposure to Online Political Information, 2004–2008." *Political Behavior* 35 (1) (2013): 113–134.

Garrett, R. Kelly, Benjamin K. Jonshon, Rachel Neo, and Aysemur Dal. "Implications of Pro- and Counter-Attitudinal Information Exposure for Affective Polarization." Presented at the Annual Meeting of the International Communication Association, London, June 2013.

Garrett, R. Kelly, and Paul Resnick. "Resisting Political Fragmentation on the Internet." *Daedalus* 140 (4) (2011): 108–120.

Geertz, Clifford. *Local Knowledge: Further Essays in Interpretive Anthropology*. New York: Basic Books, 1983.

Gensch, Dennis H., and B. Ranganathan. "Evaluation of Television Program Content for the Purpose of Promotional Segmentation." *Journal of Marketing Research* 11 (4) (1974): 390–398.

Gentzkow, Matthew, and Jesse M. Shapiro. "Competition and Truth in the Market for News." *Journal of Economic Perspectives* 22 (2) (2008): 133–154.

Gentzkow, Matthew, and Jesse M. Shapiro. "Ideological Segregation Online and Offline." *Quarterly Journal of Economics* 126 (4) (2011): 1799–1839.

Gerbner, George, Larry Gross, Michael Morgan, Nancy Signorielli, and James Shanahn. Growing Up with Television: Cultivation Processes. In *Media Effects: Advances in Theory and Research*, 2nd. ed., ed. Jennings Bryant and Dolf Zillmann, 43–68. Mahwah, NJ: Erlbaum, 2002.

Gertner, Jon. "Our Ratings, Ourselves." *New York Times Magazine* (April 10, 2005), 34–41.

Giddens, Anthony. *The Constitution of Society: Outline of the Theory of Structuration*. Berkeley: University of California Press, 1984.

Giddens, Anthony. *Social Theory and Modern Sociology*. Stanford, CA: Stanford University Press, 1987.

Gillespie, Tarleton. "Designed to 'Effectively Frustrate': Copyright, Technology and the Agency of Users." *New Media & Society* 8 (4) (2006): 651–669.

Gillespie, Tarleton. "Can an Algorithm Be Wrong? Twitter Trends, the Specter of Censorship, and Our Faith in the Algorithms around Us." *Culture Digitally* (October 19, 2011). http://culturedigitally.org/2011/10/can-an-algorithm-be-wrong.

Gillmor, Dan. *We the Media: Grassroots Journalism by the People, for the People*. Sebastopol, CA: O'Reilly Media, 2006.

Gitelman, Lisa, ed. *"Raw Data" Is an Oxymoron*. Cambridge, MA: MIT Press, 2013.

Gitlin, Todd. Public Sphere or Public Sphericules? In *Media, Ritual, Identity*, ed. T. Liebes and James Curran, 168–175. London: Routledge, 1998.

Gladwell, Malcolm. *The Tipping Point: How Little Things Can Make a Big Difference*. New York: Little, Brown, 2000.

Goerlich, Bruce. "Political Ratings—a Nation Divided?" *Thought Lobs from Goerlich's Frontal Lobe* (October 26, 2012). http://brucegoerlich.com/2012/10/26/political-ratings-a-nation-divided.

Goetzl, David. "Media Industry Can Look to U.K. for New Terminology." *TV Blog: Small Screen Big Picture.* MediaPost (August 1, 2013). http://www.mediapost.com/publications/article/205896/media-industry-can-look-to-uk-for-new-terminolog.html?edition=62934#axzz2akAw9ATq.

Goldberg, A. "Mapping Shared Understandings Using Relational Class Analysis: The Case of the Cultural Omnivore Reexamined." *American Journal of Sociology* 116 (5) (2011): 1397–1436.

Golder, Scott A., and Michael W. Macy. "Diurnal and Seasonal Mood Vary with Work, Sleep, and Daylength across Diverse Cultures." *Science* 333 (6051) (2011): 1878–1881.

Goldhaber, M. H. "The Attention Economy and the Net." *First Monday* 2 (4–7) (1997).

Goldman, Seth K., Diana C. Mutz, and Susanna Dilliplane. "All Virtue Is Relative: A Response to Prior." *Political Communication* 30 (4) (2013): 635–653.

Goldman, William. *Adventures in the Screen Trade: A Personal View of Hollywood and Screenwriting.* vol. 92. New York: Warner Books, 1983.

Gonçalves, Bruno, Nicola Perra, and Alessandro Vespignani. "Modeling Users' Activity on Twitter Networks: Validation of Dunbar's Number." *PLoS ONE* 6 (8) (2011): e22656.

Goodhardt, G. J. "Constant in Duplicated Television Viewing." *Nature* 212 (1966): 1616.

Goodhardt, G. J., A. S. C. Ehrenberg, and M. A. Collins. *The Television Audience: Patterns of Viewing; An Update.* Aldershot, Hampshire, UK: Gower Publishing, 1987.

Google. "Personalized Search for Everyone." Google Blog (December 4, 2009). http://googleblog.blogspot.com/2009/12/personalized-search-for-everyone.html.

Gottlieb, Zach. "In Online Media, Consumer Is King." *Wired* (June 29, 2010). http://www.wired.com/business/2010/06/in-online-media-consumer-is-king.

Granovetter, Mark S. "The Strength of Weak Ties." *American Journal of Sociology* 78 (6) (1973): 1360–1380.

Graser, Marc. "10 Insights from Studies of Binge Watchers." *Variety* (March 7, 2013).

Greenwald, Anthony G., and Clark Leavitt. "Audience Involvement in Advertising: Four Levels." *Journal of Consumer Research* 11 (1) (1984): 581–592.

Gunter, Barrie. *Media Research Methods: Measuring Audiences, Reactions and Impact.* London: Sage, 1999.

Habermas, Jürgen. *The Structural Transformation of the Public Sphere: An Inquiry into a Category of Bourgeois Society.* Cambridge, MA: MIT Press, 1991.

Habermas, Jürgen. "Political Communication in Media Society: Does Democracy Still Enjoy an Epistemic Dimension? The Impact of Normative Theory on Empirical Research." *Communication Theory* 16 (4) (2006): 411–426.

Hagen, Ingunn. Slaves of the Ratings Tyranny? Media Images of the Audience. In *Rethinking the Media Audience,* ed. Pertti Alasuutari, 130–150. London: Sage, 1999.

Hagey, Keach. "Creator of 'the Voice' Gets a Second Act: The Netherlands' John De Mol Was a Pioneer of Reality Television." *Wall Street Journal* (June 9, 2013).

Halavais, Alexander. *Search Engine Society.* Cambridge, UK: Polity Press, 2009.

Hale, Matthew, Erika Franklin Fowler, and Kenneth M. Goldstein. "Capturing Multiple Markets: A New Method of Capturing and Analyzing Local Television News." *Electronic News* 1 (4) (2007): 227–243.

Hall, Stuart. Encoding/Decoding. In *Culture, Media, Language,* ed. Stuart Hall, Dorothy Hobson, Andrew Lowe, and Paul Willis, 107–116. London: Unwin Hyman, 1980.

Hamilton, James. *All the News That's Fit to Sell: How the Market Transforms Information into News.* Princeton, NJ: Princeton University Press, 2004.

Hampton, K. N., L. S. Goulet, C. Marlow, and L. Rainie. "Why Most Facebook Users Get More Than They Give." *Pew Internet Report* (February 3, 2012).

Hargittai, Eszter. "Open Portals or Closed Gates? Channeling Content on the World Wide Web." *Poetics* 27 (4) (2000): 233–253.

Hargittai, Eszter. "Second-Level Digital Divide." *First Monday* 7, 4–1 (2002).

Hargittai, Eszter. "Digital Na(t)ives? Variation in Internet Skills and Uses among Members of the 'Net Generation.'" *Sociological Inquiry* 80 (1) (2010): 92–113.

Hargittai, Eszter, L. Fullerton, E. Menchen-Trevino, and K.Y. Thomas. "Trust Online: Young Adults' Evaluation of Web Content." *International Journal of Communication* 4 (1) (2010): 468–494.

Hargittai, Eszter, J. Gallo, and M. Kane. "Cross-Ideological Discussions among Conservative and Liberal Bloggers." *Public Choice* 134 (1–2) (2008): 67–86.

Hargittai, Eszter, and Yuli Patrick Hsieh. Digital Inequality. In *Oxford Handbook of Internet Studies,* ed. William H. Dutton, 129–150. Oxford: Oxford University Press, 2013.

Hargittai, Eszter, and Eden Litt. "The Tweet Smell of Celebrity Success: Explaining Variation in Twitter Adoption among a Diverse Group of Young Adults." *New Media & Society* 13 (5) (2011): 824–842.

Harrigan, Nicholas, Palakorn Achananuparp, and Ee-Peng Lim. "Influentials, Novelty, and Social Contagion: The Viral Power of Average Friends, Close Communities, and Old News." *Social Networks* 34 (4) (2012): 470–480.

Hart, William, Dolores Albarracín, Alice H. Eagly, Inge Brechan, Matthew J. Lindberg, and Lisa Merrill. "Feeling Validated versus Being Correct: A Meta-Analysis of Selective Exposure to Information." *Psychological Bulletin* 135 (4) (2009): 555–588.

Hartmann, Tilo. Action Theory, Theory of Planned Behavior and Media Choice. In *Media Choice: A Theoretical and Empirical Overview*, ed. T. Hartmann, 32–52. New York: Routledge, 2009a.

Hartmann, Tilo, ed. *Media Choice: A Theoretical and Empirical Overview*. New York: Routledge, 2009b.

Hasebrink, Uwe, and Hanna Domeyer. "Media Repertoires as Patterns of Behaviour and as Meaningful Practices: A Multimethod Approach to Media Use in Converging Media Environments." *Participations: Journal of Audience & Reception Studies* 9 (2) (2012): 757–779.

Hasebrink, Uwe, and Jutta Popp. "Media Repertoires as a Result of Selective Media Use: A Conceptual Approach to the Analysis of Patterns of Exposure." *Communications: The European Journal of Communication Research* 31 (3) (2006): 369–387.

Hayes, Tom. 2008. *Jump Point: How Network Culture Is Revolutionizing Business*. New York: McGraw-Hill.

Hays, Sharon. "Structure and Agency and the Sticky Problem of Culture." *Sociological Theory* 12 (1994): 57–72.

Hecht, Brent, and Darren Gergle. "The Tower of Babel Meets Web 2.0: User-Generated Content and Its Applications in a Multilingual Context." Paper presented at CHI 2010, Atlanta, GA, April 2010.

Hecht, Brent, and Emily Moxley. 2009. "Terabytes of Tobler: Evaluating the First Law in a Massive, Domain-Neutral Representation of World Knowledge." Presented at the 9th International Conference on Spatial Information Theory, Aber Wrac'h, France, September 21–25, 2009, 88–105. New York: Springer.

Heeter, Carrie. "Program Selection with Abundance of Choice—a Process Model." *Human Communication Research* 12 (1) (1985): 126–152.

Helberger, Natali. "Diversity by Design." *Journal of Information Policy* 1 (2011): 441–469.

Hernandez, R., and S. Elliot. "Advertising: The Odd Couple vs. Nielsen." *New York Times* (June 14, 2004).

Hilbert, Martin, and Priscila López. "The World's Technological Capacity to Store, Communicate, and Compute Information." *Science* 332 (6025) (2011): 60–65.

Hindman, Matthew. *The Myth of Digital Democracy.* Princeton, NJ: Princeton University Press, 2009.

Hirsch, Paul M., and Daniel M. Gruber. Digitizing Fads and Fashions: How Technology Has "Glocalized" the Market for Creative Products. In *Handbook on Creative Industries*, ed. Candace Jones and Mark Lorenzen. Oxford: Oxford University Press, 2014.

Hitt, Jack. "Multiscreen Mad Men." *New York Times* (November 21, 2008).

Holbert, R. L., R. K. Garrett, and L. S. Gleason. "A New Era of Minimal Effects? A Response to Bennett and Iyengar." *Journal of Communication* 60 (1) (2010): 15–34.

Holbert, R. Lance, Owen Pillion, David A. Tschida, Greg G. Armfield, Kelly Kinder, Kristin L. Cherry, and Amy R. Daulton. "The West Wing as Endorsement of the U.S. Presidency: Expanding the Bounds of Priming in Political Communication." *Journal of Communication* 53 (3) (2003): 427–443.

Hollander, Barry A. "Tuning out or Tuning Elsewhere? Partisanship, Polarization, and Media Migration from 1998 to 2006." *Journalism & Mass Communication Quarterly* 85 (1) (2008): 23–40.

Holton, Avery. "Negating Nodes and Liquid Fragmentation: Extending Conversations of Diffusion, Social Networks, and Fragmentation." *Communication Theory* 22 (3) (2012): 279–298.

Home-Office. *Broadcasting in the '90s: Competition, Choice and Quality*, ed. Secretary of State for the Home Office. London: HMSO Books, 1988.

Hotelling, Harold. "Stability in Competition." *Economic Journal* 39 (153) (1929): 41–57.

Hsu, Greta, M. T. Hannan, and Ö. Koçak. "Multiple Category Memberships in Markets: An Integrative Theory and Two Empirical Tests." *American Sociological Review* 74 (1) (2009): 150–169.

Hsu, Greta, Giacomo Negro, and Fabrizio Perretti. "Hybrids in Hollywood: A Study of the Production and Performance of Genre-Spanning Films." *Industrial and Corporate Change* 21 (6) (2012): 1427–1450.

Huberman, Bernardo A. *The Laws of the Web: Patterns in the Ecology of Information.* Cambridge, MA: MIT Press, 2003.

Huberman, Bernardo A., and Fang Wu. "The Economics of Attention: Maximizing User Value in Information-Rich Environments." In *Proceedings of the 1st International Workshop on Data Mining and Audience Intelligence for Advertising,* 16–20. San Jose, CA: ACM, 2007.

Iyengar, Shanto. Laboratory Experiments in Political Science. In *Handbook of Experimental Political Science,* ed. James N. Druckman, Donald P. Green, James H. Kuklinski, and Arthur Lupia, 73–88. New York: Cambridge University Press, 2011.

Iyengar, Shanto, and Kyusup Hahn. "Red Media, Blue Media: Evidence of Ideological Selectivity in Media Use." *Journal of Communication* 59 (1) (2009): 19–39.

Iyengar, Shanto, Gaurav Sood, and Yphtach Lelkes. "Affect, Not Ideology: A Social Identity Perspective on Polarization." *Public Opinion Quarterly* 76 (3) (2012): 405–431.

Jackson, Maggie. *Distracted: The Erosion of Attention and the Coming Dark Age.* Amherst, NY: Prometheus Books, 2009.

James, William. *Principles of Psychology.* vol. 1. Cambridge, MA: Harvard University Press, 1890.

Jamieson, Kathleen H., and Joseph N. Cappella. *Echo Chamber: Rush Limbaugh and the Conservative Media Establishment.* New York: Oxford University Press, 2009.

Jannarone, John, and Rebecca Smith. "Super Bowl Audience Totaled 108.4 Million." *Wall Street Journal* (February 4, 2013).

Jardine, Byrony. "Retaining the Primetime TV Audience: Examining Adjacent Program Audience Duplication across Markets." Master's thesis., University of South Australia, 2012.

Jarvis, J. *Public Parts: How Sharing in the Digital Age Improves the Way We Work and Live.* New York: Simon and Schuster, 2011.

Jenkins, Henry. *Convergence Culture: Where Old and New Media Collide.* New York: New York University Press, 2006.

Jenkins, Henry, Sam Ford, and Joshua Green. *Spreadable Media: Creating Value and Meaning in a Networked Culture.* New York: New York University Press, 2013.

Johansson, Petter, Lars Hall, and Nick Chater. Preference Change through Choice. In *Neuroscience of Preference and Choice,* ed. Raymond Dolan and Tali Sharot, 121–141. London: Academic Press, 2012.

Jones, V. J., and F. H. Siller. "Factor Analysis of Media Exposure Data Using Prior Knowledge of the Medium." *Journal of Marketing Research* 15 (1) (1978): 137–144.

Jumptap. "Screen Jumping: Understanding Today's Cross-Screen Consumer." Jumptap and comScore (September 5, 2013).

Jurkowitz, Mark, and Katerina Eva Masta. "Despite Some Warning Signs, Local TV Stations Are Hot Commodities." Pew Research Journalism Project (August 5, 2013).

Katz, Elihu. "And Deliver Us from Segmentation." *Annals of the American Academy of Political and Social Science* 546 (1996): 22–33.

Katz, Elihu, Jay G. Blumler, and Michael Gurevitch. Utilization of Mass Communication by the Individual. In *The Uses of Mass Communications: Current Perspectives on Gratifications Research*, ed. Jay G. Blumler and Elihu Katz, 19–32. Beverly Hills: Sage, 1974.

Katz, Elihu, and Paul F. Lazarsfeld. *Personal Influence: The Part Played by People in the Flow of Mass Communications*. Glencoe, IL: The Free Press, 1955.

Kaye, Kate. "Welcome to the Era of the Data-Driven Programmer: Yet Algorithms Won't Replace Humans Any Time Soon." *Advertising Age* (April 2013): 8.

Keen, Andrew. *Digital Vertigo: How Today's Online Social Revolution Is Dividing, Diminishing, and Disorienting Us*. New York: St. Martin's Press, 2012.

Kim, Jinhee, and Mary Beth Oliver. "How Do We Regulate Sadness through Entertainment Messages? Exploring Three Predictions." *Journal of Broadcasting & Electronic Media* 57 (3) (2013): 374–391.

Kim, Su Jung. *Emerging Patterns of News Media Use across Multiple Platforms and Their Political Implications in South Korea*. PhD diss., Northwestern University, 2011.

Kim, Su Jung, Young Min Baek, Sung Dong Cho, and Namjun Kang. News Audience Polarization across TV and the Internet in South Korea. Paper presented at the annual meeting of the International Communication Association, Phoenix, AZ, May 2012.

Kim, Su Jung, and James G. Webster. "The Impact of a Multichannel Environment on Television News Viewing: A Longitudinal Study of News Audience Polarization in South Korea." *International Journal of Communication* 6 (1) (2012): 838–856.

Kim, Susanna. "Twitter's IPO Filing Shows 215 Million Monthly Active Users." *ABC News* (October 3, 2013). http://abcnews.go.com/Business/twitter-ipo-filing-reveals -500-million-tweets-day/story?id=20460493.

Kirkpatrick, David. *The Facebook Effect: The Inside Story of the Company That Is Connecting the World.* New York: Simon and Schuster, 2011.

Kirsch, A. D., and S. Banks. "Program Types Defined by Factor Analysis." *Journal of Advertising Research* 2 (3) (1962): 29–31.

Klapper, Joseph T. *The Effects of Mass Communication: Foundations of Communications Research.* Glencoe, IL: Free Press, 1960.

Knobloch-Westerwick, Silvia. Mood Management: Theory, Evidence, and Advancements. In *Psychology of Entertainment*, ed. Jennings Bryant and Peter Vorderer, 239–254. Mahwah, NJ: Erlbaum, 2006.

Knobloch-Westerwick, Silvia, and Steven B. Kleinman. "Preelection Selective Exposure: Confirmation Bias versus Informational Utility." *Communication Research* 39 (2) (2012): 170–193.

Knobloch-Westerwick, Silvia, N. Sharma, D. L. Hansen, and S. Alter. "Impact of Popularity Indications on Readers' Selective Exposure to Online News." *Journal of Broadcasting & Electronic Media* 49 (3) (2005): 296–313.

Krcmar, Marina, and Yuliya Strizhakova. Uses and Gratification as Media Choice. In *Media Choice: A Theoretical and Empirical Overview*, ed. T. Hartmann, 53–69. New York: Routledge, 2009.

Ksiazek, Thomas B. "A Network Analytic Approach to Understanding Cross-Platform Audience Behavior." *Journal of Media Economics* 24 (4) (2011): 237–251.

Ksiazek, Thomas B., Edward C. Malthouse, and James G. Webster. "News-Seekers and Avoiders: Exploring Patterns of Total News Consumption across Media and the Relationship to Civic Participation." *Journal of Broadcasting & Electronic Media* 54 (4) (2010): 551–568.

Ksiazek, Thomas B., and James G. Webster. "Cultural Proximity and Audience Behavior: The Role of Language in Patterns of Polarization and Multicultural Fluency." *Journal of Broadcasting & Electronic Media* 52 (3) (2008): 485–503.

Ksiazek, Thomas B., and Elaine Yuan. A Comparative Networks Analysis of Audience Fragmentation in China and the U.S. Paper presented at the Annual Meeting of the International Communication Association, Phoenix, AZ, May 2012.

LaCour, Michael J. "Balanced News Diet, Not Selective Exposure: Evidence from a Real World Measure of Media Exposure." Presented at the Annual Midwest Political Science Association, Chicago, April 2012.

Lakshminarayanan, Venkat, and Laurie R. Santos. The Evolution of Our Preferences: Insights from Non-human Primates. In *Neuroscience of Preference and Choice*, ed. Raymond Dolan and Tali Sharot, 75–91. London: Academic Press, 2012.

Lampel, Joseph, Theresa Lant, and Jamal Shamsie. "Balancing Act: Learning from Organizing Practices in Cultural Industries." *Organization Science* 11 (3) (2000): 263–269.

Lanham, Richard A. *The Economics of Attention: Style and Substance in the Age of Information.* Chicago: University of Chicago Press, 2006.

LaRose, Robert. Social Cognitive Theories of Media Selection. In *Media Choice: A Theoretical and Empirical Overview*, ed. T. Hartmann, 10–31. New York: Routledge, 2009.

LaRose, Robert. "The Problem of Media Habits." *Communication Theory* 20 (2) (2010): 194–222.

Lasswell, Harold D. The Structure and Function of Communication in Society. In *The Communication of Ideas*, ed. Lyman Bryson, 37–51. New York: Coopers Square Publishers, 1948.

Lawless, John. "The Interview: Nigel Newton; Is There Life after Harry Potter." *Independent* (July 3, 2005).

Lazarsfeld, Paul F., and Elihu Katz. *Personal Influence: The Part Played by People in the Flow of Mass Communications.* Glencoe, IL: Free Press, 1955.

Lazarsfeld, Paul F., and Robert K. Merton. Mass Communication, Popular Taste and Organized Social Action. In *The Communication of Ideas*, ed. Lyman Bryson, 95–118. New York: Harper & Row, 1948.

Learmonth, Michael. "Digitas Unveils Tool to Find Youtube Stars before They're Stars: A Long Tail of Youtube Stars Is out There, but How to Find Them?" *Advertising Age* (May 2013): 2.

Lee, Angela M. "News Audiences Revisited: Theorizing the Link between Audience Motivations and News Consumption." *Journal of Broadcasting & Electronic Media* 57 (3) (2013): 300–317.

Lee, Jae Kook. "The Effect of the Internet on Homogeneity of the Media Agenda: A Test of the Fragmentation Thesis." *Journalism & Mass Communication Quarterly* 84 (4) (2007): 745–760.

Lenhart, Amanda. "Adults and Social Network Websites." Pew Internet and American Life Project (January 14, 2009).

Leskovec, Jure, Lada A. Adamic, and Bernardo A. Huberman. "The Dynamics of Viral Marketing." *ACM Trans. Web* 1 (1) (2007): 5.

Leskovec, Jure, Lars Backstrom, and Jon Kleinberg. "Meme-Tracking and the Dynamics of the News Cycle." In *Proceedings of the 15th ACM SIGKDD International Conference on Knowledge Discovery and Data Mining*, 497–506. Paris: ACM, 2009.

Lessig, Lawrence. *Remix: Making Art and Commerce Thrive in the Hybrid Economy*. New York: Penguin Press, 2008.

Levendusky, Matthew. *How Partisan Media Polarize America*. Chicago: University of Chicago Press, 2013.

Levy, Mark R, ed. *The VCR Age: Home Video and Mass Communication*. Newbury Park, CA: Sage, 1989.

Levy, Steven. "Inside the Box." *Wired* (March 2010): 96–116.

Levy, Steven. "Power Hours: Deep inside a Google Data Center." *Wired* (November 2012): 174–181.

Lewis, Kevin, Marco Gonzalez, and Jason Kaufman. "Social Selection and Peer Influence in an Online Social Network." *Proceedings of the National Academy of Sciences of the United States of America* 109 (1) (2012): 68–72.

Lippmann, Walter. *Public Opinion*. New York: Harcourt, Brace, 1927.

Livingstone, Sonia M. *Audiences and Publics: When Cultural Engagement Matters for the Public Sphere*. London: Intellect Books, 2005.

Lohr, Steve. "The Age of Big Data." *New York Times* (February 11, 2012).

Lull, James. "The Social Uses of Television." *Human Communication Research* 6 (3) (1980): 197–209.

Mangani, Andrea. "Profit and Audience Maximization in Broadcasting Markets." *Information Economics and Policy* 15 (3) (2003): 305–315.

Manjoo, Farhad. *True Enough: Learning to Live in a Post-fact Society*. New York: Wiley, 2008.

Manyika, James, Michael Chui, Brad Brown, Jacques Bughin, Richard Dobbs, Charles Roxburgh, and Angela Hung Byers. "Big Data: The Next Frontier for Innovation, Competition, and Productivity." McKinsey Global Institute (May 2011). http://www.mckinsey.com/insights/business_technology/big_data_the_next_frontier_for_innovation.

Marewski, J. N., M. Galesic, and G. Gigerenzer. Fast and Frugal Media Choices. In *Media Choice: A Theoretical and Empirical Overview*, ed. T. Hartmann, 107–128. New York: Routledge, 2009.

Mark, Noah. "Birds of a Feather Sing Together." *Social Forces* 77 (2) (1998): 453–485.

Markillie, P. "Crowned at Last." *The Economist* 2 (2005). http://www.economist.com/node/3785166.

Marks, Jon, and Michael Hess. "Redefining Program Types Using Viewing Analysis " PowerPoint presentation for Nielsen 360. Atlanta: Turner Research, 2012.

Marwick, Alice E., and danah boyd. "I Tweet Honestly, I Tweet Passionately: Twitter Users, Context Collapse, and the Imagined Audience." *New Media & Society* 13 (1) (2011): 114–133.

Mayer-Schonberger, Viktor, and Kenneth Cukier. *Big Data: A Revolution That Will Transform How We Live, Work and Think*. Boston: Houghton Mifflin Harcourt, 2013.

McChesney, Robert W. *Digital Disconnect: How Capitalism Is Turning the Internet against Democracy*. New York: New Press, 2013.

McCombs, Maxwell E., and Donald L. Shaw. "The Evolution of Agenda-Setting Research: Twenty-Five Years in the Marketplace of Ideas." *Journal of Communication* 43 (2) (1993): 58–67.

McCullough, Malcolm. *Ambient Commons: Attention in the Age of Embodied Information*. Cambridge, MA: MIT Press, 2013.

McPhee, William N. *Formal Theories of Mass Behavior*. Glencoe, IL: Free Press, 1963.

McPherson, Miller, Lynn Smith-Lovin, and James M. Cook. "Birds of a Feather: Homophily in Social Networks." *Annual Review of Sociology* 27 (2001): 415–444.

Merton, Robert K. "The Self-Fulfilling Prophecy." *Antioch Review* 8 (2) (1948): 193–210.

Messing, Solomon, and Sean J. Westwood. "Selective Exposure in the Age of Social Media: Endorsements Trump Partisan Source Affiliation When Selecting News Online." *Communication Research* (2012).

Metzger, Miriam J., Andrew J. Flanagin, and Ryan B. Medders. "Social and Heuristic Approaches to Credibility Evaluation Online." *Journal of Communication* 60 (3) (2010): 413–439.

Miller, Claire Cain. "Google Changes Search Algorithm, Trying to Make Results More Timely." *Bits* (November 3, 2011). http://bits.blogs.nytimes.com/2011/11/03/google-changes-search-algorithm.

Miller, Claire Cain. "As Web Search Goes Mobile, Competitors Chip at Google's Lead." *New York Times* (April 3, 2013).

Miller, Claire Cain. "Apps That Know What You Want, before You Do." *New York Times* (July 29, 2013).

Milton, John. *The Works of John Milton in Verse and Prose*. vol. 4. London: William Pickering, 1851.

Morley, David. *The Nationwide Audience: Structure and Decoding*. vol. 11. London: British Film Institute, 1980.

Muchnik, Lev, Sinan Aral, and Sean J. Taylor. "Social Influence Bias: A Randomized Experiment." *Science* 341 (6146) (2013): 647–651.

Mutz, Diana C., and Lori Young. "Communication and Public Opinion." *Public Opinion Quarterly* 75 (5) (2011): 1018–1044.

Nabi, Robin L., Carmen R. Stitt, Jeff Halford, and Keli L. Finnerty. "Emotional and Cognitive Predictors of the Enjoyment of Reality-Based and Fictional Television Programming: An Elaboration of the Uses and Gratifications Perspective." *Media Psychology* 8 (4) (2006): 421–447.

Nahon, Karine, and Jeff Hemsley. "Democracy.com: A Tale of Political Blogs and Content." Paper presented at the 44th Hawaii International Conference for System Sciences (HICSS), Manoa, January 4–7, 2011.

Napoli, Philip M. *Foundations of Communications Policy: Principles and Process in the Regulation of Electronic Media*. Cresskill, NJ: Hampton Press, 2001.

Napoli, Philip M. *Audience Economics: Media Institutions and the Audience Marketplace*. New York: Columbia University Press, 2003.

Napoli, Philip M. "Audience Measurement and Media Policy: Audience Economics, the Diversity Principle, and the Local People Meter." *Communication Law and Policy* 10 (4) (2005): 349–382.

Napoli, Philip M. *Audience Evolution: New Technologies and the Transformation of Media Audiences*. New York: Columbia University Press, 2011.

Neuendorf, Kimberly A., David J. Atkin, and Leo W. Jeffres. "Reconceptualizing Channel Repertoire in the Urban Cable Environment." *Journal of Broadcasting & Electronic Media* 45 (3) (2001): 464–482.

Neuman, W. Russell. *The Future of the Mass Audience*. Cambridge, UK: Cambridge University Press, 1991.

Neuman, W. Russell, Bruce Bimber, and Matthew Hindman. The Internet and Four Dimensions of Citizenship. In *The Oxford Handbook of American Public Opinion and the Media*, ed. Robert Y. Shapiro and Lawrence R. Jacobs, 22–42. New York: Oxford University Press, 2011.

Newcomb, Horace M., and M. Paul Hirsch. "Television as a Cultural Forum: Implications for Research." *Quarterly Review of Film and Video* 8 (3) (1983): 45–55.

Nielsen. "Anywhere Anytime Media Measurement." New York: Author, 2006.

Nielsen. "Television Audience Report 2008." New York: Author, 2009.

Nielsen. "The State of Media: The Social Media Report Q3 2011." New York: Author, 2011a.

Nielsen. "Television Audience: 2010–2011." New York: Author, 2011b.

Nielsen. "Buzz in the Blogosphere: Millions More Bloggers and Blog Readers." *Nielsen Newswire* (March 8, 2012). http://www.nielsen.com/us/en/newswire/2012/buzz-in-the-blogosphere-millions-more-bloggers-and-blog-readers.html.

Nielsen. "The Cross-Platform Report: How Viewers Watch Time-Shifted Programming." *Nielsen Newswire* (January 14, 2013a). http://www.nielsen.com/us/en/newswire/2013/the-cross-platform-report-how-viewers-watch-time-shifted-programming.html.

Nielsen. "The Follow-Back: Understanding the Two-Way Causal Influence between Twitter Activity and TV Viewership." *Nielsen Newswire* (August 6, 2013b).

Nielsen. "The Full Twitter TV Picture Revealed." *Nielsen Wire* (October 7, 2013c). http://www.nielsen.com/us/en/newswire/2013/the-full-twitter-tv-picture-revealed.html.

Nielsen. A Look across Screens: The Cross-Platform Report. Nielsen (June 2013d).

Nye, Jeremy. "Tapping out an Age Old Rhythm." *Viewing 24/7* (August 22, 2012).

Ofcom. "Measuring Media Plurality: Ofcom's Advice to the Secretary of State for Culture, Media and Sport" (October 5, 2012). http://stakeholders.ofcom.org.uk/consultations/measuring-plurality/advice.

Oliver, Mary B. Affect as a Predictor of Entertainment Choice: The Utility of Looking beyond Pleasure. In *Media Choice: A Theoretical and Empirical Overview*, ed. T. Hartmann, 167–184. New York: Routledge, 2009.

Ong, Walter J. *Orality and Literacy: The Technologizing of the Word*. London: Routledge, 1982.

O'Reilly, Tim. "What Is Web 2.0: Design Patterns and Business Models for the Next Generation of Software." *Communications & Strategies* 65 (1) (2007): 17–37.

O'Reilly, Tim, and John Battelle. "Web Squared: Web 2.0 Five Years On." Web 2.0 Summit, October 20–22, 2009.

Owen, Bruce. *Economics and Freedom of Expression*. Cambridge, MA: Ballinger, 1975.

Owen, Bruce M., Jack H. Beebe, and Willard G. Manning. *Television Economics*. Lexington, MA: Lexington Books, 1974.

Owen, Bruce M., and Steven S. Wildman. *Video Economics*. Cambridge, MA: Harvard University Press, 1992.

Page, Larry, S. Brin, R. Motwani, and T. Winograd. "The PageRank Citation Ranking: Bringing Order to the Web." Stanford InfoLab (1999).

Palfrey, John G., and Urs Gasser. *Interop: The Promise and Perils of Highly Interconnected Systems*. New York: Basic Books, 2012.

Pan, Bing, Helene Hembrooke, Thorsten Joachims, Lori Lorigo, Geri Gay, and Laura Granka. "In Google We Trust: Users' Decisions on Rank, Position, and Relevance." *Journal of Computer-Mediated Communication* 12 (3) (2007): 801–823.

Papathanassopoulos, Stylianos, Sharon Coen, James Curran, Toril Aalberg, David Rowe, Paul Jones, Hernando Rojas, and Rod Tiffen. "Online Threat, but Television Is Still Dominant." *Journalism Practice* 7 (6) (2013): 1–15.

Pariser, Eli. *The Filter Bubble: What the Internet Is Hiding from You*. New York: Penguin Press, 2011.

Park, Hanwoo, George A. Barnett, and Joo Chung. "Structural Changes in the 2003–2009 Global Hyperlink Network." *Global Networks* 11 (4) (2011): 522–542.

Payne, John W., James R. Bettman, and David A. Schkade. "Measuring Constructed Preferences: Towards a Building Code." *Journal of Risk and Uncertainty* 19 (1) (1999): 243–270.

PBS. "Audience Insight 2012." Webinar sponsored by CPB, June 18, 2012.

Perkurny, Robert. Coping with Television Production. In *Individuals in Mass Media Organizations*, ed. James S. Ettema and D. C. Whitney, 131–144. Beverly Hills, CA: Sage, 1982.

Peterson, Richard A. "Understanding Audience Segmentation: From Elite and Mass to Omnivore and Univore." *Poetics* 21 (4) (1992): 243–258.

Peterson, Richard A. "Problems in Comparative Research: The Example of Omnivorousness." *Poetics* 33 (5–6) (2005): 257–282.

Pew. "Beyond Red vs. Blue: Political Typology." Washington, DC: Pew Center for the People & the Press, 2011.

Polanyi, Karl. *The Great Transformation: Economic and Political Origins of Our Time*. New York: Rinehart, 1944.

Popkin, Helen A. S. "Game of Spoilers: Social Media Is Killing DVR Culture." *NBC News*.

Potter, Robert F., and Paul Bolls. *Psychophysiological Measurement and Meaning: Cognitive and Emotional Processing of Media*. New York: Routledge, 2011.

Prior, Markus. "News vs. Entertainment: How Increasing Media Choice Widens Gaps in Political Knowledge and Turnout." *American Journal of Political Science* 49 (3) (2005): 577–592.

Prior, Markus. *Post-broadcast Democracy: How Media Choice Increases Inequality in Political Involvement and Polarizes Elections*. Cambridge, UK: Cambridge University Press, 2007.

Prior, Markus. "The Immensely Inflated News Audience: Assessing Bias in Self-Reported News Exposure." *Public Opinion Quarterly* 73 (1) (2009): 130–143.

Prior, Markus. "The Challenge of Measuring Media Exposure: Reply to Dilliplane, Goldman, and Mutz." *Political Communication* 30 (4) (2013a): 620–634.

Prior, Markus. "Media and Political Polarization." *Annual Review of Political Science* 16 (1) (2013b): 101–127.

Project for Excellence in Journalism. "State of the News Media 2006: An Annual Report on American Journalism." New York: Pew Research Center, 2006.

Project for Excellence in Journalism. "How News Happens: A Study of the News Ecosystem of One American City." New York: Pew Research Center, 2010.

Proulx, M., and S. Shepatin. *Social TV: How Marketers Can Reach and Engage Audiences by Connecting Television to the Web, Social Media, and Mobile*. Hoboken, NJ: Wiley, 2012.

Raafat, Ramsey M., Nick Chater, and Chris Frith. "Herding in Humans." *Trends in Cognitive Sciences* 13 (10) (2009): 420–428.

Rainie, Lee, and Barry Wellman. *Networked: The New Social Operating System*. Cambridge, MA: MIT Press, 2012.

Ray, Michael L. Marketing Communication and the Hierarchy of Effects. In *New Models of Communication Research*. vol. 2. ed. P. Clarke, 47–176. Beverly Hills, CA: Sage, 1973.

Resnick, Paul, R. Kelly Garrett, Travis Kriplean, Sean A. Munson, and Natalie Jomini Stroud. "Bursting Your (Filter) Bubble: Strategies for Promoting Diverse Exposure."

In *Proceedings of the 2013 Conference on Computer Supported Cooperative Work Companion*, 95–100. San Antonio, TX: ACM, 2013.

Ridout, Travis N., Michael Franz, Kenneth M. Goldstein, and William J. Feltus. "Separation by Television Program: Understanding the Targeting of Political Advertising in Presidential Elections." *Political Communication* 29 (1) (2012): 1–23.

Rogers, David, and Don Sexton. Marketing ROI in the Era of Big Data. In *BRITE-NYAMA Marketing in Transition*. New York: Columbia University Business School, 2012.

Romero, D., W. Galuba, S. Asur, and B. Huberman. "Influence and Passivity in Social Media." In *Proceedings of the Machine Learning and Knowledge Discovery in Databases European Conference (ECML PKDD 2011), Athens, Greece, September 5-9*, 2011, 18–33. New York: Springer.

Rosen, Jay. "The People Formerly Known as the Audience." *Huffington Post* (June 30, 2006). http://www.huffingtonpost.com/jay-rosen/the-people-formerly-known_1_b_24113.html.

Rosen, Jeffrey. "The Right to Be Forgotten." *Stanford Law Review Online* 64 (2012): 88.

Rosenstein, A. W., and A. E. Grant. "Reconceptualizing the Role of Habit: A New Model of Television Audience Activity." *Journal of Broadcasting & Electronic Media* 41 (3) (1997): 324–344.

Rossman, Gabriel, Nicole Esparza, and Phillip Bonacich. "I'd Like to Thank the Academy, Team Spillovers, and Network Centrality." *American Sociological Review* 75 (1) (2010): 31–51.

Rubin, Alan M. "Television Uses and Gratifications: The Interactions of Viewing Patterns and Motivations." *Journal of Broadcasting & Electronic Media* 27 (1) (1983): 37–51.

Rubin, Alan M. "Ritualized and Instrumental Television Viewing." *Journal of Communication* 34 (3) (1984): 67–77.

Rubin, Alan M. The Uses-and-Gratifications Perspective of Media Effects. In *Media Effects: Advances in Theory and Research*, 2nd ed., ed. J. Bryant and D. Zillmann, 525–548. Mahwah, NJ: Erlbaum, 2002.

Rubin, Alan M. The Uses-and-Gratifications Perspective of Media Effects. In *Media Effects: Advances in Theory and Research*, 3rd ed., ed. Jennings Bryant and Mary B. Oliver, 165–184. New York: Routledge, 2008.

Ruggiero, T. E. "Uses and Gratifications Theory in the 21st Century." *Mass Communication & Society* 3 (1) (2000): 3–37.

Rust, Roland T., Wagner A. Kamakura, and Mark I. Alpert. "Viewer Preference Segmentation and Viewing Choice Models for Network Television." *Journal of Advertising* 21 (1) (1992): 1–18.

Salganik, Mark J. "P. S. Dodds, and D. J. Watts. "Experimental Study of Inequality and Unpredictability in an Artificial Cultural Market." *Science* 311 (5762) (2006): 854.

Samuelson, Paul A. "A Note on the Pure Theory of Consumer's Behaviour." *Economica* 5 (17) (1938): 61–71.

Savage, Mike. "The Musical Field." *Cultural Trends* 15 (2/3) (2006): 159–174.

Schmidt, Eric, and Jared Cohen. *The New Digital Age: Reshaping the Future of People, Nations and Business.* New York: Knopf, 2013.

Schoenbach, Klaus. "'The Own in the Foreign': Reliable Surprise—an Important Function of the Media?" *Media Culture & Society* 29 (2) (2007): 344–353.

Schoenbach, Klaus. Trap Effect. In *The International Encyclopedia of Communication,* ed. Wolfgang Donsbach, 5176–5178. Malden, MA: Blackwell, 2008.

Schoenbach, Klaus, and Edmund Lauf. "Another Look at the 'Trap' Effect of Television—and Beyond." *International Journal of Public Opinion Research* 16 (2) (2004): 169–182.

Sears, David O., and Jonathan L. Freedman. "Selective Exposure to Information: A Critical Review." *Public Opinion Quarterly* 31 (2) (1967): 194–213.

Segal, David. "The Dirty Little Secrets of Search." *New York Times* (February 12, 2011). http://www.nytimes.com/2011/02/13/business/13search.html?pagewanted =all&_r=0.

Sengupta, Sonini. "For Search, Facebook Had to Go beyond 'Robospeak.'" *New York Times* (January 28, 2013). http://www.nytimes.com/2013/01/29/business/ how-facebook-taught-its-search-tool-to-understand-people.html?ref=technology &amp%3B_r=&nl=technology&emc=edit_tu_20130129&_r=0.

Sewell, William H. "A Theory of Structure: Duality, Agency, and Transformation." *American Journal of Sociology* 98 (1) (1992): 1–29.

Sharp, Byron, Virginia Beal, and Martin Collins. "Television: Back to the Future." *Journal of Advertising Research* 49 (2) (2009): 211–219.

Shaw, Aaron, and Yochai Benkler. "A Tale of Two Blogospheres: Discursive Practices on the Left and Right." *American Behavioral Scientist* 56 (4) (2012): 459–487.

Shifman, Limor. "An Anatomy of a Youtube Meme." *New Media & Society* 14 (2) (2012): 187–203.

Shih, Clara. "What's a 'Like' Worth? Ask Facebook's Graph Search: Facebook Search Graph Optimization Becomes as Important as Google Seo." *Advertising Age* (February 14, 2013).

Shirky, Clay. *Here Comes Everybody: The Power of Organizing without Organizations.* New York: Penguin Press, 2008.

Shirky, Clay. *Cognitive Surplus: Creativity and Generosity in a Connected Age.* New York: Penguin Press, 2010.

Short, James E. *How Much Media? 2013: Report on American Consumers.* Los Angeles: Institute for Communications Technology Management, University of California, 2013.

Silver, Nate. *The Signal and the Noise: Why So Many Predictions Fail—but Some Don't.* New York: Penguin Press, 2012.

Simon, Herbert A. "Rational Choice and the Structure of the Environment." *Psychological Review* 63 (2) (1956): 129–138.

Simon, Herbert A. Computers, Communications and the Public Interest. In *Computers, Communications, and the Public Interest*, ed. M. Greenberger, 40–41. Baltimore: Johns Hopkins Press, 1971.

Simon, Herbert A. Rationality in Psychology and Economics. In *Rational Choice: The Contrast between Economics and Psychology*, ed. Robin M. Hograth and Melvin W. Reder, 25–40. Chicago: University of Chicago Press, 1986.

Simon, Herbert A. *Administrative Behavior.* 4th ed. New York: The Free Press, 1997.

Singer, Natasha. "Data Protection Laws, an Ocean Apart." *New York Times* (February 2, 2013).

Singer, Natasha. "Your Online Attention, Bought in an Instant." *New York Times* (November 17, 2012).

Slater, Michael D. "Reinforcing Spirals: The Mutual Influence of Media Selectivity and Media Effects and Their Impact on Individual Behavior and Social Identity." *Communication Theory* 17 (3) (2007): 281–303.

Sloan Commission on Cable Communications. *On the Cable: The Television of Abundance.* New York: McGraw-Hill, 1972.

Slovic, Paul. "The Construction of Preference." *American Psychologist* 50 (5) (1995): 364–371.

Smith, Aaron. "Why Americans Use Social Media." Pew Internet & American Life Project (November 2011).

Smith, Aaron. "Smartphone Ownership—2013 Update." Pew Internet & American Life Project (June 5, 2013).

Starr, Paul. *The Creation of the Media: Political Origins of Modern Communications.* New York: Basic Books, 2004.

Stecklow, Steve, and Julia Angwin. "House Releases "Do Not Track" Bill." *Wall Street Journal* (May 7, 2011). http://online.wsj.com/article/SB1000142405274870399270 45 76307261709717734.html.

Steinberg, Brian. "To Goose TV Audience, Scripps Uses the Web." *Advertising Age* (March 5, 2013).

Steiner, Christopher. *Automate This: How Algorithms Came to Rule Our World.* New York: Portfolio/Penguin Press, 2012.

Stone, Daniel F. "Ideological Media Bias." *Journal of Economic Behavior & Organization* 78 (3) (2011): 256–271.

Stones, Rob. *Structuration Theory.* Basingstoke Hampshire, UK: Palgrave Macmillan, 2005.

Straubhaar, J. D. "Beyond Media Imperialism: Asymmetrical Interdependence and Cultural Proximity." *Critical Studies in Media Communication* 8 (1) (1991): 39–59.

Straubhaar, J. D. *World Television: From Global to Local.* Thousand Oaks, CA: Sage, 2007.

Streeter, Thomas. "The Cable Fable Revisited: Discourse, Policy, and the Making of Cable Television." *Critical Studies in Mass Communication* 4 (2) (1987): 174–200.

Stroud, Natalie J. *Niche News: The Politics of News Choice.* Oxford: Oxford University Press, 2011.

Sundar, S. S., and C. Nass. "Conceptualizing Sources in Online News." *Journal of Communication* 51 (1) (2001): 52–72.

Sunstein, Cass R. *Republic.com 2.0.* Princeton, NJ: Princeton University Press, 2007.

Sunstein, Cass R. *Going to Extremes: How Like Minds Unite and Divide.* New York: Oxford University Press, 2009.

Surowiecki, James. *The Wisdom of Crowds: Why the Many Are Smarter Than the Few and How Collective Wisdom Shapes Business, Economies, Societies and Nations.* New York: Doubleday, 2004.

Swisher, Kara. "Social Media + Pop Culture = ?" *Wall Street Journal* (June 3, 2013).

Tam, Donna. "Facebook Processes More Than 500 Tb of Data Daily." CNET (August 22, 2012). http://news.cnet.com/8301-1023_3-57498531-93/facebook-processes-more -than-500-tb-of-data-daily.

Taneja, Harsh. "Mapping an Audience Centric World Wide Web: A Departure from Hyperlink Analysis." Paper presented at the Association for Education in Journalism and Mass Communication, Washington, DC, August 2013.

Taneja, Harsh, and Utsav Mamoria. "Measuring Media Use across Platforms: Evolving Audience Information Systems." *International Journal on Media Management* 14 (2) (2012): 121–140.

Taneja, Harsh, James G. Webster, Edward C. Malthouse, and Thomas B. Ksiazek. "Media Consumption across Platforms: Identifying User-Defined Repertoires." *New Media & Society* 14 (6) (2012): 951–968.

Tavakoli, Manouche, and Martin Cave. "Modelling Television Viewing Patterns." *Journal of Advertising* 25 (4) (1996): 71–86.

Tepper, Steven J., and Eszter Hargittai. "Pathways to Music Exploration in a Digital Age." *Poetics* 37 (3) (2009): 227–249.

Tewksbury, David. "The Seeds of Audience Fragmentation: Specialization in the Use of Online News Sites." *Journal of Broadcasting & Electronic Media* 49 (3) (2005): 332–348.

Tewksbury, David, and Jason Rittenberg. *News on the Internet: Information and Citizenship in the 21st Century.* Oxford: Oxford University Press, 2012.

Thompson, Clive. "If You Liked This, You're Sure to Love That." *New York Times Magazine* (November 21, 2008a). http://www.nytimes.com/2008/11/23/magazine/ 23Netflix-t.html?pagewanted=6.

Thompson, Clive. "Is the Tipping Point Toast?" *Fast Company* 122 (2008b): 74–105.

Thompson, Clive. *Smarter Than You Think: How Technology Is Changing Our Minds for the Better.* New York: Penguin Press, 2013.

Thorson, E. "Changing Patterns of News Consumption and Participation." *Information Communication and Society* 11 (4) (2008): 473–489.

Tobler, W. R. "A Computer Movie Simulating Urban Growth in the Detroit Region." *Economic Geography* 46 (1970): 234–240.

Trilling, D., and K. Schoenbach. "Challenging Selective Exposure: Do People Expose Themselves Only to Online Content That Fits Their Interests and Preferences?" Paper presented at the WAPOR 65th Annual Conference, Hong Kong, June 2012.

Trilling, Damian, and Klaus Schoenbach. "Patterns of News Consumption in Austria: How Fragmented Are They?" *International Journal of Communication* 7 (2013).

Turow, Joseph. *Breaking Up America: Advertisers and the New Media World*. Chicago: University of Chicago Press, 1997.

Turow, Joseph. *Niche Envy: Marketing Discrimination in the Digital Age*. Cambridge, MA: MIT Press, 2006.

Turow, Joseph. *The Daily You: How the New Advertising Industry Is Defining Your Identity and Your Worth*. New Haven, CT: Yale University Press, 2012.

Tversky, Amos, and Daniel Kahneman. "Judgment under Uncertainty: Heuristics and Biases." *Science* 185 (4157) (1974): 1124–1131.

Vaidhyanathan, Siva. *The Googlization of Everything (and Why We Should Worry)*. Berkeley: University of California Press, 2012.

Valentino, Nicholas A., Antoine J. Banks, Vincent L. Hutchings, and Anne K. Davis. "Selective Exposure in the Internet Age: The Interaction between Anxiety and Information Utility." *Political Psychology* 30 (4) (2009): 591–613.

Vallone, R. P., L. Ross, and M. R. Lepper. "The Hostile Media Phenomenon: Biased Perception and Perceptions of Media Bias in Coverage of the Beirut Massacre." *Journal of Personality and Social Psychology* 49 (3) (1985): 577–585.

Van Alstyne, M., and E. Brynjolfsson. "Global Village or Cyber-Balkans? Modeling and Measuring the Integration of Electronic Communities." *Management Science* 51 (6) (2005): 851–868.

Van Dijck, José. "Users Like You? Theorizing Agency in User-Generated Content." *Media Culture & Society* 31 (1) (2009): 41.

Van Eijck, K., and K. Van Rees. "The Internet and Dutch Media Repertoires." *IT& Society* 1 (2) (2002): 86–99.

van Rees, Kees, and Koen van Eijck. "Media Repertoires of Selective Audiences: The Impact of Status, Gender, and Age on Media Use." *Poetics* 31 (5–6) (2003): 465–490.

Vanderbilt, Tom, and Willa Paskin. "The Platinum Age of TV." *Wired* (April 2013).

Varian, Hal R. Revealed Preference. In *Samuelsonian Economics and the Twenty-First Century*, ed. Michael Szenberg, Lall Ramrattan, and Aron A. Gottesman. Oxford: Oxford University Press, 2006.

Vasterman, Peter L. M. "Media-Hype Self-Reinforcing News Waves, Journalistic Standards and the Construction of Social Problems." *European Journal of Communication* 20 (4) (2005): 508–530.

Vermeulen, Frederic. "Foundations of Revealed Preference: Introduction." *Economic Journal* 122 (560) (2012): 287–294.

Vidmar, Neil, and Milton Rokeach. "Archie Bunker's Bigotry: A Study in Selective Perception and Exposure." *Journal of Communication* 24 (1) (1974): 36–47.

Vogel, Harold L. *Entertainment Industry Economics: A Guide for Financial Analysis.* 8th ed. Cambridge, UK: Cambridge University Press, 2011.

Vorderer, Peter, Christoph Klimmt, and Ute Ritterfeld. "Enjoyment: At the Heart of Media Entertainment." *Communication Theory* 14 (4) (2004): 388–408.

Waisbord, Silvio. "MCTV Understanding the Global Popularity of Television Formats." *Television & New Media* 5 (4) (2004): 359–383.

Waller, V. "Not Just Information: Who Searches for What on the Search Engine Google?" *Journal of the American Society for Information Science and Technology* 62 (4) (2011): 761–775.

Wallerstein, Andrew. "Netflix Series Spending Revealed." *Variety* (March 8, 2013).

Waterman, David. *Hollywood's Road to Riches.* Cambridge, MA: Harvard University Press, 2005.

Watts, Duncan J. *Everything Is Obvious: Once You Know the Answer; How Common Sense Fails.* New York: Penguin Press, 2011.

Watts, Duncan J., and Steven H. Strogatz. "Collective Dynamics of 'Small-World' Networks." *Nature* 393 (6684) (1998): 440–442.

Watts, Duncan J., and Peter Sheridan Dodds. "Influentials, Networks, and Public Opinion Formation." *Journal of Consumer Research* 34 (4) (2007): 441–458.

Webster, James G. "Audience Behavior in the New Media Environment." *Journal of Communication* 36 (3) (1986): 77–91.

Webster, James G. "Beneath the Veneer of Fragmentation: Television Audience Polarization in a Multichannel World." *Journal of Communication* 55 (2) (2005): 366–382.

Webster, James G. "Audience Flow Past and Present: Television Inheritance Effects Reconsidered." *Journal of Broadcasting & Electronic Media* 50 (2) (2006): 323–337.

Webster, James G. The Role of Structure in Media Choice. In *Media Choice: A Theoretical and Empirical Overview*, ed. T. Hartmann, 221–233. New York: Routledge, 2009.

Webster, James G. "User Information Regimes: How Social Media Shape Patterns of Consumption." *Northwestern University Law Review* 104 (2) (2010): 593–612.

Webster, James G. "The Duality of Media: A Structurational Theory of Public Attention." *Communication Theory* 21 (1) (2011): 43–66.

Webster, James G., and T. B. Ksiazek. "The Dynamics of Audience Fragmentation: Public Attention in an Age of Digital Media." *Journal of Communication* 62 (2012): 39–56.

Webster, James G., and Patricia F. Phalen. *The Mass Audience: Rediscovering the Dominant Model*. Mahwah, NJ: Erlbaum, 1997.

Webster, James G., Patricia F. Phalen, and Lawrence W. Lichty. *Ratings Analysis: Audience Measurement and Analytics*. 4th ed. New York: Routledge, 2014.

Webster, James G., and Jacob J. Wakshlag. "A Theory of Television Program Choice." *Communication Research* 10 (4) (1983): 430–446.

Weinschenk, S. *100 Things Every Designer Needs to Know about People*. Berkeley, CA: New Riders, 2011.

Wellman, Barry. "Is Dunbar's Number Up?" *British Journal of Psychology* 103 (2) (2012): 174–176.

WFA/EACA. *Guide to Organizing Audience Research*. Brussels: World Federation of Advertisers and European Association of Communications Agencies, 2008.

Whiting, Susan. "The Additive Effect of Tablet Reading." Economist Group (July 19, 2012).

Wildman, Jeff. "Edgerank: A Guide to Facebook's Newsfeed Algorithm" (2013). http://edgerank.net.

Wildman, Steven S. One-Way Flows and the Economics of Audiencemaking. In *Audiencemaking: How the Media Create the Audience*, ed. James S. Ettema and D. C. Whitney, 115–141. Thousand Oaks, CA: Sage, 1994.

Wildman, Steven S., and Stephen E. Siwek. *International Trade in Films and Television Programs*. Cambridge, MA: Ballinger, 1988.

Williams, Bruce A., and Michael X. Delli Carpini. *After Broadcast News: Media Regimes, Democracy, and the New Information Environment.* Cambridge, UK: Cambridge University Press, 2011.

Williams, Raymond. *Culture and Society, 1780–1950.* New York: Columbia University Press, 1958.

Williams, Raymond. *Television: Technology and Cultural Form.* New York: Schocken Books, 1974.

Wohn, D. "Yvette, and Eun-Kyung Na. "Tweeting about TV: Sharing Television Viewing Experiences via Social Media Message Streams." *First Monday* 16 (3) (2011): 1–29.

Wonneberger, Anke. "Coping with Diversity: Exposure to Public-Affairs TV in a Changing Viewing Environment," PhD thesis, University of Amsterdam, 2011.

Wonneberger, Anke, Klaus Schoenbach, and Lex van Meurs. "Dimensionality of TV-News Exposure: Mapping News Viewing Behavior with People-Meter Data." *International Journal of Public Opinion Research* 21 (1) (2012): 87–107.

Wonneberger, Anke, Klaus Schoenbach, and Lex van Meurs. "Dynamics of Individual Television Viewing Behavior: Models, Empirical Evidence, and a Research Program." *Communication Studies* 60 (3) (2009): 235–252.

Wonneberger, Anke, Klaus Schoenbach, and Lex van Meurs. "Tuning Out? TV News Audiences in the Netherlands 1990–2010." Presented at the 61st Annual Meeting of the International Communication Association, Boston, May 2011.

Wonneberger, Anke, Klaus Schoenbach, and Lex van Meurs. "Staying Tuned: TV News Audiences in the Netherlands 1988–2010." *Journal of Broadcasting & Electronic Media* 56 (1): 55–74.

Wonneberger, Anke, Klaus Schoenbach, and Lex van Meurs. "How Keeping up Diversifies: Watching Public Affairs TV in the Netherlands 1988–2010." *European Journal of Communication* (December 2013): 646–662.

WPP. "GroupM Forecasts 2012 Global Ad Spending to Increase 6.4% U.S." Press release, London.

Wright, David. "Making Tastes for Everything: Omnivorousness and Cultural Abundance." *Journal for Cultural Research* 15 (4) (2011): 355–371.

Wu, Fang, and Bernardo A. Huberman. "Novelty and Collective Attention." *Proceedings of the National Academy of Sciences of the United States of America* 104 (45) (2007): 17599–17601.

Wu, Fang. D. M. Wilkinson, and B. A. Huberman. "Feedback Loops of Attention in Peer Production." Paper presented at the International Conference on Computational Science and Engineering, CSE '09, August 29–31, 2009.

Wu, S., J. M. Hofman, W. A. Mason, and D. J. Watts. "Who Says What to Whom on Twitter." Paper presented at the International World Wide Web Conference, Hyderabad, India, March 28–April 1, 2011.

Yang, Jaewon, and Jure Leskovec. "Patterns of Temporal Variation in Online Media." In *Proceedings of the Fourth ACM International Conference on Web Search and Data Mining*, 177–186. Hong Kong: ACM, 2011.

Yim, Jungsu. "Audience Concentration in the Media: Cross-Media Comparisons and the Introduction of the Uncertainty Measure." *Communication Monographs* 70 (2) (2003): 114–128.

YouTube. "Statistics." http://www.youtube.com/t/press_statistics.

Yuan, Elaine J. "The New Multi-Channel Media Environment in China: Diversity of Exposure in Television Viewing." PhD diss., Northwestern University, 2007.

Yuan, Elaine J., and James G. Webster. "Channel Repertoires: Using PeopleMeter Data in Beijing." *Journal of Broadcasting & Electronic Media* 50 (3) (2006): 524–536.

Zajonc, Robert B. "Attitudinal Effects of Mere Exposure." *Journal of Personality and Social Psychology* 9 (2) (1968): 1.

Zajonc, Robert B. "Mere Exposure: A Gateway to the Subliminal." *Current Directions in Psychological Science* 10 (6) (2001): 224–228.

Zaller, John. "A New Standard of News Quality: Burglar Alarms for the Monitorial Citizen." *Political Communication* 20 (2) (2003): 109–130.

Zaslow, Jeffrey. "If Tivo Thinks You Are Gay, Here's How to Set It Straight." *Wall Street Journal* (November 26, 2002).

Zillmann, Dolf. Mood Management in the Context of Selective Exposure Theory. In *Communication Yearbook*, ed. M. E. Roloff, 103–124. Thousand Oaks, CA: Sage, 2000.

Zillmann, Dolf, and Jennings Bryant, eds. *Selective Exposure to Communication*. Hillsdale, NJ: Erlbaum, 1985.

Zimmer, Ben. "Who First Put 'Lipstick on a Pig'?" *Slate* (September 10, 2008).

Zuckerman, Ethan. "Serendipity, Echo Chambers, and the Front Page." *Nieman Reports* 62 (4) (2008): 16.

Zuckerman, Ethan. *Rewire: Digital Cosmopolitans in the Age of Connection*. New York: Norton, 2013.

INDEX